# WILLIAM MARSHAL

THE MEDIEVAL WORLD

*Editor: David Bates*

Already published

CHARLES THE BALD

Janet Nelson

CNUT

The Danes in England in the Early Eleventh Century

M.K. Lawson

WILLIAM MARSHAL

Court, Career and Chivalry in the Angevin Empire 1147–1219

David Crouch

KING JOHN

Ralph Turner

INNOCENT III

Leader of Europe 1198–1216

Jane Sayers

THE FRIARS

The Impact of the Early Mendicant Movement on Western Society

C.H. Lawrence

ENGLISH NOBLEWOMEN IN THE LATER MIDDLE AGES

Jennifer C. Ward

# WILLIAM MARSHAL
## Court, Career and Chivalry in the Angevin Empire 1147 – 1219

David Crouch

LONGMAN
London and New York

**Longman Group UK Limited**
Longman House, Burnt Mill, Harlow,
Essex CM20 2JE, England
*and Associated Companies throughout the world*

*Published in the United States of America*
*by Longman Inc., New York*



First published 1990
Second impression 1993

**British Library Cataloguing in Publication Data**

Crouch, David, 1953–
William Marshal: court, career and chivalry
in the Angevin Empire 1147 – 1219 – (The medieval world).
1. England. Social life, 1154 – 1399. Biographies
2. Title II. Series
942.03′03′092′4

ISBN 0-582-03787-5 CSD
ISBN 0-582-03786-7 PPR

**Library of Congress Cataloging in Publication Data**

Crouch, David.

William Marshal: court, career, and chivalry in the
Angevin Empire, 1147 – 1219 / David Crouch.
p. cm.—(The Medieval World)
Includes bibliographical references.
ISBN 0–582–03787–5.—ISBN 0–582–03786–7 (pbk.)
1. Pembroke, William Marshal, Earl of, 1144?–1219.
2. Great Britain—History—Angevin period, 1134–1216.
3. Knights and knighthood—Great Britain—Biography.
4. Regents—Great Britain—Biography.
5. Chivalry.
I. Title II. Series
DA209.P4C73 1990
942.03′4′092 dc—20 [B] 89–29171 CIP

SET IN 10.5/12 Linotron 202 Baskerville
Produced by Longman Singapore Publishers (Pte) Ltd.
Printed in Singapore

# CONTENTS

# MAPS AND FIGURES

# EDITOR'S PREFACE

In terms of what we can expect in the medieval period, William the Marshal is a man about whom we can know a great deal and a man whose career is a ready vehicle to illustrate twelfth and thirteenth century aristocratic society. The verse *Histoire de Guillaume le Maréchal* is the first medieval 'biography' of a layman who was not a king. Through it we are given insight into the world of the courts of the Angevin Empire and the political and social milieu which surrounded kings Henry II, Richard I and John, into tournaments and what we often call chivalry, and into the companionship and notions of loyalty and good conduct which permeated aristocratic society. We also follow the remarkable rise to wealth and power of a younger son of a middling aristocratic family and observe his role during the collapse of the Angevin Empire, the civil wars of John's reign and the turbulent affairs of Anglo-Norman Ireland.

David Crouch does justice to this story in a lively and appealing narrative. His William the Marshal is a great warrior and a superb practitioner of the contemporary codes of chivalric conduct as we now understand them. This means that he was a master of the science of war and that he could conceal his purposes behind a mask of politeness in order to translate his military abilities into wealth and prestige. Dr Crouch's Marshal is a courtier, a politician and, in the last decade of his life, a magnate. What especially sets Dr Crouch's study apart from other books on William the Marshal is his command of the full range of the sources. He has collected the Marshal's charters, documents which sometimes question the accuracy of the *Histoire*, and which give us numerous insights into the entourage which surrounded the great magnate. We perceive through them a society which was scarcely one of lords and vassals at all, where conditions approximated to what is conventionally called 'Bastard Feudalism'. We understand better social relations between clergy and laity, the essential sources of noble wealth and power, the importance of family connections, and the nature of love, loyalty and politics. Dr Crouch tells us a good story and his commentary on the aristocratic society of William Marshal's age is a major contribution to the social history of the Middle Ages.

# PREFACE

In writing this book, I have incurred a number of debts. I must acknowledge first the help of David Bates, who came to me with the idea for the book, and neatly shepherded the resulting flock of words into several well-ordered folds. Thanks are also due to others who have contributed ideas and suggestions: Adrian Ailes, David Carpenter, Steve Church, Lindy Grant, Sandy Heslop, Tom Keefe, Derek Keene, Chris Lewis, Tom McNeill and Jeffrey West. Any remaining errors and obscurities are my own doing. Eric Hemming's endeavours while my research assistant must be warmly acknowledged. The forbearance of my wife while writing this book was constant and generous.

The staff of a number of record repositories and libraries gave me material assistance: notably the British Library, the Public Record Office at Chancery Lane, the Archives Nationales in Paris, Somerset and Wiltshire Record Offices, and Birmingham Central Reference Library. Of a wholly different order has been the contribution of the Institute of Historical Research, which hosted for four years the research project from which the material for this book has been drawn. I gratefully acknowledge the immense debt owed to Professor Michael Thompson, Dr Alice Prochaska and their staff in the Institute's administration and library, in furthering my research. The Economic and Social Research Council provided the funds for computer support of the project. Lastly, I must thank the Leverhulme Trust, whose remarkable generosity has principally funded the research out of which this book has resulted, and without which it would not have been possible.

*London*
September 1989

**TO LINDA AND SIMON**

. . . . .

# INTRODUCTION

William Marshal, Earl of Pembroke (or 'the Marshal' as he was generally known in his own lifetime)[1], was born at some time around 1147 in Wiltshire, or perhaps Berkshire, in the reign of King Stephen. We do not know precisely when or where because his family was not then important enough for the fact to be thought worth mentioning by anyone. He was the fourth son (the second by his second marriage) of John Marshal, a court officer and minor baron, a man well connected but not overly wealthy. From these small beginnings William rose in his seventy-two or so years of life to be a great earl and marcher lord in Wales and Ireland, a man of European celebrity and until his final illness, protector of England and the person of its boy-king Henry III.

The Marshal lived a life of an epic scale, and nothing was more suitable after his death in 1219 than that his sons and followers should commission a poem in the vein of a great romance to celebrate it. The *Histoire de Guillaume le Mareschal*, as it is generally called, is an astonishing survival, even in the imperfect copy which survives: a Middle French poem of 19,214 lines in rhyming couplets all celebrating the life of one remarkable man. It names its author as one John, a man who had known the Marshal himself in his prime, and who had travelled widely on the Continent in tournaments and warfare, but of whom nothing more is known. John seems to have worked on the poem for several years, collecting anecdotes and written submissions of eyewitnesses for the purpose. He even did a little research in the household archives of the Marshal family to assist him in the earlier, more obscure, period of the elder Marshal's life. His

1 The various names by which William Marshal was known are treated fully in Appendix II.

upkeep was met by money from the Marshal's eldest son, the second Earl William, and one of the executors of the old earl's will, John of Earley. He completed it after 1226 (for the later part of it, at least, was written after the death of the Earl of Salisbury in that year) and before John of Earley's death in 1229 (for it talks of him as a living man). John's poem is (with one exception) the only surviving biography of a man of that time of any dignity less than a king.[2] It is our chief source for much of what we know of aristocratic life in the period, especially warfare and the tournament, and one of the key sources for Anglo-French politics of the twelfth and early thirteenth centuries. It has never been translated into English, although at present the Anglo-Norman Text Society is preparing a new edition to fill the gap.

. . .

## OLD WORK AND NEW QUESTIONS

The *Histoire* allows us to present to the modern reader a biography of a man of the High Middle Ages in more detail than any other of his lay contemporaries below the rank of sovereign prince (we know contemporary churchmen far better from their letter collections, autobiographies and biographies). His career was important politically: from 1189 he was a leading actor in the history of England and France. His biography is also an important social document for military and aristocratic life in the High Middle Ages. So it should be no surprise that this book is not the first attempt to tell the Marshal's story; it is in fact the fourth in English.[3] Of its three predecessors the best (and weightiest) by far is that by the American scholar Sidney Painter. I have no hesitation in acknowledging a great debt to his work, not least in inspiration. It is well written, and based on sterling research, but it was published over fifty years ago. Much work on

2 The exception is the memoir of his own life composed by Philip de Navarre (or Novara), a French baron in Outremer, in the mid-1220s (the very time when the *Histoire* being composed), but this fragment would seem to have been little more than an accumulation of his notes for his later history of his times, see, *Mémoires*, ed. C Kohler, (C.F.M.A., 1913).

3 The three predecessors are: T L Jarman, *William Marshal, First Earl of Pembroke and Regent of England* (Oxford, 1930); S Painter, *William Marshal* (Baltimore, 1933); J Crossland, *William the Marshal: the Last Great Feudal Baron* (London, 1962).

both aristocratic society and political events of the Marshal's lifetime has built up since 1937, and new questions have since been asked by historians.

What are these new questions? Painter's picture of William Marshal has been taken as the portrait of a typical baron of his age: illiterate and socially clumsy; well-disposed in general but still grasping; primitively religious; sophisticated only in the technicalities of war. Yet paradoxically Painter also portrays his Marshal as respecting the emerging code of chivalry, loving fair play and worshipping the ideal of woman (though not at ease with the real creature). It is remarkable how this stereotype of the 'bold, bad baron'[4] (to quote a recent commentary on English liberty by a distinguished early modernist) lingers, even amongst historians who are supposed to beware of stereotypes; and because the Marshal biography is the only one of its kind, Painter has to take much of the blame for this.

The Marshal, in my view, was by no means typical. To begin with there has been sufficient work done recently to indicate that the Marshal was unusual amongst his fellow magnates in being a complete illiterate, not even able to read French, let alone Latin.[5] This single fact may have helped to distort our views of the level of sophistication of the aristocracy of his day, as it is difficult to avoid taking the Marshal as typical. But, on the other side of the coin, it is not often remembered that his biography was the work of a layman. His biographer may not have been technically *litteratus* as the thirteenth century understood it (for that word was applied to those educated in Latin), but he could clearly write, if only in the vernacular. The Marshal was also not typical in being so exclusively military in his interests. Most of his fellows amongst the court aristocracy were administrators first, and soldiers second, sometimes a long way second. But the Marshal was a captain and soldier by talent and inclination, and an administrator and judge only when he had to be. There are other question marks over the Marshal as Painter has reconstructed him for us. The degree of chivalry he displayed is one question, another is the level of sophistication of his warmaking. Painter would have granted that he was a talented and thoughtful soldier, but a recent study by Mr John Gillingham

4 Christopher Hill in *The Guardian* 15 July 1989.

5 M T Clanchy *From Memory to Written Record* (London, 1979), 175–201.

elevates his generalship to a higher plane than that.

Lastly, and for me most importantly, there is the question of the Marshal's basic political conduct, and indeed the nature of the political world in which he operated. For Painter he was an honest, engaging character; not particularly bright, but straightforward enough. He was a feudal lord who built his power on the ties of homage between him and his men. His success was a matter of being a useful soldier and being lucky in his friends and patrons. To me this is a regrettable misinterpretation of the sources. Rereading the *Histoire* in the light of the recent study by Professor Stephen Jaeger, it seems clear to me that the Marshal was one of the great practitioners of courtliness of his age. His political conduct was studied, sophisticated and devious. Nor was the world in which he rose to the top so uncomplicated as Painter wished it to be. The Marshal's England was long past the stage when feudal knight service was important. For him power was achieved by attracting independent, influential men into his following, and making alliances with his equals at court and in the country. His was a world where feudalism was already bastardized, a world of shifting political affinities. This was why he was so often able to defy King John; the court was so riddled with his friends that none of the magnates would assist the king against him. Those who held land from the Marshal by knights' service provided him with money, when he could get it out of them, and did not in general give him political and military assistance.

The other significant work on the Marshal is in French, by the eminent medieval scholar and academician, Georges Duby.[6] His is in many ways a fine book, or at least a well written one: his passages on the Marshal's death-bed and tournament career are models of how a historian should seek to write, be he French or English. But as a biography the book has many deficiencies. It is based on a perceptive reading of the *Histoire* and nothing else. Duby preferred to rely on the historical notes of Paul Meyer, the editor of the text of the *Histoire*, without much heeding even what Painter had to add to Meyer's monumental researches. As a consequence he makes numerous errors of chronology and genealogy which sadly devalue his work. Duby is also less than well instructed on English political and social life. Like Painter

6 *Guillaume le Maréchal, ou le meilleur chevalier du monde* Paris, 1984 trans R Howard *William Marshal, Flower of Chivalry* (London, 1986).

he is not critical of the *Histoire*, except in a literary sense. He too has some axes to grind, he is convinced of the Marshal's limitations, he sees him as a simple warrior carried far beyond his sphere. Duby's work, if rich in insight, fails to provide any serious rethinking of the man's career nor does it present any new evidence, indeed in total it is downright misleading: he takes from the *Histoire* that which confirms his preconceptions about aristocratic society and ignores the rest. Perhaps no historian is entirely guiltless of this, but Duby's Marshal is a warning of how selective historical writing can distort the evidence in a most unacceptable way.

Apart from the *Histoire* there is one other source for the Marshal's career which has till now been ignored. Neither Duby nor Painter employ the other main source for the Marshal's career, or at least his later career: the Marshal's own charters, of which at least sixty-seven survive in archives scattered across Ireland, Britain and northern France. These, as I will explain, give a picture of the Marshal's activities which differs from that of the *Histoire*; they show us, amongst other things, the Marshal as businessman and estate-manager, an aspect of his character entirely overlooked by Duby, although not ignored by Painter. Most importantly, they allow us to analyse the nature of his political following. The *Histoire* is a mirror of the emotional bonds between the Marshal and his men; but the charters are a microscope that enable us to look much deeper into their material nature.

. . .

## THE PROBLEMS OF THE SOURCES

One of the main problems about the biography of the Marshal is how far the *Histoire* is to be trusted. This is particularly true of what it has to say about the early period of the Marshal's career. At a later stage, when the Marshal gained in fame and wealth, there is more by other authors with which to compare it. But here the author had no more to go on than his own hazy conceptions of the events of the reigns of Stephen and Henry II in England and France, some few early written records he had seen (a tally of ransoms from the 1170s and a tournament roll of 1180), and the Marshal's own recollections of his early life as remembered by his family and friends. These autobiographical fragments, curiously, would seem to be for the most part unexceptionable.

The Marshal, at times clearly a garrulous old man, had a nice line in self-mockery and obviously told a story well, the fact that, no doubt, he repeated them over and again may have fixed them in the family mythology. These stories do not always portray the Marshal in a favourable light, and so the element of truth in them may be high.

'A history which is true should have perforce nothing in it of falsity', says the pious author of the *Histoire*. He did not on that account try to avoid the odd half-truth or evasion when it suited him. He left gaps in the Marshal's story. He was reticent about his political career from 1170 to 1183, when the Marshal was in the centre of events, but in the disreputable entourage of Henry II's eldest son, Henry. Again, there is a curious ignorance shown by the *Histoire* about the Marshal's immediate family. Although we hear a lot about the Marshal's father (a favourite subject of his stories, apparently) we hear little of the fate of his brothers, Walter and Gilbert (who had died before 1166), and the *Histoire* gives a distorted picture of how the Marshal estate descended through the family. The career of William's brother John Marshal barely features in the *Histoire*, although there is good evidence that John was very important to him in the reign of Richard. There is every reason to believe that William was for a long time estranged from his siblings, which led to his silence on the subject. As a result the author of the *Histoire* fills in the gap with passages of pure fiction, particularly his treatment of the sad deaths of Walter and Gilbert Marshal.

The element of identifiable fiction in the *Histoire* is a warning that we must treat it carefully. Apart from its obvious bias towards its subject, it is written in a literary tradition that must have distorted its truth. Although it is unique in its content and aims, it is far from unique in its form. It is written in the tradition of French epics and romances whose known pedigree stretches back to the beginning of the twelfth century in England, with the epic, *The Song of Roland*. In one particular instance, the portrayal of tournaments, it has been pointed out by Larry Benson that the *Histoire*'s account of certain of them seems to have been inspired directly by the writings of Chrétien de Troyes, a half-century before. A good example of this romantic influence is the description of William Marshal with which the author provides us. Phrases such as, 'He was so noble a man that he might have been taken for the emperor of Rome!', do not in fact tell us much, but even when the poet seems to get more specific he cannot be trusted. The key to this is, I regret to say, the size of the Marshal's crutch. 'He had a crutch as large, and a stature as striking, as only a gentleman could have.' Large crutches, an obviously desirable feature in a horse-riding society, were regarded as a badge of male aristocratic beauty. We find such a feature praised as early as *The Song of Roland*. In a romance composed in the household of the Earl of Warwick some ten to twenty years before the *Histoire*, a popular work called *Gui de Warewic*, one of Guy's great friends, Count Thierry of Guaremaise, is described in just such terms as the Marshal: well made, tall in stature with a large crutch. The Marshal was held to have been a handsome man when he was young, so his biographer describes him according to the conventional, contemporary canons of what a young, handsome man should look like (except he was not a blond, as heroes normally were).

Does the same apply to the author's descriptions of events? This is a disturbing question for a historian, and not an easy one to answer. It is however probable that to a degree the poet–biographer did allow his stock of epic verse to intrude into events, particularly the early events of the Marshal's life. There is a distinct change of gear in the pace of the *Histoire* after the Marshal joins Henry II's household in 1186. Names and events then begin to come thick and fast, digressive anecdotes grow few. The reason for this is given us by the author himself: he was drawing on the (probably written) memoirs made for him by (amongst others) John of Earley, the West Country knight who was the Marshal's ward and body squire from 1187, and household knight after 1194. Of all the *Histoire*, the tournament scenes in the Marshal's bachelorhood are the most suspect. He wins the prize and ransom far too often for my comfort. The hero's winning of the prize in the tournament was a stock romantic episode, such as in Chrétien de Troyes' *Erec and Enide*, a romance of the 1170s, where the eponymous hero overrides all opposition in the tournament to celebrate his marriage and in the end 'everyone on both sides said that by his lance and shield he had become victor in the tournament'.[7] Perhaps the Pembrokes were sneering at the pretensions of the Warwicks, pointing to a real-life hero in their family tree, not a myth. Guy of Warwick is described on occasion as 'the best knight in all the world', and this is the title appropriated by the *Histoire* to William Marshal.

7 Trans D D R Owen in *Arthurian Romances* London 1987 30.

If this were so, then the Warwicks had the last laugh, for *Gui de Warewic* went on to be one of the most popular romances in England for several centuries, while the *Histoire* had no circulation in the Middle Ages.

This book is not therefore just a biography of William Marshal and a survey of his times, it is also an attempt to disentangle at least the historical problems posed by the *Histoire*. One need not be unduly pessimistic about the task. There is much with which to compare it and although John, the Marshal's biographer, had prejudices, in general they are well advertised: he bitterly loathed King John, for instance, and the king does not appear to any advantage in the work (except when he is said to have died extolling the Marshal's virtues with all but his last breath). The *Histoire* studiously avoids mentioning John's creation of the Marshal as Earl of Pembroke and the remarkable number of grants with which he favoured him. If such prejudices are understood then the work can be used to some effect, and whatever its faults it is undeniably a brilliant window on to contemporary life and customs. It brings alive the courtly world of the late twelfth and early thirteenth centuries as do few other sources.

*Chapter 1*

# CHILDHOOD AND SQUIREHOOD

. . .

## JOHN MARSHAL: FATHER AND SON

William was born around 1147 into the middle of a war: the civil war between the supporters of Stephen and Mathilda that wasted England between 1139 and 1153. In a way, it was in warfare that he was conceived. John Marshal, his father, and Sybil of Salisbury, his mother, were married to seal a pact between John and Sybil's brother Patrick, Earl of Salisbury, who was John's rival for power in Wiltshire. Even William's name may have been a political stratagem. It recalled his mother's eldest brother, William of Salisbury. He had died three or four years before William Marshal was born.

Civil wars are evil affairs. The war of Stephen's reign was grimmer than most. It came after the reigns of the first three Norman kings, peaceful and prosperous for the most part in England, once the time of conquest and colonization had ended. People had come to regard peace and strong royal government as the natural order of things. In 1135 Stephen seized the crown. He was a man of strong feelings and good intentions, but little judgement. He could not manage his nobility. He did not know how to stand aloof from his barons, confident and unapproachable. He did not know how to use fear to keep them uneasy, nor favour to entice them into his court. Like all the worst kings, he played favourites. Within two years there was a breakdown of the balance between court factions. The estranged barons took their differences to the country, and those opposed to the king found a ready-made cause in Mathilda, the late King Henry's only surviving legitimate child. The result in England was the 'Anarchy' as it is now called. Memories of this evil time were still strong some three generations later, when the Marshal's biographer wrote that there was 'neither peace, understanding, agreement nor justice, so cruelly and long was war carried on'.[1]

But the civil war was not without compensations for a man of a certain sort. John Marshal was just the type who could take advantage of the peculiar advantages the Anarchy offered. He was cool-headed, whether in battle or bargaining, ruthless in his ambition and a hero to his followers and knights. He knew how to reward and how to punish, when to attack and (less common in such a man) when to retreat. To his son, William, he could not have been more than the memory of a strong man, fearfully scarred on the face by battle, a man he believed to be all-powerful, capable of riding into the king's camp where he was held hostage and riding away with him to his mother. From his father he expected protection, from his mother, close in her chambers, he had love and care. William never saw his father after his childhood, and would have seen little enough of him then. But he remembered stories of his father's prowess that the women, his brothers, and the servants would have told him. He would remember the awe that gathered about such a paterfamilias. His cunning was legendary, his military skill in castle building and tactics a marvel to his contemporaries.

So it is that the first part of William's biography, the *Histoire*, is dominated by John Marshal. The biography is honest enough about John's origins. 'Though he was neither earl, nor baron of great resources, his largesse so abounded that men marvelled at it'.[2] He was the hereditary royal master-marshal. As such he was a dignified enough man, and in King Henry I's reign he lived in a court where he could find some opportunity to further himself, in a modest way. In 1130 we know that he was able to dispose of large sums of money to pay for his succession to his father's office and buy control of the marriage of a Wiltshire heiress. His landed endowment was small. He owned houses on the corner of what was later to be called Jewry Street in Winchester, not far from the royal castle and palace, place of his duty. Elsewhere there were lands held from the king in Somerset and Berkshire. The family centre in Henry I's days would have been at Hamstead Marshall, in the Kennet valley in Berkshire, close to the Wiltshire border. Here there was a hall and other houses within a large enclosure, which John Marshal transformed into an earth-and-timber castle in Stephen's reign.

1 *Histoire* ll. 128–31.

2 *Histoire*, ll. 32–35.

Apart from these possessions, John and his father were able, like other royal ministers, to pick up pieces of land from powerful barons who thought them worthy of attracting into their orbits; so John had scattered lands in Herefordshire of the Candos family, in Oxfordshire of the Arsic family, and in Wiltshire of the Salisbury family. There were fees besides from the bishops of Exeter, Winchester and Worcester, and the abbot of Abingdon. In 1130 his total lands were assessed, for the purpose of a tax exemption as thirty-five and a quarter hides, about the amount a prosperous minor baron might hold.

John's great days began with the death of King Henry I in 1135. The king's nephew, Stephen, hastened across the Channel, and with the help of his brother, the bishop of Winchester, and the money and weight of London, was crowned king before the other nobles of the court had finished debating possible alternatives. Although the *Histoire* says that John joined Mathilda 'without hesitation',[3] we know from other sources that he promptly accepted King Stephen, along with almost everybody else who had frequented Henry I's court. Stephen exerted himself to reward prompt allegiance; nowhere more so than in the south-west of England. Here he feared (groundlessly as it turned out) the opposition of Earl Robert of Gloucester, King Henry's eldest bastard.

Early in the reign John Marshal received custody of the royal town and castle of Marlborough, along with other lands in north Wiltshire at Wexcombe and Cherhill, which he was still holding at the king's pleasure at the end of the civil war. With Wexcombe he acquired for his own profit the court of the large hundred of Kinwardstone or Bedwyn, south-east of Marlborough.[4] This windfall transformed him into a castellan of some power. Marlborough, at that date a timber-and-earth castle on a strong site with an impressive motte, commanded the route along the Kennet valley across the downs from London to Earl Robert's centre of Bristol. John may have been expected to watch the road from the west, but the king's generosity also made him the most formidable

3 '*sanz faille*': *Histoire*, l. 47.

4 We know he had Marlborough in 1138; the likelihood is that he had the lands and hundred too. He first appears with Wexcombe and Cherhill along with Marlborough in the Pipe Roll of 1156: but lands called *terris datis* (distributed lands) in the early Pipe Rolls of Henry II were frequently royal concessions of earlier grants of Stephen, *Red Book of the Exchequer*, ed. H Hall (3 vols) Rolls Series 1889 II 664.

man in north-east Wiltshire, with command of the Kennet valley and the downlands between Swindon and Hungerford. Littered with the ominous and mysterious relics of the neolithic past, the downs overlook wide stretches of the surrounding country. Even in those days the hills were bare, cropped by thousands of sheep. From the window of a train from Paddington to the west, they can still look haunted and formidable on a dark afternoon at the year's end. In the 1140s the menace would have been real. John Marshal's squadrons of mercenary knights issued regularly from the defiles of those grey hills, demanding tribute and obedience from all the lowlanders who had no protector of their own.

When in 1138 Earl Robert was finally driven into revolt by King Stephen's suspicions and plots, John Marshal, along with others in the earl's reach, had a difficult decision to make. For example, Milo, sheriff of Gloucester, who had done well out of the king's attempts to ring in the earl with royalists, but he crossed unhesitatingly into Earl Robert's camp. John's actions were more ambiguous. He provisioned his castle of Marlborough and another he had acquired or built at Ludgershall, which blocked the road from Marlborough to Salisbury.[5] He must have hesitated a little too long in supporting the king, for when Mathilda landed in Sussex in September 1139, we find that the king was engaged in a siege of Marlborough, his patience with his marshal clearly at an end. When war broke out in earnest between the royalists and Angevins (that is, followers of the counts of Anjou, Lat: *Andegavia*) in the autumn of 1139 John may have learned enough caution to give his nominal support to Stephen. In practice, however he must have sat secure on the downs and done little but recruit and retain knights, and make his presence felt by those among his neighbours whom he could overawe.

Some of his neighbours had to be treated gingerly. The Salisbury family, who were later to be so important in the life of William Marshal, were richer and more powerful than John, holding Salisbury castle as hereditary castellans and sheriffs. They were at this time loyal to the king, and he had more to fear from them, as the greatest baronial house in Wiltshire, than the Earl of Gloucester. Certainly, early in 1140, the well-informed chronicler, John of Worcester, believed that John Marshal was still a supporter of the king, and that it was in the king's interest

5 The author of the *Gesta Stephani* mentions John's talent for castle building. There are signs of hasty fortifications at the family home of Hamstead Marshall at this time, later strengthened into a powerful motte and bailey castle.

that he had artfully trapped in Marlborough one Robert fitz Hubert, a rogue Flemish mercenary captain of Robert of Gloucester, who had seized Devizes. On the other hand, a royalist prelate who wrote a history of the reign, the *Gesta Stephani* (the Deeds of Stephen), was equally sure that early in 1140 John was an ally of Earl Robert. It was by no means impossible that John was playing a twofold game, nominally the king's man, but keeping up friendly relations with dangerous neighbours of the other side. Earl Robert's friendship would have protected his Somerset estates. But he needed to stay for a while within the royalist camp, while the king and his allies were still dangerous to him. Stephen's reign can provide many examples of such quicksilver loyalties.

By early 1141, however, John had definitely changed sides. It was not just that Earl Robert had captured the king in battle outside Lincoln in the February of that year. King Stephen, who never mastered the intricacies of policy and people, had attempted towards the end of 1140 to impose a Breton governor on Wiltshire. The stranger had been angrily set on and driven out by the united Wiltshire barons. Under such provocation, it would not have been hard then for John and his neighbours, the Salisburys, to go over to Mathilda, and both John and the aged Walter of Salisbury were acting as her agents in Wiltshire after the capture of the king.

Marshal family legends told of John's many adventures and enterprises in Mathilda's service. How much is legend, and how much truth is difficult to say. But at least one had substance to it. John was pictured as the hero of the siege of Winchester late in 1141; the *Histoire* tells us that he managed Mathilda's escape from the king's army, obliging her to ride astride on the retreat to Ludgershall, so she could spur on her horse, rather than keep her escort back by riding side-saddle, as a noblewoman should. When the royalists closed in he fought a desperate rearguard action near the nunnery of Wherwell.[6] He took refuge in the abbey church and his pursuers tried to flush him out by setting the church alight. But he would not leave, and threatened to kill the knight who had made it into the church with him when he suggested giving themselves up. He stayed put even when molten lead began to cascade down from the roof of the tower where he was hiding; he was splashed, burned and lost an eye. His pursuers gave him up as a charred corpse, but once they were gone he staggered out and stumbled home to Marlborough on foot, a journey of twenty-five

6 The *Gesta Stephani* informs us that Wherwell abbey had been converted by the Angevin forces into a temporary fort to protect their retreat northwards.

miles, a whole day's march. Here there is some evidence, other than tales of the hall, to suggest that the episode in Wherwell abbey might well have happened. The burning of a nunnery to flush out a rebel leader was likely to receive more than local attention. The Worcester chronicle mentions one John, a partisan of the Earl of Gloucester and Mathilda, who was chased into Wherwell abbey church after the rout; who would not come out even when the nunnery was fired around him. The chronicle does not make this John the architect of Mathilda's escape, but it gleefully mentions that she was forced to the indignity of riding astride.

Another thing that the *Histoire* mentions at this time which can be borne out from other sources, is a local war that arose between John Marshal and the new head of the rival family of Salisbury, Patrick. For us this clash has some relevance, for one of its indirect results was William Marshal himself. There is every reason to believe that the Marshals and Salisburys really did come to blows in Stephen's reign, but the exact time and nature of the conflict is impossible to establish. In its account, the *Histoire* places the affair immediately after the siege of Winchester in 1141, and calls Patrick an earl and a follower of Stephen. But Patrick was created Earl of Salisbury by Mathilda, not Stephen, and not until after 1144; while in 1143, Patrick's elder brother, William, was noted as supporting Mathilda. Setting aside the *Histoire* then, what other indications there are tell of a date in the mid-1140s.[7] In 1144 the *Gesta Stephani* depicts John Marshal at the height of his power, dominating the region, indifferent to his excommunication, exacting services from churchmen within his reach and compelling their attendance at his court.[8] The conflict that upset his hegemony would have happened after that, maybe around 1145 or 1146. It would have been in the middle of the long period of the desultory stalemate between Stephen and Mathilda that followed

7 It is by no means impossible that Patrick changed sides to support Stephen after his recovery in 1141; we have no evidence either way, and family splits are known elsewhere. But it is unlikely that whatever side he was on, Patrick could have been acting so decisively until after 1143 when his brother William died. Until then William had been the active leader of the family (Walter, their father, did not die until 1147, but age or illness would seem to have crippled him long before then and he confided the running of his estates to his sons).

8 This comment of the *Gesta* is borne out by the chronicle of Abingdon abbey, Oxon., which names John Marshal as one of its four chief oppressors in Stephen's reign: the abbey had a concentration of lands in Berkshire neighbouring John Marshal's castle of Hamstead.

Winchester. We can dismiss Stephen's part in it altogether. It was purely local power politics; perhaps sparked by a dispute over Ludgershall, a Salisbury family manor commandeered by John as a castle site. There may be some truth in the Marshal source which talks of aggressive raids by Patrick, which John resisted. Patrick's eventual success might explain the willingness of Mathilda to grace him with an earldom. Beating down John Marshal would have been the first step to securing Wiltshire. We find Earl Patrick busy in 1147 campaigning south of Salisbury against another local rival, the bishop of Winchester: was this another stage in the same campaign?

Despite his reverse, John Marshal escaped utter humiliation. In twelfth-century power politics, as in war, combat was rarely to the death; siege and stratagem were more popular. The final confrontation was avoided wherever possible. John was left with a way out. He must become Patrick's man and marry his sister, Sybil. There was a difficulty with this, for John had been married for many years to another lady, Adelina, by whom he had two sons.[9] But in those days such an obstacle could be overcome, if the lady's kin and the Church were willing. Both were apparently satisfied. The probable grounds for the separation was the convenient discovery of a relationship between Adelina and John within the prohibited degree of kinship. This was beginning to be a popular way of terminating marriages amongst the aristocracy in the mid-twelfth century. The aristocracy was so closely intermarried by then that it was not always difficult to discover that the wife you wished to set aside was, alas, a cousin anyway up to the fifth degree. Since we know that the two sons of the first marriage were not bastardized by the separation between John and Adelina, this seems to be how the matter was resolved, for such separations left the children of the annulled marriage legitimate.[10] The first marriage was, whatever the case, set aside. Adelina was honourably remarried to an obscure character, by name Stephen Gay. Her eldest son by John, Gilbert, was later to have his mother's lands, and a share of his father's.

9 Her identity is not fully established. Painter suggested that she was the heiress of the Wiltshire baron, Walter Pipard, for the control of whose marriage John was paying the king in 1130, but that cannot be assumed to be the case automatically, even though one of her sons carries the name of her putative father. For her remarriage see *Regesta Regum Anglo-Normannorum* III *1135–1154*, ed. H A Cronne and R H C Davis, Oxford 1969 no. 339.

10 *Glanvill*, ed. G D G Hall, London, 1965 68.

John Marshal settled back into his old life with his new wife after this unwelcome incident: ruling his lordship on the downs, begetting more children and watching the road that led from Windsor and Reading to the west. Sybil of Salisbury gave him four more sons: John and William before the end of Stephen's reign, then Anselm and Henry, and three daughters besides. With all going so well, and the ferocity of the civil war dying down, John Marshal then became perhaps a little over-confident. At some time in or soon before 1152 he attempted to strengthen his control of the Kennet valley approaches by advancing eastwards from his castle of Hamstead Marshall and establishing a new outpost at Newbury, where the road from Reading crossed the north-south route from Oxford to Winchester. This brought on him the full attention of King Stephen, who appeared without warning outside Newbury and began a determined siege. The constable of Newbury was low on supplies and men. Although he beat off the attempt of the royalists to storm the castle, he could not hold out long against a blockade. He was granted a day's grace to consult with John Marshal about surrender. John asked for more time, but the king would only grant this if he had in return one of the Marshal's sons as a hostage against trickery. John agreed and sent to the king his youngest son, William.

So it is that the young William Marshal first appears as an actor in these pages. In 1152 he would have been four or five years old. It is impossible to be sure because we do not know precisely when he was born. Earlier writers have favoured a date around 1143 but from my reconstruction of events, we have his parents marrying *c.*1145, an elder brother appearing *c.*1146 at the earliest, leaving William to appear no earlier than 1147, a date of birth that is indicated by other evidence (see below). This would fit in with his own memories of the events he witnessed as the *Histoire* records them. He had by then a certain physical dexterity; he could recall some of the events himself, though did not realize their significance at the time; and, as we shall see, he had the ability to play games happily with someone else.

His father had no intention of keeping his agreement with King Stephen. He reinforced his garrison at Newbury with provisions and determined men, and then refused to surrender it. The king's advisers ('criminal and craven men' as the *Histoire* has it) wanted William hung in front of the castle. When this was made known to his father, he merely observed to the messenger that he still had the hammers and anvils to make more and better sons. What are we to make of this stunning paternal indifference? Was the slaughter of an infant a matter of such indifference in the twelfth century? Plainly not. Those who advised the king to do it were called by the derisory name *losengiers*, meaning 'deceivers'. The *Histoire* makes much of the unsuspecting innocence of the young William, and the horror of the doom that was hanging over his head. The writer expects his readers to share with him the enormity of the deed that was being contemplated. What is difficult to understand is the indifference of the father, the 'true and loyal' John Marshal. It may be, as has been suggested, that twelfth-century society would have admired the hard-faced practicality of such a father, even if it did not sympathize with it. For them the guilt of the killing of the boy would lie then with the king, not indirectly with the father for his indifference. On the other hand, the king obviously expected John to keep to his agreement because he had his son. The twelfth century shared with us the idea that the emotional link between father and son was a potent security. Gerald of Wales, writing later in the century, tells the lurid story of a father who castrated himself at the demand of an enemy who held his son over the edge of a tower, rather than see him dropped to his death. John Marshal had no feelings of that strength (his 'hammers' were not expendable), but that did not make him an unnatural father, by our lights or those of his day. In the imagery of the *Histoire*, he was gambling for high stakes. That he won might indicate how well he knew his opponent. He had had two busy years at the court of King Stephen in England and Normandy between 1136 and 1138. He had been intimate with the king, the sole witness to some of his charters. His gamble with his son's life might not have been so daring if he were convinced that Stephen would never take the forfeit.

So when young William was escorted to the gallows and placed on a siege catapult, no-one took any notice in the garrison, whatever the private alarms of the Marshal household back at Marlborough or Hamstead. Even dangling the boy over the opening of a wicker shield before the castle gate had no effect on the constable: a great millstone was hurled down on the royal troops regardless. Little William, doggedly innocent, called back over his shoulder wanting to know what sort of funny game it was to be hung out of a window. After a few futile attempts to convince the garrison that the boy was to die, the king gave in. William was too young to serve around the household, but the king kept him by him; the first of many monarchs to be prey to William's confident charm, enjoying his artless and amusing prattle. William later told the story of how the king condescended to play a game of 'knights' with him in his flower-strewn pavilion, a sort of play tournament with straw men.

It is difficult to know when William was reunited with his family. Newbury castle eventually fell to the king, who moved on to the more important Angevin stronghold of Wallingford. It was his determined assault on Wallingford that led to the final confrontation between royalist and Angevin in England. Duke Henry of Normandy, Mathilda's son, arrived in England at the urgent pleas of his party. One of those who joined his army in the West Country was John Marshal. The barons wanted peace and, after prolonged negotiations, Stephen recognized Henry as his heir in November 1153. Both pledged to return the landed situation to what it had been when Henry I died. It may not have been until then that William returned to his mother, for the *Histoire* talks of a long stay with the king and his release after a general peace was negotiated in the kingdom, in which all grudges were forgotten and men were satisfied with what had always been theirs.

William made another début in the two years immediately after Stephen died and Henry II succeeded in 1154. This was his first appearance in a charter. In or soon before 1156 his father parted with the Somerset manor of Nettlecombe to Hugh de Ralegh. The price was the service of one knight, a horse, two dogs and eighty marks in cash (£53 6s. 8d.). Hugh had also written into the charter the consent of John's wife and his sons, amongst them William, now perhaps nine years old. His half-brothers, Gilbert and Walter, and his full brother John had payments of gold and horses for their consent, William nothing.[11] He was still youngest and least, and we know from what happened later that his father did not plan that he would have a share of the family's lands after he died.

Perhaps in 1156 John's affairs were already taking a downward turn, which is why he was willing to sell off Nettlecombe. Henry II kept him with him in his first tour of his kingdom as king, in 1155 and 1156, but he is not found thereafter at court and in 1158, when Henry II was preparing to leave for France, John lost Marlborough castle. He did not lose everything. He kept his exemption from tax, his marshalship, the hundred of Kinwardstone and the royal

11 *Collectanea Topographica et Genealogica* II London, 1835 163–4. The grant was confirmed by Henry II in 1156 at Bridgenorth.

manors of Cherhill and Wexcombe, but the abrupt resumption of Marlborough shows that the king regarded him, as he regarded many others of the older generation of Angevin supporters, as a man not worth courting, and possibly dangerous. In 1163, a chronicler tells us that John came under a black cloud of the king's anger. He had been dabbling in a current aristocratic craze, attempting to make sense of the fictitious prophecies of Merlin which were then the subject of much attention. John rashly let it be known that according to Merlin, Henry II would not return again to England after he left for his campaign against Toulouse in 1158; the loss of Marlborough obviously rankled.[12] Henry returned in 1163, and John's speculation looked then very much like treason. John only recovered the king's favour by acting as his inglorious stooge in the persecution of Becket in 1164.[13]

It was in these fading years, as John Marshal grew older and the court hostile, that some provision was made for young William. The *Histoire* claims that at some time, probably early in the 1160s John contacted his 'cousin german' William de Tancarville, the Chamberlain of Normandy (often known as 'the chamberlain of Tancarville'), and arranged that William should cross to Normandy to be schooled in the Tancarville household as a *gentil home* (a man of family).[14] There is no other evidence that John Marshal and the Tancarvilles were related, and it may well be that the *Histoire* got it wrong. There *is* evidence that the relationship was in fact between the Salisbury family and the Tancarvilles. So it might well be that William's fostering in Normandy was made possible by his mother's family, even if the suggestion came from his father.[15] William was already adolescent when he took leave of his

12 Ralph de Diceto, *Ymagines Historiarum* in *The Historical Works of Master Ralph de Diceto* ed. W Stubbs (2 vols) Rolls Series 1876 I 308.

13 For John Marshal's involvement in the Becket affair, see M Cheney, 'The Litigation between John Marshal and Archbishop Thomas Becket in 1164: A Pointer to the Origin of Novel Disseisin?' in *Law and Social Change in British History* ed. J A Guy and H G Beale Royal Historical Society London, 1984 9–26. The deduction about John's opportunism in the affair is mine, not Mrs Cheney's, and seems to follow from John's problems in 1163.

14 It is worth mentioning that William Marshal was not the only cousin to whom William de Tancarville gave a helping hand. He provided the marriage portion by which his cousin Beatrice could marry a local knight in the Pays de Caux, *Chartes du Prieuré de Longueville*, ed. P le Cacheux S.H.N. 1934 50.

15 Lands and houses in Rogerville and Rames (Seine-Maritime, canton St-Romain-de-Colbosc) were held by Edward of Salisbury, Earl Patrick's

weeping mother, sisters and brothers. By then he was tall enough to ride a horse. Straight-grown, brown-haired and – if the *Histoire* is to be believed – handsome, he rode off to Tancarville attended (as was customary) by another young aspirant (unnamed) who was to be a companion and friend, there was also a serving man. When he returned his mother would be a widow, and his two older half-brothers would be dead. The marshal would then be his brother, John, and the elder marshal would be lying in a tomb in Bradenstoke priory.

We do not know if William Marshal loved his father; it is rare indeed that the conventional family piety of the Middle Ages can be penetrated. Later he made pious grants for his parents' souls, but so did others who we know loathed their father, such as the sons of Henry II. The chief purpose of the father in the medieval aristocracy was not to be loved, but to protect and provide, to school and to dominate. John Marshal was a formidable model for his son: astute, physically powerful, an easy companion in the royal chambers, and a cool warrior in the field. In his days as castellan of Marlborough he was no coarse bandit. He was more of a baron than a robber. He played the great game of politics with talent and perception, rising rather than falling amongst the factions of civil war. Giving ground when defiance would be quixotic, he still ended up on the winning side. So far as his limited resources allowed, he was a generous patron of the church: a benefactor of abbeys and priories, particularly Bradenstoke priory, the Salisbury family foundation and mausoleum in Wiltshire, where he was buried himself. He shared the aristocratic fascination of his day with the Knights Templar, to whom he devoted his manor of Rockley in Wiltshire when William was a boy of nine or ten. We may look to him for the beginnings of

grandfather, of the honor of Tancarville in the early part of the reign of Henry I, J le Maho 'L'apparition des seigneuries châtelaines dans le Grand-Caux à l'époque ducale' *Archéologie Mediévale* VI 1977 21. Edward of Salisbury appears in two charters of William (I) de Tancarville, one the foundation charter of the abbey of St-Georges-de-Boscherville. Edward was a benefactor to the abbey in Normandy. This appearance of a Salisbury–Tancarville link may well bespeak a marriage between the families, perhaps between Edward and a daughter, sister or aunt of William (I) de Tancarville. The Salisbury lands in Normandy would then be the girl's marriage portion. William (I) de Tancarville was very active in England in the reign of Henry I, with lands in Edward's Wiltshire, and also in Gloucestershire and Rutland, with a Marcher lordship in Gwent. For these see *Monasticon Anglicanum* VI pt 2 1066–67; *Llandaff Episcopal Acta, 1140–1287*, ed. D Crouch, South Wales Record Society V, 1988 no. 28.

William's fruitful acquaintance with the crusading orders. John Marshal was the first great exemplar of lordship in his son's life, and even at the distance of centuries we will see, in his strengths and weaknesses, how the son drew himself in some aspects from the pattern of his father.

. . .

## WILLIAM DE TANCARVILLE: THE 'GOOD MASTER'

At the age of thirteen or fourteen William Marshal came to Normandy and entered a new world, even though Normandy was the land of his fathers. William had known only England, and it may be that for him, as for other Anglo-Norman noblemen, English was the language of his mother's chamber. But William must also have been taught French, or he would never have been able to talk to King Stephen during his time as hostage. We can only guess at the homesickness and disorientation that he would have experienced: perhaps akin to what the historian Orderic Vitalis, when an old monk and scholar in the 1140s, recorded that he felt when he left his birthplace of Shrewsbury to enter the Norman monastery of St-Evroult as a novice in the days of King William Rufus.

William's biographer has little to tell us of the years spent in the Tancarville household. William must have been uncommunicative on the subject. All that we know is one of those self-deprecatory stories which must stem from the man himself, how all he was known for at that time was sleeping, eating and drinking a lot. 'Scoff-food' (*gaste-viande*) was his nickname in the Tancarville household, where it was alleged he slept when there was nothing to eat. The Chamberlain was said to have predicted great things for him nonetheless. One thing we can be sure that he received in those years was first-class military training. The Chamberlain of Tancarville was known throughout Europe as one of the grander patrons of knighthood. The size of his military retinue was famous, or notorious. To Henry II's clerk, Walter Map, around 1180, the chamberlain was 'a man of noble race, a remarkable soldier, manly . . . he is the father of knights'; it was his custom to ride everywhere with a great retinue of them.[16] The Chamberlain was a man of ancient lineage (as Normans went),

16 Walter Map *De Nugis Curialium* ed. M R James revised edn Oxford 1983 488.

wide possessions, and great generosity. He held three castles: the powerful fortress of Tancarville with the square, stone keep his grandfather had built, rising from a promontory on the north bank of the estuary of the Seine; Hallebosc, or Albosc, a lesser stronghold some seventeen kilometres inland to the north; and Mézidon in Central Normandy, above the valley of the Dives. His baronies of Tancarville and Hallebosc made up most of the Pays de Caux between Le Havre and Lillebonne.[17] Even William Marshal's uncle, the Earl of Salisbury, could not command such resources. William's placing in the Chamberlain's household was for him a great thing, and whichever side of his family placed him there, they found for him the best training available both in soldierly skill and courtly graces. The Chamberlain was then in the prime of life, not yet tainted with the rebellion that soured his later career, an ideal knightly patron.

William may have learned the skills of the hunt in the forest of Tancarville, hawking in the marshes of the Seine estuary, the discipline of arms in the great bailey of the castle, and to sing (once his voice allowed) in the chambers of his lord's wife. These were things that every young aristocrat must know.[18] One thing we can be fairly sure that he did not learn was his letters. Literacy (that is, the ability to read Latin) began to be seen as a desirable part of a young baron's education in the reign of Henry I. William's father's generation contained many paragons of educated laity: Earl Robert of Gloucester for one. John Marshal himself had some interests wider than warfare, for he was said to have had some acquaintance with the writings of Geoffrey of Monmouth or one of his imitators. While William was in the Tancarville household the justiciar of England was Robert, Earl of Leicester, a man who wrote letters on philosophy to learned Cistercian abbots, read treatises on astronomy, and consulted bishops on the problems rich men might encounter entering heaven. A little later, the seneschal of Normandy was William fitz Ralph, famous for

17 For the baronies of the Tancarville family in Normandy see le Maho 19–23; for Mézidon, *Complete Peerage* x appendix F 50–1. The Tancarville lands in Normandy answered for ten knights to the duke in 1172, with 94¾ knights' service at the lord's own disposal, F M Powicke *The Loss of Normandy, 1189–1204* Manchester 1913 353.

18 Hawking, hunting and the discipline of arms were what was taught in Henry II's household late in the 1150s to an Italian youth sent by Pope Adrian IV to England for a knightly education, see *The Letters of Arnulf of Lisieux* ed. F Barlow Camden Society 3rd ser LXI 1939 18–20.

personally examining charters in law cases in his court at Caen. On one occasion he detected a forgery produced before him, to the horror of the guilty party. But different virtues were courted at Tancarville. William Marshal's biography betrays no evidence that he ever aspired to anything more than physical and military proficiency. He was, however, well acquainted already with clerks and chaplains from a very early age: his father employed at least two, and his youngest brother Henry was destined for the Church. His entire career shows an awareness of the value of literacy and accounting skills, but he employed those who had them, he did not have them himself. He was being fitted out for a career as a professional soldier, and the omission is understandable. We will see later that he was quick to take into his service clerks of his own once he had the need for them; before then he would borrow his master's. His accomplishments in Latin were probably no more than the basics required of a layman: the Lord's Prayer, the Ave Maria, and the creed, which he would have learned, as like as not, from his mother or the household chaplains, or both. Biblical stories and tales of saints, particularly warrior saints, would have been stored in his memory from an early age as would have been some family history. French (Romance) literature was a rising interest of his generation. Here he would have gained acquaintance with, and perhaps memorized, a whole range of gestes and lesser romances: epic tales of Normandy and Britain's past, of Charlemagne, Roland and the Twelve Peers, and the legendary deeds of the Roman emperors. With them he would have taken in a mass of ideas that are best summarized as 'chivalry', the developing aristocratic code of behaviour.

One other necessary skill for survival had to be acquired in the Tancarville household: courtliness. This had as much to do with self-preservation as mastering his sword and lance. The lord of Tancarville was surrounded by a great retinue of knights, squires and servants, greater and lesser. Even a humble squire might find himself the object of envy and plot. The *Histoire* is full of the doings of the Marshal's detractors, who cropped up everywhere he went to discredit him with his current master. This persecution was no mere literary convention to explain the rough patches in his career. At Tancarville his kinship with the lord, and the lord's evident satisfaction in the boy's looks, humour and address, brought on him the envy of others who were competing for the rewards of their master's favour. Some just may not have liked him: an engaging personality and good looks can produce in some people a powerful aversion, rooted in self-hatred. The biography says that William coped with these rivals in the approved manner of courtly heroes: enduring backbiting in silence, behaving with modesty, and confounding envy by great deeds. This may well be so, his line in self-deprecation is a very good example of this form of defence. He was filing down the teeth of persecution by jokes against himself – a ploy which is still to be found alive and well in the playgrounds of the schools of England, as every teacher knows.[19] He was sent to Tancarville because 'much did he need a good master to educate him'.[20] William de Tancarville did his duty by him. In his over-populated retinue William learned, as no doubt his father had intended, all that was necessary for a household knight to know. Not merely the physical skills, but some of the political ones too.

William's father died some time in 1165, before September. In his testament he made no known provision for William. His lands were divided between his two surviving eldest sons: Gilbert and John. Gilbert himself died only months after his father, leaving all the Marshal inheritance in the hands of the younger John. William did not return for the obsequies of his father and half-brother, as far as we know. Indeed the *Histoire* has nothing to say on his father's death. Even more strangely, it places the deaths of both his half-brothers, Gilbert and Walter, in their parents' lifetime, and betrays no knowledge of the family succession arrangements. Such things were obviously not talked about amongst the later Marshals, and may have been forgotten. And if there were a reason for this it must be because these important events in England touched not at all on young William in Normandy, where his career was not dependent on his brothers but on his relations with the Chamberlain, his master.

In 1166, when his brother John was taking on the headship of his family and government of their lands, William was fast approaching the end of his squirehood. At some time in 1167, perhaps with a batch of companions, he was knighted by William de Tancarville. William's knighting was not the great festival it would have been if he had been a young baron. William de Tancarville's own knighting in Stephen's reign had been a solemn and lavish occasion, with a week of festivities ending in his

19 On the subject of courtliness in aristocratic education, see C S Jaeger *The Origins of Courtliness* Philadelphia 1985 211ff, 257–68.

20 *Histoire* l. 736.

reception with a great crowd of kinsmen and knights by the abbot of the family monastery of St-Georges-de-Boscherville in solemn procession at the abbey door; he was received as the abbey's protector, and offered his sword on the high altar, which he and his friends redeemed by great gifts.[21] William had to be satisfied with much less. The ceremony was carried out when he was twenty-years-old after perhaps as many as six years in the Tancarville household.[22] It was carried out when the chamberlain was on campaign on Normandy's northern border, in garrison at Neufchâtel-en-Bray. The ceremony is simply, perhaps shamefacedly, described by the *Histoire*. In his new cloak, William had a sword girded to his side by his master, and received a ritual blow on his shoulder – the dubbing. There may have been a vigil, a bath, and a subsequent mass and feast, all occasional features of the ritual of becoming a knight, but we hear nothing of them. So he entered into what was already being described in his time as the 'order' of knighthood with very little fuss, considering how great an ornament to it he was to become.

21 This information can be reconstructed from a charter in the Archives départementales de la Seine-Maritime, 13 H 15, printed in A. Deville *Essai historique et descriptif sur . . . l'abbaye de St-Georges-de-Boscherville* Rouen 1827, 73–6.

22 The question of the Marshal's age at his knighting is difficult to resolve because of the obscurity of the relevant passage in the *Histoire*, which says (ll. 772–3) *Mès l'om dist que vint anz enters/Fu il ben eskuers* that is 'It is said that he was twenty whole years a fine esquire'. If 'esquire' refers to his training at Tancarville then this is obvious nonsense. Paul Meyer, the first editor of the text thought *vint* was a misreading for *huit* (eight), but since he placed the knighting incorrectly in 1173 and thought that William had been born in 1143, this contorted the chronology unbearably, and Meyer confessed that he was confused by the text here. If, however, we take it to refer to William's age, applying 'squirehood' to the whole passage of his life before his knighting, then the reference does make at least chronological sense.

*Chapter 2*

# THE HOUSEHOLD KNIGHT

The twelfth century was the first medieval century to know the sorry plight of distressed gentlefolk. Western society had, by then, discovered standards of display which the man of blood had to live up to, or fall in dignity. When William Marshal had become a knight these standards of style, dress and display were not as elaborate as they were to become in his later days,[1] but they still required that he have three horses (a sumpter for his baggage, a palfrey for riding about, and a big-boned war-horse for the tournament and battle); the long, rich cloak of a gentleman; and the ironmongery of war (a hauberk and hood of mail, mail and plate leggings and a helmet). William Marshal was in the tidal reaches of aristocracy, a younger son with no resources other than his wits. He knew how a man of good family should live, eat, dress and spend, but did not have the means to keep up with his more fortunate fellows. In his time there was a social beach to be swept down by the ebb tide of poverty. He might well have known the sad story of Hugh Poer, whom his father would have met at Stephen's court. He too was the younger son of a baron, but had been raised briefly to the earldom of Bedford, then tumbled to common knight and total obscurity in a few years.

William was a man with a dignity to support, and for such a man his dignity was a great burden. He was one of the Honourable Georges and Honourable Johns of his day. Since his father had not been inclined to reserve him a share of his lands, his options were limited. If he had not gone on to seek his fortune he had only one

1 The *Histoire* notices this elaboration of expectations between the 1160s and the 1220s when it describes William leaving his family for France with no more than a friend and a manservant: 'in those days people were not so proud; the son of a king rode out with a cloak rolled up behind him, with but a squire, who did not expect a pack-horse', *Histoire* ll. 763–8.

other resort: his family home. He would have had to live on in his brother's hall, to grow old, unmarried, in hopes of something turning up, but at least keeping up appearances in the glow of the nearness to a great relation. On occasion the sources allow us glimpses of such men. Geoffrey du Neubourg, the fourth son of Earl Henry of Warwick, was, like William Marshal, brought up in Normandy by a relation, this time an adult brother. In Stephen's reign he returned to England to live off his eldest brother, Earl Roger of Warwick. When Roger died in 1153, Geoffrey 'the earl's uncle' lived on at Warwick in his nephew's household, occupying a place in his charter witness lists. Geoffrey was still there in the 1170s, when William Marshal was making his way in the world, and by then was in his sixties. He never married nor had land. He must have had some money from the earl, or the family would have been embarrassed by his poverty. It may even be that he had a high old time, like one of P.G. Wodehouse's drones, but we do not know. His sort of existence does not sound very attractive. Yet there were enough of these aristocratic supernumeraries around in William Marshal's day to acquire a group name in English law-books; they were the 'hearth sons'.

William Marshal did not choose to seek a living from his brother, John, in 1167. Why he did not do so is something of a puzzle. It may be that some personal difference was responsible for this, or at least a determination that he could do better. On the other hand, there is some evidence that his brother could not have done much for him immediately after their father's death, even if he had wanted to. John Marshal was under age when the elder John died, and spent a period of as much as a year in royal wardship, his lands in the custody of the rapacious royal officer, Alan de Neuville.[2] But by 1167 John must have been free and of full age, and William now had some claim on his brother. He must have known that by then he was the heir to John's lands and office, at least until John produced legitimate children. But this did not persuade him to go home, as others we know of did in his circumstances. There was therefore only one course open to him, his family had given him but one possible profession, arms, and he had to pursue it.

Fighting had been a way of life for a man for many centuries before William's time. What was new in the twelfth century was the nature the calling had assumed. Armed bands had surrounded

2 We know of this from the recollection of a Wiltshire jury of 1201, *Curia Regis Rolls* I 424.

great men since the Late Empire, but in the mid-twelfth century in Western Europe such bands had been refined into the *mesnie* (the word comes from that Latin word *mansio*, meaning household, but the usual Latin equivalent in the twelfth century was *familia*), the military household. Kings and great barons recruited men of mixed backgrounds into their service, but all were trained and disciplined to the same degree. They were uniformly equipped at their lord's expense in armour and trappings, bearing his device or colours. The earliest such unit of which we get a close glimpse was the household guard of King Henry I of England. He employed several hundreds of horsemen, formidably skilled and organized. Some were landed men with a penchant for war; others were royal bastards; some were younger sons or heirs in search of profit, glamour and opportunity; others again were men of obscure birth with no other resource than their sword and strong arm.[3] It is certain that Henry I's *mesnie* was not the first such band, it had its predecessors under earlier Norman kings and dukes, but it is unlikely that they would have been as well organised as his. In his day the *mesnie* was a separate department of the royal household, under its constables and marshals, each soldier receiving pay. Such *mesnies*, whether in the service of the King of England or of France, or of the lesser French princes, were bodies of soldiers unique in Western Europe since the collapse of the Late Imperial army. Indeed contemporaries compared the royal *mesnie* favourably with Caesar's legionaries' adopting a certain self-satisfaction. The *mesnie* had high morale, and cultivated specialized military skills, but above and beyond this, it had its own military rituals and respected a code of behaviour that was growing more and more elaborate. Later it was to become known as chivalry (literally 'what the horse soldiers did').[4] By William Marshal's day it was by living like the horse soldiers did that set a *gentil homme* apart from any other free man. It is by his biography that we are able in part to trace the growth of this aristocratic code.

3 M M Chibnall 'Mercenaries and the *familia regis* under Henry I' *History* LXII 1977 15–23.

4 Such a meaning is evoked by the *Histoire*'s use of the word *chevalerie*, as when the royal garrison at Winchester in 1141 rode out daily 'for to do *chevalerie*' (*Histoire* ll. 174–8): meaning manly deeds of horsemanship and arms.

. . .

## THE DEVICE OF TANCARVILLE

A settled position in someone's *mesnie* was what William Marshal was looking for in 1167. In many ways he was in the same position as a contemporary graduate after the close of the last examination booklet. He was free, but free to starve as much as prosper, at the mercy of the job market. There were thin pickings for young knights, and what was to be had depended on luck and notice. Failure meant a return to kick his heels in the family home, whether he was welcome or not. At this point in his life William would have been ticking off in his mind the possible openings his network of kinship offered him. The wider circle of kinship did not play much of an active part in twelfth-century society. Family affections, then as now, embraced little more than the nuclear family we acknowledge today: uncles, aunts, perhaps first cousins, were the remotest relations a man was expected to cherish. However, when a man increased in wealth and needed followers, it seems to have been the general rule to look to kinsfolk. As Abbot Samson of Bury St Edmunds discovered, alleged kinsfolk were not shy of waylaying him on his return from his blessing as abbot, seeking places. Samson resisted their pleas, but certainly later took on those of his kin who he thought had the talent to be of use to him. Kin were not necessarily trustworthy, or even grateful, but medieval society valued blood, and believed it strengthened the link between lord and man, patron and client.[5]

In 1167 William Marshal had hopes of a postgraduate career in the Tancarville household, but for reasons that are unclear this was ultimately to be denied him. However, to begin with, luck was with him. In 1167 the rivalry between Henry II of England and Louis VII of France brought him some short-term employment in the form of a small border war. If we take up Sir Richard Southern's image of north-west Europe as a French cultural empire, then it was an empire with two rulers. First and foremost was Louis, in theory. He was not a king of great capacities; his attainments were as modest as his resources. But if he lacked vision, he did not lack the single-minded doggedness that is sometimes almost as good. He also had a knack of making important friends and engaging men's affections. He was the

5 Raymond le Gros, an Anglo-Welsh settler in Ireland, was escorted by a *mesnie* of knights in 1176 whose special feature was that all its members were his kinsfolk, a point that seems to contemporaries to have enhanced its military usefulness.

underdog, and as a result he had the applause of the disinterested. On the other hand, Henry was the shogun of the cultural empire. He had the cunning and intellect that Louis lacked, an abundance of ruthlessness and ambition. He also had the edge in territory and wealth. Louis, however, was his overlord in France, and had the moral high ground. He could sit on his dignity and know he had the tactical advantage in any confrontation.

In 1167 Louis and Henry came to blows for the first time for over five years. The years when William had been a squire in the Tancarville household had been years of peace. But trouble in the Auvergne and Louis's support for the exiled Thomas Becket, under his protection at the abbey of Pontigny, led to conflict. If William had thought about it, he could have reflected that his father had played a part in putting Becket where he was, a banner at the head of Louis's secular ambitions.

The King of France could only attack Henry II on one side of Normandy, down the Seine valley from Paris, or in the lands on either side of it, the Vexin to the north or the Méresais to the south. It was a broad front, but by the mid-twelfth century was well screened with castles. Another road into Normandy was on the north-east frontier, facing Flanders and Picardy. Here the king had to attack by proxy, for Flanders and Picardy were dominated by another great man at this time, a man who played no small part in William Marshal's career, Count Philip of Flanders. His influence spread much further than Flanders, across northern France, south of the Somme, to the very borders of the king's domain around Paris. What was more, his brother Matthew was lord of the rich maritime county of Boulogne. These two great men, along with a lesser auxiliary, the Count of Ponthieu on the Norman border, allied with King Louis in 1167. They camped on the borders of Normandy with a large army, threatening to break across it anywhere along its fifty kilometres length. A Norman force was based at Neufchâtel-en-Bray deep within the frontier to counter any incursion. The Norman marcher lord, the Count of Eu, along with the Earl of Essex, the Constable of Normandy, and William de Tancarville led the defending army. It was in camp with this force, in the early stages of the campaign, that William Marshal was knighted.

Neufchâtel was one of an inner line of fortresses along the river Béthune, built to defend the northern approaches to the Norman capital, Rouen. It was some twenty-five kilometres from the Norman border to north and east. As such it was a good base to await an expected onset, if its direction was uncertain. The way that the *Histoire* and the historian, Gervase of Canterbury, describe the ensuing campaign, it would seem that the thrust when it came still took the Normans off balance. The invaders reached Neufchâtel with almost no warning. The border counties of Eu and Aumale were already lost before the Chamberlain and his colleagues were aware of their danger. Gervase tells us that the county of Eu was looted and burned by the Flemings. This probably means that the enemy entered Normandy across the river Bresle, between Eu and Blangy and spread out in several parties to waste and pillage. It would have been the main column, commanded by Count Matthew of Boulogne, that surprised the Normans at Neufchâtel.

The Normans were in total disarray when news reached them of the imminent descent of the Flemings. The Count of Eu wandered about, unarmed, his imagination undoubtedly warning him what was happening to his estates and revenues. We know from other sources that he was impoverished by the pillaging of his county, and later had to raise money to pay the knights and serjeants he enlisted for the campaign by confiscating the treasure of his abbey of Le Tréport.[6] Other Normans rode off in an undisciplined attempt to meet the enemy before they forced a passage into the town. The young Earl of Essex and a few men had the presence of mind to head for the bridge outside what seems to have been the town's west gate. Here the road ran out over a ditch into a faubourg, or suburb, then called the Chaussée d'Eu (nowadays perhaps, the area called St-Vincent). The Chamberlain of Tancarville was not so headlong in the crisis. He stumped about the castle dragooning together a company of his men, including William. Together they rode down to the bridge. The excitement of the day carried William away. He forgot himself, and was on the point of passing his master when the Chamberlain halted him with the jovial cry of: 'William, get back! Don't be hasty! Let the knights get through!' The putdown seems to have been one of the Marshal's favourite stories in later life. But, characteristically, he did not fail to add that despite the rebuke he let a few of his elders get by, and then spurred on his horse and got near the front again.

6 *Cartulaire de l'abbaye de St-Michel du Tréport*, ed. P Laffleur de Kermaingant (Paris, 1880), 63–4. The count took two rich gospel books, two thuribles, a gilded silver chalice and over two dozen vestments, and pawned them. On his death-bed, a few years later, he regretted his action and compensated for it by an annual rent.

At the bridge, the Chamberlain's company joined up with the Earl of Essex and almost immediately encountered mounted Flemings pouring into the suburbs of Neufchâtel. The leading ranks of each side spurred into a charge in the street of the Chaussée. William's lance was broken by the shock of the meeting of the hemmed-in ranks, but he laid about with his sword to some good effect. Despite the Normans' efforts they were pushed back by the press of the enemy to the bridge. A general mêlée developed in the crush before the bridge as Count Matthew committed new forces to break into the town. For a while the struggle swayed about as the Normans, helped by the townsfolk, pushed back in their turn. At some point William's luck ran out. A party of Flemish foot soldiers got hold of an iron hook from the roadside – a fire precaution to pull down burning thatch from the surrounding houses. They used it to catch William on his shoulder and struggled to pull him down and take him. He pulled free, but in the meantime his horse was wounded to its death. Fortunately, the battle had swept by and the Flemish forces were withdrawn, Count Matthew perhaps unwilling to prolong the skirmish into a risky general action, once he had lost the advantage of surprise.

As a first taste of the excitement of battle, William's experience that day might have been worse. For what it is worth, the *Histoire* tells us that Normans, captured French and Flemish, and townspeople alike were all agreed that he had distinguished himself. An idea corresponding to our 'man of the match' was known then and was the culmination of every tournament. William might have done better, however, had he remembered what the more experienced knights knew. War in the twelfth century was not fought wholly for honour. Profit was there to be made – and the men who must make it were precisely those in William Marshal's position: the household knights with no other resource. His failure to convert his valour into more tangible benefits was a sad failing in one in his position. His elders were not slow to remind him of this.

The evening was given over to a celebration of the sort familiar to anyone who has been in the bar of a rugby club after a home win; an evening of drink, loud laughter, reminiscence and practical joking of a peculiarly unsubtle sort. The Earl of Essex called down to William.

> 'Here Marshal! I'd like a gift for love of you and reward'.
> 'Willingly! What?'

> 'Give me a crupper, or at least an old collar'

The request for a gift of assorted items of saddlery rather puzzled William, for, as he said, he had never owned such things in his life, but used his lord's.

> 'Oh? But Marshal, what are you saying? You had forty or sixty of them – yet you refuse me so small a thing!'.[7]

There was a general belly laugh around the hall at William's expense. It penetrated the elation and exhaustion of the day, and entered his store of instructive stories with which he regaled his eventual biographers, when they were squires needing instruction, no doubt. The point of the earl's joke was that William had failed to profit by his chances. His calling was now arms, its fees were the ransoms and equipment of the men he defeated. He had acted the hero, and although his efforts were ungrudgingly respected, his lack of realism – given his circumstances – was not.

In November 1167 peace was made between the two kings. Peace was a problem for a man in the position of the young William Marshal. It was especially unwelcome in 1167 for the skirmish at Neufchâtel had lost him his expensive war-horse, which left him as much a knight as an admiral would be without a fleet. The Chamberlain, on his return home, decided to economize on his retinue. He let it be known that those of his knights who wished to go off in search of fortune would have free licence from him. This was tantamount to giving notice to such knights as he did not particularly pick out, to quit his hall. William Marshal was meant to go too, but his cousinship to the Chamberlain made an outright command to leave difficult, but hints were dropped. No support was given to him to replace his horse. He had to sell the new cloak he had for his knighting. With the twenty-two shillings this raised William bought a passable mount, a rouncy, a squire's horse, but with no money for a pack-horse, the new war-horse had to double as the transport for his armour and baggage, while he rode his palfrey. While his fortunes were still undecided, his luck resurfaced. News reached Tancarville of a tournament in Maine. The Chamberlain decided to participate and as a result William's fortunes took a turn for the better. The Chamberlain was now willing to retain him for the occasion, and as a result new

7 *Histoire* ll. 1145–57.

equipment was forthcoming, and ironically and belatedly a war-horse. But the Chamberlain was a whimsical man, and he did not want William Marshal to feel too convinced of his continuing goodwill. He deliberately left him out when the horses were given out to the other knights. When William reminded him of his promise, a horse was forthcoming. It was a fine horse, but wild. We are told that William needed all his skill to break in his Bucephalus.

The tournament was a particular success for William. His performance was once again remarked upon; more important, he made three captures, one an important courtier of the King of Scotland. Ransoms of horses and money gave him some independence, and the Chamberlain was happy to let him go off immediately to a second tournament a few days' ride away. Again, William distinguished himself. On his return to Normandy he went back to Tancarville – for he still wore the colours and device of the Chamberlain. Here he got leave to cross the Channel and return to England. The Chamberlain willingly bid him farewell, with an amiable jibe that he should not stay too long there. England (despite the military tumult of Stephen's reign) had acquired, or maybe retained, a reputation as a dull place for knights fond of active exercise. Henry II did not allow tournaments there, and those barons and knights who had a taste for the sport had to cross to the Continent. That the English were more fond of drinking and boasting than of fighting was a routine insult thrown by the Norman French at their English cousins. Twelfth-century English writers took great exception to it. Like the well-established contemporary joke that Englishmen secretly had tails hidden about them, it was one of those tedious pleasantries which marked a growing divergence in feeling between the English and Norman components of Henry II's realm. This emotional separation between peoples is a theme that surfaces again and again in the Marshal's biography.

. . .

## PATRICK, EARL OF SALISBURY

We are told that William went to England to see his family, from whom he had been separated now for five years and more. But it was one particular member of his family that he really wanted to meet, and the *Histoire* does not disguise it. He had cast off from the insecure refuge of Tancarville, hoping to find a safe harbour in

England. His uncle, Earl Patrick of Salisbury, as one of his most potent relatives, was the first port of call. He found the Earl at Salisbury late in 1167, or early in 1168, newly returned from the king's side. A campaign was being planned to subdue the rebellious Lusignan family in Poitou, one of Henry II's most troublesome provinces, and Earl Patrick was to be one of the leaders of the expedition. With a campaign in the offing, the earl readily found his courtly and confident young nephew a place in his *mesnie*. William was very soon recrossing the Channel with his uncle. The *Histoire* fails to tell us whether he found the time to see the rest of his family while he was in England.

So William embarked optimistically on his second campaign in a year, under a new banner. Just after Easter 1168, his uncle was given the task of assisting Queen Eleanor to govern Poitou. It does not seem that he had long to discover the difficulties of his position. Accounts differ as to the precise circumstances of what happened. The Angevin court historian, Roger of Howden, says that the earl was returning from a pilgrimage to Santiago de Compostella in Spain, presumably before assuming his responsibilities. This snippet may be just a device to underline the vileness of the earl's murder: the brutal assassination of a pilgrim. The *Histoire*'s more detailed account has the earl escorting the queen peacefully between castles. Both accounts, however, are clear that a party of Poitevins led by the Lusignan brothers, Geoffrey and Guy, ambushed the earl's party. When the ambush erupted around them, Earl Patrick's *mesnie* grappled for their hauberks, helmets and arms. The queen was hustled off to the protection of a nearby castle, perhaps captured Lusignan itself. The defenceless earl, wheeling about, was less lucky, a passing Poitevin knight (the Lusignans always denied it was at their orders) struck him down from behind; he died under his nephew's eyes. In a rage of anger and horror, the Young Marshal, forgetting his helmet, rode into the Poitevins, hacking at the murderers. He did not last long, for his horse was cut down and he was surrounded. He set his back to a hedgerow, and stood the Poitevins off 'like a wild boar amongst the dogs', mouthing threats and insults. Soon enough a knight got behind the hedge and struck at him through the foliage, slashing into his thigh. Felled, he was taken as a knight worth ransoming and bundled off, bleeding heavily, tied on to a mare. His dead uncle too, meanwhile, was being carried off by such of his men as survived. The corpse was laid to rest at the church of St Hilary of Poitiers, a rather more remote tomb than the Wiltshire priory of

Bradenstoke that was the mausoleum of his and the Marshal's families, where no doubt he had intended to lie one day.

William's period of captivity, the only such episode in his life, may not have lasted more than a few months, but it was not made comfortable for him. His captors carried him around with them like an awkward bundle. His wound was not treated: they wanted him to pay up his ransom and go home, though who it was they thought would pay is difficult to say. This was not the age of 'chivalry', as it later came to be. William's Poitevin hosts were desperate and dispossessed men; William was a hostage and a source of profit, not a fellow-knight in difficulties.

In the end he was freed by a means that must have surprised even him. Somehow he had come to the attention of Queen Eleanor, and whether it was a whim, or whether she had decided that William was one of the best bargains on offer in the military market-place, or whether she had admired his reckless attempt to avenge his stricken uncle, she decided to buy him free. Once pledges had been given acceptable to both parties, William was freed into her hands, and was retained in her own household. So at the age of but twenty-one, he entered the golden circle of royalty he had first glimpsed as a small boy, and had never forgotten. The author of the *Histoire* was well aware of the dramatic jolt this gave William's fortunes. He chooses this point in his narration to break into a paean of anticipated triumph: deeds of prowess, wealth and the respect and confidence of kings and princes.

What was it about William Marshal that won him so much, so easily? He was well-connected, so much is true. The Earl of Salisbury was an uncle, the Chamberlain of Tancarville and the Count of Perche close cousins (see Fig.2). His father and grandfather had been in office at the court of England for half a century. But success needed to be founded on more than the web of kinship. He had luck in an abundance that would have ensured him a marshal's baton from Napoleon. But it was the man himself that counted. He was no deep thinker, and as far as we can tell his educational level was below the ideal for an aristocrat of his day. What he did have was a practical intelligence, and the assurance to make quick, confident decisions. His attempts at sophistry, where the *Histoire* preserves them, are little more than stubborn and shallow attempts to justify his own self-interest. The mental assurance was complemented by physical co-ordination and confidence. He was undoubtedly a big, healthy and prepossessing man, a fine athlete and horseman. This mixture of quick wit and hand made him as perfect a warrior as he was to become in time a commander. The crown of his fortune was that he had an open face, a ready humour and an underlying alertness for his own advantage that made him as natural a courtier as he was a soldier. The Queen of England, as good a judge of a male animal as might be found in mid-twelfth century France, was bound to be impressed. William's face was his fortune.

. . .

## THE ROYAL HOUSEHOLD

For the next fifteen years of his life William was dependent on the fees and wages of the various Plantagenet royal households of which he was a member; these and the profits he amassed on his own account on the tournament circuit. For six years more, besides, he was still what he would have called a *bacheler* (or if he was in a particularly carefree, sword-tossing mood, a *bacheler leger*), a retained knight and professional soldier. Until 1170 he remained with the queen; in that year he transferred to the household of her eldest surviving son, Henry, and in 1186 he entered the retinue of the old king himself. He would be forty-three years old before the royal *mesnie* stopped being the focus of his career. These years were the years of his prime, and, what was more, he spent them doing what he deeply loved. Even allowing for the bias of his biography, the bare chronology of his career demonstrates that he was valued and respected and never short of employment by the greatest of his world. After 1168, money was easy and he had no responsibility to anyone but himself, except in his latter days to his own squires and retainers. In old age he could not let a campaign pass without pushing himself forward, a boy again, even to the extent of becoming a nuisance to a new generation of bachelors. His old age must have been a time of gnawing regret to him: a world class sportsman grown old and stiff, sentenced forever to the club bar and committee room. Golf and bowls might be the consolation that history now offers such men; for him it would have been hawks and hounds (although, oddly, no source mentions his enjoyment of the hunt).

It is very curious that we hear little from the *Histoire* of what happened to him in these the best years of his life. Only two incidents of any political importance are recorded by his biography between 1170 and 1182; we know far more of his childhood and apprenticeship in arms. There are reasons for this. The men who provided details of his life for his biographer, John, did not really get to know him till the very end of the period. But over and above this is the fact that much of what happened in this period was less than creditable to him considering what his later career was. He participated in plots and scenes that were distinctly unsavoury. A mist was therefore allowed to obscure this period of his career – a golden mist full of the shapes of grand tournaments and festivities, of kings, dukes and counts of great renown.

But despite this it is possible to recover something of what was really happening at this time. The cold evidence of charters and the sardonic chronicles of Roger of Howden give a very different picture of the Marshal's world, particularly when he was in the court of the king's son between 1170 and 1183. When the Marshal was placed in the household of Young Henry (as he was often called) the boy was fifteen, newly crowned as his father's associate-king (hence he is also often called the Young King). He was an engaging youth, generous, likable, and determined to be liked. His most formidable quality was his charm; it won him friends and a loyal following. But charm is a useless commodity in the political market-place unless stiffened with more solid virtues. Henry had none, he was feckless, and had an uncheckable humour which had to say the funny line on his lips with no thought of the consequences. He never learned the sort of courtliness a king must practise, charm and accessibility tempered by caution and suspicion; no mask was before his face. When the archbishop congratulated him on his coronation, saying that he had been raised to an equality with his father, he denied it, for, he said, he was the son of a king, and his father only the son of a count. He was a creature of irrepressible whim, choosing one day in Normandy in 1172 to eject from a packed dinner everyone who was not called William (which being the commonest Norman name left him still with numerous guests, including his *carissimus*, his most intimate intimate, William Marshal). But he was also fretful and peevish, particularly about his lack of money and responsibility. He wanted a land to rule, as he wore a crown, but demonstrated little of the capacity that would have enabled him to wear the diadem with credit.

William Marshal became one of the household knights of this gilded youth, as much a companion as a guard. We are told by the *Histoire* that he was given especial responsibility to tutor the boy in arms. Literary and charter sources mention just such figures in the education of the greatest amongst young aristocrats.[8] There is supporting evidence elsewhere for his closeness to the boy king. Young Henry's charters reveal a permanent group of some eight knights in his entourage, and of these William is invariably placed first, with the only exception of Peter fitz Guy, the Young King's seneschal in the 1170s. This inner retinue, the *mesnie privée* as it was often called, contained a majority of Normans, with two Englishmen: William himself and Simon de Marisco. Some of the eight were from minor baronial families; the Normans, Adam d'Yquebeuf and Robert de Tresgoz, were like William in expectation of succession to the family lands. We glimpse besides these men, a much larger group of squires surrounding the knights, men like Henry Norreis, a sycophantic hanger-on of the Marshal, who was the unintentional cause of his downfall. But above both these and the knights were a group of glittering young magnates who moved in and out of the Young King's court, men who enhanced the glamour and fashion of his following. Chief among them was Robert, Count of Meulan, a man in his late-twenties when the Young King was crowned. He was the greatest magnate in Normandy, and a cousin of the King of France, but had been excluded from the favour of Henry II, for unknown reasons. Others were less substantial men, but still more than common knights: Judhael de Mayenne, Baldwin de Béthune, and John des Préaux.

In this rich and glamorous gathering were abundant opportunities for the young Marshal, and he used them. He cultivated useful friends such as like Baldwin de Béthune, brother of the great Picard magnate and Robert, advocate of Arras. Baldwin eventually received the county of Aumale, and the honest friendship between the two men was a great help to both, particularly as they inhabited a little world where enemies were common and not open. William gained a more than nodding acquaintance besides with dukes, counts and even kings, a celebrity in which the *Histoire* frequently rejoices.

The mid-twelfth century was the first great age of the lay courtier. Courtiers were nothing new at this time, but what was new was the amount of thought, and even study, that went into their careers in the households of the great. Courtly qualities were

8 Thus in the important romance of *Gui de Warewic* composed twenty or thirty years before the *Histoire*, we find the hero Guy as a youth with his 'master' Heralt of Arden who, on Guy's knighting, became his companion and friend; a relationship closely mirroring that of the Marshal and Young Henry. We also hear in the eleventh century how Robert, Count of Eu, entrusted his son John to the tutelage of his knight, Oysterland.

discussed and cultivated: a man must be cheerful, urbane, witty and wise, as well as having the innate qualities of nobility and good looks. The courtier must always be equable, not show open resentment at slights, he must wear a mask to disguise his true feelings. All these qualities were summed up in the new word the French language acquired from Latin at the beginning of the twelfth century: *courtesie*. The bare facts of his career, setting aside the bias of the *Histoire*, tell us that the Marshal must have been a very icon of courtliness, innately good-humoured, charming and amusing. With tact and a well-bridled tongue he had no need to be a master of manœuvre and dissembling. What for others was merely the carefully-constructed outer mask was for him his natural disposition. In the words attributed to King Richard of him, he was '*molt corteis*' (most courtly). His ambition rode easily beside his own disposition. His aggression and competitiveness was channelled into the tournament and warfare. After he had put off his armour and sword, he could lapse into the companionship of the household with ease. He rose effortlessly, without needing to plot, or subvert the position of others. His only danger was his own success.

The courtly world of the Plantagenets had its dark side. Courts could be ugly places, sinks of treachery and conspiracy. The greater the ruler, the more there was to be gained by intrigue and slander against one's rivals for men of few scruples. Behind the mask of some of these courtiers was deceit and treachery. There did not lack for such men at Henry II's court. It can be no coincidence that his reign produced the first great crop of satirists of the court: men such as his distinguished clerical courtiers, John of Salisbury, Peter de Blois, Gerald of Wales and, above all, Walter Map, who turned to bitter essays on the courtly life to relieve their anger and frustration at the daily pettiness and intrigue of their lives. William Marshal's biography, as well as contemporary courtly romances, contains similar sentiments, although in general his biographer is more stoic in his approach to difficulties at court. The *losengers* and *paltoners* (deceivers and traitors), who haunt the Marshal from his earliest exposure at court as a boy in Stephen's reign, were for him just one more set of opponents to be overcome, not evils to be bewailed – the Marshal was, after all, a soldier.

What applied to the court of Henry II was true to an even greater degree of that of his son, the Young King. The boy had no power or responsibilities, just time to kill in the most elegant and expensive ways his day could offer. The inhabitants of his court were young and ambitious men, and he was eager for a wealth and influence that would not be his until his father died. Time, money and a grievance added to a bright and inexperienced court could only mean trouble. Henry II realized this and in a desultory, abstracted way did something to damp it down. Smothering the problem with money for amusement and display in fact did little to help, for there was never enough for his son, and attempted economies only provided more grievances. Picking sensible men to fill positions at his son's court was another way. In 1170 William Marshal's apparent steadiness would seem to have secured him his tutorship to the Young King. Yet Henry II could not prevent his son taking on men more to his own liking. The clerks the elder king placed with his son would be truest to his interests. The staff of the Young King's miniature chancery in fact depended on the father for their advancement in the church hierarchy. This section of his son's household may have been intended to be Henry II's hold on his son's wilder political activities. If this were so he miscalculated badly.

Royal and baronial households by the twelfth century had two broad departments: the lay household, the *mesnie* and the officers of the hall, and the clerical household (called the Chancery in the royal households and those of certain great magnates). In general there seems every reason to believe that the two sections got on very well together. Clerks and knights were after all usually men of the same class and shared certain interests. There are numerous examples of lords displaying great affection for their household clerks and chaplains, lavishing rewards on them and their relations, just as they did on their knights. Even in the Young King's household, William Marshal could enjoy a good working relationship with his master's kitchen clerk, Wigain, who kept for him a running tally of his tournament wins in the 1170s and 1180s. Literacy was in great demand in the twelfth century, and deeply respected by an aristocracy that aspired to learning. It was an age of earnest religion amongst laymen. But still, there were two distinct departments in the households of the great, and their respective members were sharply distinguished by different dress, education, skills and ideals. There was at least the potential for anticlericalism, and in the Young King's household there was every necessary ground for an unhappy schism. There is good evidence from the writings of John of Salisbury of a feeling of clerical contempt for the knight in Henry II's efficient household.

Henry's son, the feather-brained lord devoted entirely to military pleasures, held the ring between, on the one hand, an arrogant young *mesnie* and, on the other hand, senior clerks with loyalties elsewhere, and no useful work to do.[9] It was hardly to be wondered at that the two must conflict, and the Young King would fail to keep them apart.

In 1173, the Young King's irritation with his father's restraints on his power and purse led him to rebel and ally himself with the King of France. All of the knights who can be identified as his intimates from his charters, joined him. They appear in a list of rebels drawn up by Henry II's government and preserved in Roger of Howden's chronicle. William Marshal appears along with them, his first appearance in a surviving contemporary history. But it is notable that the boy's then chancellor, Richard Barre, and Walter, the royal chaplain, as well as the Young King's chamberlain and usher, his father's appointees, promptly defected to Henry II. Richard was of a Buckinghamshire knightly family, had received promotions to archdeaconries from Henry II, and had been one of his ambassadors to the Pope on the dangerous mission to Rome after the murder of Becket in 1170. It was inconceivable that such a man could have much sympathy with his nominal master's cause, and would return in such a crisis to his true lord.[10]

Later, in 1176, after the failure of the rebellion and the Young King's reinstatement, Howden tells us of his vice-chancellor, Adam (the then chancellor, Geoffrey, Henry II's eldest bastard, did not reside with the household, perhaps wisely). Adam did not like what he saw going on at Young Henry's court, and 'as he owed everything to the lord king (i.e. Henry II) who had found him a place with his son' he attempted to inform on him by letter, in secret. Unfortunately for him his intrigue was discovered. The Young King and his intimates tried Adam for his life, and the death sentence was being pondered when a friendly bishop stepped in and saved the hapless clerk. Nonetheless, Adam was whipped naked through the streets of the Norman town of Argentan and incarcerated, until Henry II intervened and had him transferred to the friendlier custody of Hyde abbey in Winchester. No wonder, perhaps, that William Marshal did not speak over-much of his long residence in such a menagerie, except of his

9 See G Duby *The Three Orders* trans A Goldhammer Chicago 1980 263–8.

10 For the career of Richard Barre see R V Turner, 'Richard Barre and Michael Belet' *Medieval Prosopography* VI (1985) 12–34.

glorious tours of the tournament fields. Who knows but that the tournament may have seemed for him a place of freedom; above him the empty sky rather than the roof timbers of the packed hall, around him the hoarse bellows of combat rather than the whispers of conspiracy behind stone arcades. No need for the courtier's mask of mannered indifference under a helmet, he could let his animal spirits and aggression rip. The *Histoire* records the position he was in when he was off the sports field. Speaking of his appointment by Henry II to be his son's companion and tutor it says,

> There did not lack men to tell the father: 'My lord! The boy you entrusted to those masters did such and such; because of them he goes completely over the top! The day before yesterday he had 500 pounds, today it is all gone. Soon it will be 1,000 pounds. He will waste and make off with everything you have!'.[11]

As William grew in intimacy with the Young King, it became clear that he had no friend in Henry II, and his entire livelihood depended on a fickle youth, in a court riven with faction and laced with informers.

For a long time the Marshal trod the tightrope of favour with confidence and success. It probably helped that he was unaware that there was a chasm below his feet. In 1173 during the rebellion against Henry II, while the Young King's *mesnie* was awaiting an onset by his father's forces raiding into the Ile-de-France, it was to William that the Young King turned to knight him. This William did gladly, though it would not have gained him the friendship of Henry II, who, we are told, had reserved that honour for Louis VII of France as a matter of policy. Still, there would have been nothing to look for in that quarter in any case. The Young King's addiction to the tournament guaranteed William perpetual favour, so long as he did not become the object of factional hatred. Unfortunately, in the early 1180s, a clique formed against him in the military household. He became a victim of his own success.

Perhaps the events of 1180 are the key to this fall from grace. In the previous year the Young King had represented his father at Reims when Louis VII's son and heir, Philip, was crowned as associate-king of France. Henry had borne the crown of France ahead of Philip in the procession, and had shouted '*Vive le roi!*' along with the rest of the nobles present. The Young King then

11 *Histoire* ll. 1975–84.

attended the subsequent tournament at Lagny, some seventeen kilometres east of Paris, to advertise the munificence of the new French king. William Marshal's name featured high amongst those who participated at Lagny, in a list that the *Histoire* preserves embedded in its text. Here for the first time he appeared as a knight *portant banière*, that is, he had gained sufficient wealth and prestige to raise his own banner as leader of a company of knights who wore his colours. This must have been the occasion when he first displayed his own bearings. Individual devices, the prototypes of heraldic arms, were at that date reserved for counts, barons and a few more famous knights. We know from the thirteenth-century artist–historian, Matthew Paris, that William Marshal adopted a banner half-green, half-yellow, featuring a red lion rampant.[12] Ever the courtier, the Marshal, like many other prominent royal followers, chose to incorporate in his design the lion device that had been associated with the English kings since the reign of Henry I.

He had now left his former colleagues in the *mesnie* far behind, and they resented it. Perhaps they had resented it since 1173 when the Marshal had knighted the eighteen-year-old king, but now he was so obviously set socially above them they chose to move. A cabal was formed of, appropriately, five members. The *Histoire* chooses to be coy about who they all were, but it does at least name the two leaders, Adam d'Yquebeuf and Thomas de Coulonces. Adam had much in common with William Marshal in origins and expectations, he even shared a connection with the Tancarville household. He had served the Young King as long as had the Marshal, and had attained a high position in the *mesnie*, but nowhere near that of the Marshal. It may well be, therefore, that we should look to envy as the root cause of the plot against William, as the *Histoire* suggests. But it also mentions another cause when it pictures the cabal attempting to entice other reluctant members of the *mesnie* into their web. It was inappropriate, they said, that the Marshal should be set above the rest of them, equal with dukes and counts, when they were Normans, and he was English. We will see in a later chapter from what source the *Histoire* acquired that particular prejudice, but for now it might be observed that the use of such an argument, however ineffectual it was, did not augur well for the future unity of Henry II's realm.

According to the *Histoire*, the plotters adopted two lines of

12 In heraldic parlance: *party per pale or and vert, a lion rampant gules.*

attack. The Marshal, they said, was haughty and arrogant to the point of *lèse majesté* (treason). When the Young King went into action alongside the Marshal in tournaments, the Marshal's own followers had raised the cry 'God for the Marshal!', and scooped up prisoners and ransoms for their master, and not the king. But more subtle, difficult and insidious was their supposed allegation that William had slept with the Young King's wife, Margaret, daughter of Louis VII. Such a titillating rumour must spread uncontrollably in the crowded life of the royal household. It was soon known to William's friends, and then to the Marshal himself. But there was not much he could do to stem its spread, and so he chose to keep a dignified silence.

The allegation of adultery with a queen that the *Histoire* presents us with as the chief cause of its hero's fall from grace creates some difficulties for us. Not the least of these is the fact that it is an allegation that a number of fictional epic heroes had to contend with. Tristan's encounter with King Mark of Cornwall's wife led to his overthrow at court. In the English romance, *Gui de Warewic*, written in the Marshal's lifetime, the hero is accused by the evil seneschal of the Emperor of Constantinople of just such an unfounded crime, and temporarily withdrew from court, but unlike the Young King, the emperor did not give the charge any countenance.

Another problem is that, unfounded or not, the allegation did tend to enhance the Marshal's status in a seedy sort of way. He had been thought worthy to knight a king, and now was thought capable of having seduced a queen, or at least of having been thought worthy by her of seduction. The fictional precedent of Lancelot comes to mind: hero and adulterer. On the other hand, it cannot be denied that such things really did happen in twelfth-century society. In 1182 memories would still have been fresh of the sensational events at the court of Flanders only seven years earlier when Count Philip had discovered one of his *mesnie* in a secret liaison with his wife. The culprit had been denied a hearing and ignominiously executed: beaten by the household butchers and hung head down in a sewer until he suffocated.

We cannot therefore tell for sure whether the allegation of adultery was ever really made against the Marshal. For me, the most telling evidence against it is that if it was made, the Marshal survived it suspiciously easily. One would expect that a sexual encounter with his lord's wife would have raised some genuine Plantagenet passion in the allegedly cuckolded Young King when he got to hear of it. All we find in the *Histoire* is a description of a period of royal coldness to William, that William found deeply wounding, but which did not get in the way of the Young King continuing to employ him as team manager on the tournament field. No other source mentions the affair at all, which is a little odd in such a well-documented age which had a taste for salacious gossip. Only Roger of Howden provides what might be a speck of confirmation, when he reports that early in 1183 the Young King sent his wife to her brother, King Philip, and does not explain why. But an innocent explanation might be found in the other events of that time. The Young King was preparing war against his brother, Richard. He might well have been sending his wife out of the way of a coming conflict. In the face of such ambiguous evidence I would put down the allegation of adultery with Queen Margaret as an invention of the author of the *Histoire*, derived from contemporary romances and maybe subsequent, erroneous gossip; a distraction from the more difficult accusation of *lèse majesté*.

William distanced himself from the king, whatever the cause of his disgrace. First he stayed with friends, but was soon recalled for the purpose of a tournament in the Ile-de-France. At the dinner afterwards, says the *Histoire*, the Count of Flanders publicly lectured the Young King on the stupidity of quarrelling with the Marshal; to no good effect. In the meantime Henry II had got to hear of the rumours of the estrangement. He was rather more pleased than otherwise; the *Histoire* has the honesty to admit that William was by then seen by the elder king as one of the least desirable of his son's companions. When a little later William attempted to appeal to Henry II at Caen at his magnificent Christmas court of 1182, his suggestion of a battle to prove his innocence was brushed off. This was not the only time in his career that the Marshal challenged his detractors to prove their accusations in battle with him. He was to do it again before John in 1205 and 1210, when charges of treason hung over his head. It was as if the very threat of a physical encounter would absolve him of suspicion; a clean act of the body to override the dark and dirty insinuations of wicked and envious minds. The *Histoire* puts a grand speech into the Marshal's mouth by way of reply, which we may well doubt was ever spoken. He had been denied justice. He must leave the Plantagenet lands and find a more welcoming place to live. A false accusation had been made and his accusers did not dare to lift their heads, yet still he suffered wrong. So a safe conduct to the frontier was given him, and he and his men departed south to the county of Perche, leaving behind him his relieved and exulting enemies.

The Marshal no doubt at this point thought, or at least feared, that his prestigious connection with the English royal house had come to an end. At any rate he must have worked up a plan to guard against the worst that might happen. He was now thirty-five years of age. He was still in his prime, and in a man so practised and active, would not have lost any of his prowess. But thirty-five is a time to look both back and forwards. Balanced on the mid-point of man's alloted span, it is a time to begin to think of a colder future. 'He that ever hopes to thrive, must begin by thirty-five'. The Marshal would have taken the moral in Johnson's verse. In the event, he reverted to the strategy of his younger days. He sought the tournament field, advertising his availability. But at the same time he kept in touch with subsequent doings at the Young King's court. Baldwin de Béthune undertook a correspondence with him, although William needed a clerk to read to him what Baldwin sent.

He passed into the region of Paris and found a tournament in mid-January some kilometres east of the city. If finding employment was his plan, he could not have done better. The *Histoire* talks of dukes and counts outbidding each other for his service and there is some confirmation that this really happened, for although the *Histoire* says he regretfully declined the offers, there is other evidence that he accepted a particularly tempting one. Unlike the author of his biography, the Marshal did not know that he would be recalled to the Young King in a couple of months. He was at a loose end, unemployed and still landless; his brother might easily marry and produce an heir. When so great a patron as Count Philip of Flanders offered him a substantial fee to retain his service, he took it gratefully. Recently it has been discovered to have been the rents of a quarter of the Flemish city of St-Omer, one of the count's personal estates.[13]

As the Marshal was quietly ending his days as a simple *bacheler*,

13 That the Marshal possessed a fee in Flanders was known to Painter (*William Marshal* 49 and n.), and he made the logical connection that this fee must have been acquired in 1182, when the Marshal was free and his friend Philip was still count. The location of the fee in St-Omer is mentioned in an inquest long after William's death, along with the information that he exchanged it with the Count of Guines (a potentate of the area around St-Omer) before 1204 for the count's English estate of Trumpington, Cambs, see PRO KB26/146 m 9. For the status of St-Omer as comital demesne, see a charter in *Les chartes de*

a counter-conspiracy was under way at the court of his former master. Circumstances favoured a reconciliation. In January 1183 the sons of Henry II fell out amongst themselves, Henry and Geoffrey taking on Richard. In February, Young Henry, for only the second time in his life, put his household on a war footing. At this point he was vulnerable to the blandishments of William's friends at court. Everyone seemed to interest themselves in his recall, even Geoffrey de Lusignan, whom the Marshal still blamed for his uncle's death fourteen years before. Obligingly, the triumphant Yquebeuf faction promptly discredited itself by arguing against war as soon as it became apparent that Henry II was going to move in to support Richard against his brothers. William was hastily recalled from Paris to resume his position at the head of the Young King's *mesnie*.

The campaign seems to have already been well under way when William returned to his young master, preceded by letters of safe conduct and recommendation from King Philip and others at the French court to Henry II, taking the Marshal's part in the late differences. These apparently stood him in good stead with the elder king, who signalled his willingness that the Marshal resume his old position in his son's household. Along with Baldwin de Béthune, William rejoined the king late in the season of Lent. They were received honourably, and maybe with relief, for the campaign was not going well. Young Henry, his brother Geoffrey, and a party of rebel Poitevins were established near Limoges, threatened by Henry II and Richard. Money was desperately short to maintain the mercenaries who made up the Young King's army. To find it, he had ordered the forced seizure of the treasures of surrounding monasteries, and on a gathering tour, early in June, Young Henry contracted dysentery; out of sheer pique with his father, according to the implacable Howden. Weakening rapidly, he was carried by his household back to his base at the castle of Martel, near Limoges. The father was informed but would not come, sending only a ring in token of forgiveness. He

*St-Bertin* ed. D Haigneré (4 vols) St-Omer 1886–90) I 188. There is the alternative suggestion that the Marshal had the fee in St-Omer in 1197 when he was on an embassy to Count Baldwin. He is said to have done the count good service in battle when he was in Flanders and it is possible that the St-Omer fee was a reward for that. But on the other hand his stay there was brief, and service in battle was rewarded usually by gifts of ransoms or money, not rents.

had been shot at by his sons' crossbowmen earlier in the campaign (by mistake, they said).

On 7 June it was apparent that the Young King was dying, and so the solemn medieval pomp of death was begun. On that day he was confessed privately in his chamber by the bishop of Cahors and an abbot, prostrating himself naked on the floor in agony before the bishop's crucifix. He renounced his recent actions and received the sacrament. Four days later, before his retinue, the Marshal among them, he made a public confession and received the last rites. As frequently happened in those days, he made his testament as one of his last conscious acts when it was evident that everything was nearly played out and there would be no recovery. He had at some time had a Crusader's cross stitched to his cloak and was evidently now troubled by the lightness with which he had taken the vows. Not only the *Histoire*, but two historians also record that at the last he committed the cloak to William Marshal 'his most intimate friend' to take to the Holy Sepulchre in Jerusalem as fulfilment of the vow. As an extravagant display of repentance he had himself taken from his bed and laid on one of ashes, with a stone pillow, a hair shirt on his back and a noose about his neck. Clasping or kissing the ring that his father had sent him as a token of peace, he lapsed into unconsciousness and died soon after.[14]

Whatever the grief and hopelessness of the occasion, the Marshal had received his first lesson in how a great man must die. For him it would be some thirty-six years before he would need to put it into practice. Unfortunately he also got a first taste of the chaos that follows the death of a king. The Young King had died penniless, and had left some pressing debts. The Marshal was promptly seized by a company of Basque or Spanish mercenaries demanding their arrears of pay. It took all his personal authority for them to take his pledge that the debt would be paid. In the meantime the corpse was prepared for the long journey to Rouen, where the Young King had requested burial. Its bowels, brain and eyes were removed, the body packed with salt and stitched into bull's hide. A lead coffin and pall were found and the cortège moved off in procession in fine weather. At the monastery of Vigeois, its prior recorded that the late king's entourage was so impoverished that a collection at a requiem on an overnight stop

14 For the death scene, see particularly Geoffrey, prior of Vigeois *Chronicon Lemovicense*, in *Recueil des Historiens de France* XVIII 216–20. It is Geoffrey who favours us with the description of William Marshal as the king's *carissimus*.

there raised but twelve pence (which the Young King's chaplain filched). A friendly abbot had to provide the candles about the bier, and the knights had to be fed by the priory's charity.

Heading north, the cortège crossed Poitou and Anjou, leaving the dead king's internal organs to be interred at the priory of Grandmont, a favourite house of Henry II, and, ironically, one of those monasteries the Young King had recently pillaged. But now they were faced with more difficulties. It is not often that we encounter 'public opinion' in the Middle Ages, but in a rudimentary way it existed and expressed itself, frequently through popular religious movements. The common people of that region of France were already in a state of excitement. The depredations of the bands of mercenaries employed by the late Henry amongst others had sparked off a resistance movement. For a month or two before Henry died men had been banding together under the inspiration of a carpenter called Durand, who was said to have been inspired by a vision of the Virgin. Under his leadership companies of 'peace-men' clothed in white cloaks, and supported by local knights and the Church, took on and routed the Brabançons and Navarrese who were terrorizing their land. Odd though it may seem, the Young King's death must have tapped this same vein of popular emotion. However silly and feckless he had been, he was not his father and hopes had grown about his succession, which would lift the harsh gloom of the present. Now this longed-for event would not happen and a regret infected all levels of society. In those days such a regret would be expressed by claims for the sanctity of the lamented deceased, and acclamations of miracles at his bier, or tomb. Over a decade later, such claims would be made in London after the execution of William Longbeard, a city magnate who had been credited with a desire to improve the lot of the poorer citizens.[15] The same claims to sainthood were made in the French countryside for Young Henry, and for the same reasons: an expression of the grief of the inarticulate for lost and buried hopes. Cures were claimed at overnight stops, lepers were cleansed by touching the bier, a column of light appeared above the coffin at night. The historian, William of Newburgh, accused 'certain people' of fostering this nascent cult either to justify the son's campaign against his father or to claim that God had accepted his final penitence. At Le Mans the countryside was so feverish that the bishop halted the cortège,

15 C N L Brooke and G Keir *London, 800–1219* London 1975 48–9.

and the Young King was buried at the cathedral along with one of his household squires who had sickened and died on the way. The dean of Rouen had later to claim the body with a royal warrant to get it to the dead king's chosen resting place in his cathedral, where it was buried well over a month after his death.[16]

William Marshal undoubtedly played a part in these tumultuous scenes, for the *Histoire* tells us that he escorted the corpse to its grave. It is, however, unclear whether he was one of those who were promoting the excitement. Probably he was not, because the *Histoire* begins to signal a *rapprochement* with King Henry the father even before the Young King's death. After the burial of his late master, he sought out Henry II, characteristically taking in a money-raising expedition to a tournament on the way to court. The Marshal found the king softened towards him. There is no doubt that Henry had been shaken by his eldest son's death, and he knew besides the nature of his son's last command to William. Henry undertook to retain the Marshal in his household when he returned, and to demonstrate his earnestness took two of the Marshal's horses as a guarantee of his return to him. He then conferred a purse of one hundred Angevin pounds on the Marshal for his expenses. The *Histoire* dryly notes that a single one of the horses the king kept was worth that much, but doubtless the Marshal would have seen the advantages of the bargain. After a visit to his family in England, the Marshal took ship for the Holy Lands, and there he stayed for over two years, two of the final few years of the Latin kingdom of Jerusalem.

The *Histoire* is silent as to what William did there, save that he accomplished his mission and did as much in two years as others did in seven. A cynic might conclude from this turn of phrase, and then silence, that the Marshal, in that case, had done very little. This would be unjust. Before he left, William had been the witness

16 For the cult of Young Henry the most judicious source is William of Newburgh *Historia Rerum Anglicanum* in *Chronicles of the reigns of Stephen, Henry II and Richard* (4 vols) Rolls Series 1884–89 I 234; and the most revealing a sermon by Thomas de Agnellis, archdeacon of Wells, 'On the death and burial of Young King Henry' in *Radulphi de Coggeshall Chronicon Angicanum* ed. J Stevenson Rolls Series 1875 263–73. Thomas fulsomely advocated the sanctity of the Young King, and made no secret of his connection with Henry's mother, who had been imprisoned in England for many years by her husband when her son died. It is likely enough that she and the Young King's friends were the 'certain people' supporting the cult referred to by William of Newburgh, rather than the Capuciati of Berry and the Limousin. For this movement see Duby *The Three Orders* 327–36.

of the last gloomy weeks of a wasted young life. We do not need the assurances of the *Histoire* to know that he was deeply moved. For all his undoubted ambition and worldliness, William took the cross and the road eastwards from which so many did not come back. By no stretch of the imagination could this be interpreted as a career move or a manœuvre. He went to discharge his duty to his dead lord and to God. In his last days he was to reveal to his knights that he had been smitten in the East with thoughts of his own mortality, thoughts black enough to cause him to buy the cloth to lay on his own bier, and to make an informal commitment to end his days amongst the Templars and be buried in a Templar house. The Marshal had a spiritual life (although the *Histoire* does not rhapsodize about it). We must believe that what he saw and did in Palestine satisfied a longing deeper than the thirst for wealth and fame that had pushed him so far. He did not need to talk about it. The twitterings of his vague successes in the East are his biographer's vanity, not his own.

*Chapter 3*

# THE MAKING OF A MAGNATE, 1186–1205

. . .

## THE HOUSEHOLD OF HENRY II, 1186–89

William returned from the East to pick up the threads of his career at some time in 1186. He found the king in Normandy, in his hunting lodge of Lyons-la-Forêt.[1] He was welcomed and found the king as good as his word; he was retained to serve in the military household of Henry II, still then the most potent ruler in Christendom. He found several familiar faces in the royal retinue: Peter fitz Guy, Gerard Talbot and Robert de Tresgoz, also sometime members of the Young King's household. The king was now sixty-three years of age, with two legitimate sons left to him. Richard, the Count of Poitou and his presumed heir, was approaching thirty; John, the youngest, was nearly twenty: recently he had been made Lord of Ireland, but his father's attempt to give the title reality had come to grief ominously on the young man's incompetence.

The next few years were busy ones. William was constantly engaged on active military service. The tournament makes no further appearance in his life (except when, as regent, he banned one in 1217). War, counsel and command were now his daily business, and the *Histoire* gives us accounts of his campaigns rich in detail. Indeed the *Histoire* is now an altered creature. It abandons its anecdotal, patchy approach and we begin to get a more methodical, less embroidered picture of its subject's life and

1 Following Meyer, Painter has William returning to court in 1187, because 'a little after he returned' the True Cross was lost to the Saracens. However, he must have left for the East early in 1184 at the latest, and was there, according to the *Histoire*, for two years. This would bring him back, by his biography's reckoning, in 1186. In the spring of that year Henry was at Gisors, in the vicinity of Lyons-la-Forêt, whereas his itinerary does not place him there in 1187, when he was mostly in England. We should probably take the *Histoire's* vague expressions of the passage of time as loosely as its author intended them. The year 1187 could be 'a little after he returned' in that case.

times. This is largely because the *Histoire's* informants, particularly John of Earley, the Marshal's squire and ward, were taken into the Marshal's own small household during this time. But also it is describing events less far removed from the days when it was composed. The author's own memories and those of his contemporaries could be tapped.

However, this does not mean that the *Histoire* is to be wholly trusted in its account after 1186. The Marshal is its central character, and by magnifying him (as in a Romanesque sculpture), all the other characters about him are dwarfed. The picture of indispensable royal aide and general that the *Histoire* contrives to project has its element of truth. A loyal servant by temperament and family tradition, William was probably the king's most reliable and accomplished captain and his importance grew towards the end as the fabric of Henry II's Continental government loosened and slid into ruin in the face of the king's growing illness, internal rebellion and the aggression of Philip II of France. But the king's business was not principally war. Within the world of the court William Marshal was but a small creature as yet. He did not have the sources of external power, the lands and followings, that made bishops, earls and barons men of note. He was not of the king's own generation, and all his skills as a courtier could not make up for the lack of a common experience that gave the older men at the court of an ageing king such an advantage. He could not talk of old triumphs and failures, or reminisce about the old battles and conspiracies. Indeed in some of the more recent ones he had been on the wrong side. His face was a new one; it fitted, but that was all.

Sources outside the *Histoire* give a truer picture. The Marshal appears in the acts of the last years of the reign infrequently and in a junior position, on occasion alongside another promising newcomer, the young administrator and justice, Geoffrey fitz Peter, whose career paralleled his own in many ways.[2] The two were to become allies at court, and there is some evidence of friendship. Rewards began to come the Marshal's way, as they did Geoffrey's. One of the most economical means of royal patronage was the granting of wardships: the keeping of the lands and persons of under-age boys or female heirs, whose custody belonged to the king if their fathers held their lands directly from the Crown. One of the first grants that William had was the keeping of the fifteen- or sixteen-year-old John of Earley (but not

2 See, R.V. Turner *Men Raised from the Dust* Philadelphia 1988 35–70.

his lands), son of William of Earley, a minor baron of Somerset and Berkshire and royal chamberlain.[3] He took John into his household as his squire; it is probable that he was given also the right to marry him off to whoever he pleased. There is a pattern to some of the other grants. In 1187 he had the grant in England of the large royal estate of Cartmel in Lancashire, between Lake Windermere and Morecambe Bay. At about the same time he was given the keeping of one of the king's female wards, Heloise of Lancaster, the heiress of the barony of Kendal in Westmorland, which neighboured Cartmel to the east. The plan was, it seems, to raise William to the standing of a baron in the north of England. He could, if he so wished, have married the lady of Kendal, and then her lands would have been his and the heirs he had from her. It would have brought him to a level with his elder brother, John Marshal, and have been a handsome reward enough. The barony of Kendal spread across Westmorland, Lancashire and the West Riding of Yorkshire and as lord of Kendal he would have had castles, the priory of Cockerham, and great tracts of forest.[4]

Circumstances did not in the end favour this alliance. The Marshal and the lady remained 'just good friends' as the *Histoire* puts it with a certain anachronistic tact. Events began to gather a speed in 1188 that would have left neither the king nor William with time to plan marriage alliances. The king's relations with Count Richard, his heir, were no more successful than they had been with the Young Henry, and for the same reason: the king would not resign into Richard's hands any more power than he could get away with. Richard could count on the support of Philip II of France in any confrontation with his father, the same way as the Young King had counted on Louis VII, and Philip was assiduous in raising doubt in Richard's mind about Henry's ultimate intentions. A rumour that Henry intended to cut Richard out of the succession and make John his heir, most likely started in Paris. It began to circulate at a critical time. Henry II had been subject to recurrent and serious illness since 1182, and an arduous and successful campaign against Philip in the course of 1188 had exhausted his mind, body and finances. But as peace seemed on the point of being made at the end of the year, a storm over the succession blew up. Philip artfully proposed that he would

3 For William and John of Earley, see below, pp. 195–6.

4 For the extent of the royal lordship of Cartmel (an area of 28, 747 acres) and the barony of Kendal see, *Victoria County History of Lancashire*, viii, 254; W Farrer *Lancashire Pipe Rolls and Early Charters* (Liverpool 1902), 389–90.

relinquish the lands in dispute between Henry and himself to Richard, providing Richard married his sister, Alice, as had long been proposed, and that Richard be recognized as his father's heir. In proposing this recognition, Philip stabbed to the heart of the troubled relationship between Henry and his son, and drew blood. Henry would not answer the proposal and so Richard's active and suspicious mind drew the fatal conclusion that his disinheritance was indeed being considered. He drew off to Poitou in haste, summoning all his forces as he went.

William Marshal was one of the king's messengers who pursued Richard into Poitou, demanding that he return and talk again to his father. The *Histoire* claims that this mission of mercy was William's idea, but whether it was or not, it was abruptly abandoned when the envoys reached Amboise hot on the count's heels, and found that the night before Richard's clerks had written and sealed over two hundred letters summoning men to their master's side. A desultory border war followed through that winter and spring, with Richard actively assisting Philip. Henry II fell ill again in the New Year, and a proposed peace conference was continually postponed. The sick king languished in Anjou, the heart and centre of his domain, his family's ancestral county. The knights and barons of his household at his side may well have come to seem more important to him at this time, which must often have found him weak and fearful, for he moved to secure their allegiance more firmly. The young Gilbert fitz Reinfrid, son of a royal justice and nephew of Walter de Coutances, archbishop of Rouen, and recently appointed the steward of the royal household, was one of those favoured.[5] At some time in Lent 1189, William Marshal was asked to give up the wardship of Kendal and its lady, and it was transferred to Gilbert by a charter which William himself witnessed.[6] In this way the king would not just have rewarded young Gilbert, but gratified the powerful official

5 For the genealogy and origins of the family of fitz Reinfrid, which derived from relatively humble origins in Cornwall, and was represented at Henry II's court by the brothers Walter de Coutances (died 1207) and Roger fitz Reinfrid (died 1196), as well as Roger's son Gilbert and a host of siblings in canonries and archdeaconries in England and Normandy, see the Rouen obits printed in *Recueil des Historiens de la France* XXIII 359, 362, and the article by Kate Norgate in the *Dictionary of National Biography* under 'Walter de Coutances'. Archbishop Walter had been a member of the Young King's household at some point, alongside William Marshal.

6 *Lancashire Pipe Rolls* 395. The charter is undated, but it calls Gilbert a royal steward, which he had become only recently in 1189; the witness list parallels a

dynasty to which he belonged, and of which he was the chief heir. No slight to the Marshal was intended, however, for he had instead a promise from the ailing king of one of the greatest heiresses then in England, Isabel, the daughter and heir of Earl Richard of Striguil, with estates and claims that dwarfed Kendal. A number of others of Henry II's household had promises of great reward at this time, including the Marshal's friend, Baldwin de Béthune, who had the even greater reward of the heiress of Châteauroux in Berry.

Eventually, at the end of May 1189, when Henry was feeling better, the parties came together, but no good resulted. Henry's continued prevarication simply served to confirm for Richard the danger he was in of disinheritance. Henry, however, did not realize his own danger. Richard has been criticized for lacking subtlety, but he was a determined, perhaps brilliant, general, and he did not mitigate that quality just because he was dealing with his father. After leaving this last conference, he and Philip launched a vigorous assault on Henry as he was retreating back into Maine. Castles fell with a rapidity that can only suggest that their keepers were aware that the old king was labouring in his last illness, and that their new master was at their gates. Richard caught up with his father at Le Mans (where Henry had been born) on 12 June. Henry was accompanied by his servants and household guards but no army. The barons of Normandy had been summoned to join Henry, but had halted at Alençon, troubled by the combination of King Philip and Count Richard, and reluctant to proceed.

King Henry was now in a very difficult position. Richard and Philip made a determined advance on Le Mans, and despite attempts to block the passage of the river Huisne, their troops succeeded in penetrating the suburbs of the city. Henry was almost taken in the process; he had been surprised by the French scouts while out watching the movements of his enemies. He departed Le Mans in haste with his guards, leaving the city in flames, and its castle to fall to the French. The pursuit was hot behind him. William Marshal and a few others were left to delay the pursuers. It seems that the Marshal had in mind his father's

similar grant to the royal usher, Walter, datable to 1188 x 89 (the symbol 'X' indicates a date range within which an event took place but which cannot be narrowed down); also it is addressed to Count Richard, something that a prudent beneficiary might well have asked for if the king was ailing, and Richard the next heir.

tactics against a raid by King Stephen on Ludgershall in the 1140s. Count Richard, unarmed except for an iron cap so as to ride all the faster, was leading the party of pursuers plainly thinking that his father's men were routed. The Marshal waylaid him with a party of the royal *mesnie*. The ambush was unexpected, and could have been fatal for the count. The Marshal himself, fully armed, rode him down. Richard, finally realizing his position and recognizing his assailant, shouted out that he was unarmed and that it would be an evil deed so to kill him. The Marshal cursed him, lowered his lance point, and killed the count's horse, calling on the devil to despatch Richard himself. This reverse halted the pursuit and the king proceeded at a more leisurely pace to his great fortress of Chinon on the Vienne, within the borders of the Angevin province of Touraine.

Even before he reached Chinon, it was evident that Henry had made his last rally. His spirits sank, he failed to assemble such forces as he had available, and consented to a last bitter interview with Philip and Richard. He rose with great pain from his bed for a conference near Tours and accepted the terms which were dictated to him by Philip (to his credit, embarrassed to find how feeble and wretched his adversary had become). Henry then returned to Chinon and what was to be his deathbed, although to the end he hoped to recover and revenge himself. The end was not long in coming. He fell into a stupor and delirium on hearing that his beloved son, John, had joined Philip and Richard against him, and after three days of incoherent semi-consciousness, died attended by none but his menial servants on 6 July. His corpse and chamber were stripped before the knights of his *mesnie* learned of his death. They found it cold and stiffening in an empty room, black blood staining the nostrils and mouth from a final paroxysm. For decency's sake, one of his knights cast his cloak over the dead king.

The *mesnie* did what it could and had the body prepared and dressed in its royal robes. William Marshal attempted to get the seneschal of Anjou to open the treasury of Chinon to scatter the customary alms to the poor, but the seneschal stubbornly refused. This must have all seemed depressingly similar to William to the shabby aftermath of Young Henry's death. The day after the king's death his bier was escorted by the *mesnie* and the barons of Anjou and Touraine downriver to the Loire valley and the abbey of Fontevrault, a house of nuns particularly favoured by Henry II. There the body was received and lay in state till the arrival of

Count Richard.

William did his last duty to his master, and followed the body to Fontevrault. There, with the rest of the *mesnie* and household, he awaited the arrival of the count. His situation was not a happy one. He and everyone else knew how he had covered Henry's retreat from Le Mans, and the expectations of the men standing around waiting with him at the abbey were that his career in royal service had ended. Several, we are told, rather generously offered to settle a modest competence on him to tide him over. William had now only his rents in St-Omer and the land of Cartmel, if the new king let him keep even that. He had let Kendal go earlier in the year, and had not had time to take possession of the heiress of Striguil.

. . .

## LORD OF STRIGUIL

If those at Fontevrault could have known what plans were forming in Count Richard's head as he rode to join them, they would not have needed to commit themselves so hastily to William's future upkeep. The count, soon to be king, was already turning in his mind the execution of the grand plan that was to become the Third Crusade. To quit his new kingdom for several years and yet ensure its safety in his absence was already his great concern. Before he even reached Fontevrault he must have decided that William Marshal was to be part of that plan. Richard meant to secure England by raising such men as he knew were tested, capable, and above all loyal, to great power in the kingdom and leave them to guard it for him. William Marshal, whose loyalty to his current lord was his most famous quality, was to be one of them: there was to be no small-mindedness about the ambush outside Le Mans.[7]

The count arrived at the abbey. The author of the *Histoire*, in one of his most telling asides, recalls either his own or one of his source's impressions of Richard on the point of becoming the most powerful king in Christendom. 'If you ask whether he looked joyful or wrathful when he came, there is no-one who knows who can tell if he were joyful, sad, remorseful, grieving or cheerful.' Here was the pattern courtly king, standing impassive beside the

7 Roger of Howden remarks how the count retained all the servants of his father who he knew to be true men (*fideles*) and these he rewarded each according to their desserts; he treated with contempt those who had abandoned his father, *Gesta Henrici Secundi* II 72–3. The *Histoire* lists some of these deserving men as Baldwin de Béthune, Reginald fitz Herbert and Reginald de Dammartin.

corpse of his father whom he could with justice have been said to have harried to his grave, if not driven to his death. But there was no emotion in his face. Whatever his eyes saw was not allowed to speak to his heart. By such acts of self-control were great kings set apart from common humanity.[8]

Richard left the church and summoned William Marshal to him, along with the Manceaux magnate Maurice de Craon, presumably as a witness. According to the *Histoire* the count first teased the Marshal with attempting to kill him on the road from Le Mans, and when the Marshal indignantly protested that if he had been aiming at Richard he would have struck him and not considered it a crime, Richard let be and pardoned him. William and a colleague were to be sent immediately to England on a mission, the nature of which the *Histoire* does not reveal. At this point members of the dead king's household, apparently standing around within earshot and perhaps rather gratified at the turn events were taking, protested to the count that his father had given William the heiress of Striguil. The count corrected them. His father had only promised the girl to William: *he* was giving her to him. Others still in expectation of reward were also relieved of their anxieties, the *Histoire* provides an instructive list of them. But this could not have been all that Richard bestowed on William at Fontevrault, for on his subsequent journey to England William paused in the Pays de Caux to take possession of certain unnamed estates which can only have been the portion of the lands of the Giffard family to which his wife-to-be was also heir. The Marshal must have left Fontevrault armed with a sheaf of Richard's writs directing various bailiffs and officers to surrender their charges to the Marshal.

There remained little more to be said. Following the funeral William took to his horse and rode north to Normandy and the Channel coast. He seized the opportunity of taking charge of the Giffard lordship of Longueville en route to Dieppe, and awaited his servants' news that they had found him a boat at the port at

8 Henry of Huntingdon writes in a similar vein about Henry I of England nearly a century before this, 'he was a deep dissimulator and his mind was unreadable', see 'Epistola de contemptu mundi' in *Historia Anglorum* ed. T Arnold (Rolls Series 1879) 300. Chrétien de Troyes, the apostle of courtliness, writing in the 1170s pictures the courtly king, Erec of Brittany, on hearing of his father's death thus: 'Erec's sorrow was far greater than he showed to the people; but grief is not becoming in a king, and it is not seemly for a king to show sorrow', *Erec et Enide* ed. M Roquez Classiques françaises du moyen age 1952, ll. 6466–9.

St-Vaast-d'Equiqueville, a Giffard manor east of the town.[9] This would have been the first time the Marshal had spent a night under a roof that he could have called his own. Before the end of July he was in England. He sought out first his patron of long ago, Queen Eleanor, newly released from her years of captivity at Winchester. He delivered to her whatever message Count Richard had entrusted him with and then took to the road again, heading for London and the girl, Isabel of Striguil. Another writ eventually delivered her from the Tower into his hands (despite some cavilling by the justiciar, Ranulf de Glanville) and they were married with no delay in the city.

Such alliances were the occasions of great festivity in the twelfth century. When Isabel's great-aunt had married a local baron at Chepstow priory some forty years before, all the barons and prelates of the country roundabout had been there. Ten days of festivities had ended in a great cavalcade up the Wye valley to her new home at Monmouth.[10] The Marshal arrived in London dusty and without the sort of money to afford such a display. However, he did at least find it easy to raise credit. The prominent city magnate and financier, Richard fitz Reiner, with whom he was staying was willing and eager to lend sufficient sums to allow the marriage to take place in appropriate state. William's credit rating had improved rapidly since he was last in England. The Marshal was to cultivate several such contacts in London, where in the end he kept his own financial agents. The marriage done, William retired to Surrey, where he had borrowed the house of a friend, Enguerrand d'Abenon, at Stoke Daubernon, and there he commenced life as a married man, awaiting the arrival of Richard in England.

We have little knowledge of the nature of that life. We know his wife was still very young when they married (she could not have been older than twenty), and that he was uxorious (they produced ten children in all, and she was pregnant before 1189 was out). It may be that William had looked for sexual satisfaction before his marriage amongst the prostitutes who had their place in contemporary court life. The alleged liaison with the Young King's wife

9 St-Vaast-d-Equiqueville appears in a later grant by William Marshal to Longueville priory as (at least in part) his demesne manor, *Chartes de Longueville*, 105 and n.

10 The marriage of Rohese de Clare can be reconstructed from charters granted to Monmouth priory to celebrate the event, printed in T Madox, *Formulare Anglicanum* London 1702 no. 400.

certainly hints that he was known to be a man not unattracted by women. But since he produced no bastards that he acknowledged in the later part of his career, it may well be that he had till 1189 either kept a rein on his sexuality or, perhaps, used very careful women of the camp. Bastards were a great asset for a baron: girls could be used to form alliances with lesser families; boys made knights, clerks or stewards whose loyalty to their fathers had to be total. If William Marshal had been a man like his elder brother and had openly taken a mistress, we would know about it. Our day and age, cursed by Freud, has a tendency to underestimate the extent to which a willing celibacy could be a feature of lay life in the Middle Ages.

In 1189 William Marshal became, by right of his wife, Lord of Striguil. It is often wrongly said that he also became Earl of Pembroke. In 1189, and for over a decade afterwards, Pembroke was in the hands of the king, for Henry II had confiscated it from Isabel's father, Earl Richard, in 1153 or 1154 and never let it go. The earldom of Pembroke had been created for Isabel's grandfather in 1138 as a reward by King Stephen. When Earl Richard succeeded in 1148 he was only a child and it was easy for Henry II to reclaim Pembroke from him, almost certainly on the grounds that it had been a royal estate alienated by Stephen which was rightfully his under the peace settlement of 1153.[11] Earl Richard had then to settle for his father's honor of Striguil, which had been given to his family in the days of Henry I and therefore could not lawfully be touched. Earl Gilbert of Pembroke had also enjoyed the possession of the castles of Orbec and Meullers in Normandy, and we find the Marshal later holding them, so his wife brought him them too.

'Striguil' was a contortion of an earlier Welsh name for what we now call Chepstow castle. This formidable cliff-top fortress still dominates the lowest bridging point on the river Wye before it meets the Severn. The name Striguil was applied to the castle and to the honor, the great estate, that depended on it. In 1189 this was a scattering of 65½ knights' fees in several English counties, and several large manors kept in the lord's hand (in 'demesne' as it is

11 For the royal hold on Pembroke and other points see MT Flanagan 'Strongbow, Henry II and the Anglo-Norman Intervention in Ireland' in *War and Government in the Middle Ages: Essays in honour of J O Prestwich*, ed. J Gillingham and J C Holt Woodbridge, 1984 63–70, and comments in D Crouch, 'Strategies of Lordship in Angevin England and the Career of William Marshal' in *The Ideals and Practice of Medieval Knighthood* II ed. C. Harper-Bill and R Harvey Woodbridge, 1988 16–18.

called). But the core of the lordship was in south east Wales, in Lower Gwent, or Netherwent. Here the lord of Striguil controlled most of the lowlands along the Severn estuary between the Usk and Wye, as well as the forest of Wentwood that overlooked the flats. Earl Richard had added to this rump of his father's lordship by a successful campaign against his Welsh neighbour, Iorwerth, lord of Caerleon. He had taken from Iorwerth the castle and lordship of Usk at some time before 1170. Gwent therefore was the seat of Richard's earldom, not Pembroke, and around 1173 he recognized this by dropping the title 'Earl of Pembroke' which he had kept up to remind the world of his claims; afterwards he was 'Earl of Striguil'.

Earl Richard had conquered Leinster in Ireland in 1170–71, but this too was not immediately given to the Marshal in 1189; it was still being held by Count John, the new king's brother. He did not give it up on William's marriage, and in the winter of 1190 the Marshal had to solicit the king for his intervention in getting John to release it. John was reluctant to do this, for in the years of his wardship of Leinster he had, as was not uncommonly done, used it to endow many of his own men. Not unreasonably, he doubted that the Marshal would leave them be if he ever got control of the lordship. Eventually John had the tenure of his butler, Theobald, recognized in Leinster, but the king would allow him no more. Then the Marshal had the problem of how to administer Leinster. He would not go there himself – it was too far from the warm centre of things where the king was – and any emissary of his would be ineffective. But a representative was sent, the otherwise unknown Reginald de Quetteville, to stake the Marshal's claim: 'God help him!' says the *Histoire*. He was utterly ineffectual, as might reasonably have been expected. It is very much to be doubted that the Marshal exerted any effective control over his Irish estates for ten years and more after he received them.

So, in 1189, William Marshal became a magnate, but by no means as great a magnate as Sidney Painter believed. He was ruler of one of the flatter, and therefore richer, Marcher lordships. Here he was lord of two powerful stone fortresses (Chepstow and Usk), and overlord of other lesser castles; he was patron of an abbey (Tintern) and two priories (again, Chepstow and Usk), but in England he held precious little other than the potential to make money that the services of sixty-five and a half knights' fees gave him. The fat demesne manors of Weston in Hertfordshire and Parndon and Chesterford in Essex that were part of his honor were, until she died, in the hands of his mother-in-law, Eve 'the Irish countess' widow of Earl Richard and daughter of Dermot, king of Leinster. From this we can see why King Richard was prepared to add to Striguil half of the great Giffard lordship in Normandy and England, an arrangement confirmed by charter in November 1189.[12] Otherwise the Marshal could have complained with justice that he had not exchanged much of immediate value for Kendal.

Richard was willing to consolidate William's power in the Southern Marches even further. He allowed William to buy control over the office of sheriff of Gloucester, and with it Gloucester castle and the Forest of Dean. This bodily extended the Marshal's influence as a magnate eastwards across the Wye up the Severn valley. It constructed a bloc of power that the region had not seen since the disgrace of Earl Roger of Hereford in 1155. It may be that Sidney Painter was right to suggest that the king so raised the Marshal in order to use him to counter the power of his brother, Count John, to whom Richard had given the heiress and estates of the earldom of Gloucester, with control of Bristol and the Marcher lordships of Glamorgan and Newport. On the other hand, the Marshal's actions were so ambiguous towards John in the king's absence, that we might suggest just as plausibly that as things turned out the Marshal and his brother became, in effect, part of Count John's affinity in the area.

William had married the daughter and heir of an earl, but that did not necessarily make him an earl himself. It had long been accepted in England, before the Conquest indeed, that the king alone might create an earl. The earldoms that were created in England and Wales after the Conquest were hereditary and their creations were acts of royal patronage. But royal control had gone further than that and, strictly speaking, a man might not call himself 'earl', even if his father had been one before him, until he had been invested with his earldom by the king. What this involved by William's day was the belting by the king of a sword

12 The Earl of Hertford brought forward a claim to the Giffard lands when Richard arrived in England. The matter was settled amicably by dividing them, and a copy of the king's grant of his half to Earl Richard of Hertford survives, *Cartae Antiquae Rolls, 11–20* ed. J.Conway Davies Pipe Roll Society 1960 165–6. Earl Richard was given the chief Giffard seat in England, and William the corresponding chief seat in Normandy: Longueville and its honor south of Dieppe. In England, William's chief Giffard possessions were his manors of Caversham, Oxon, and Long Crendon, Bucks, which otherwise compensated for his lack of demesne in England.

around the new earl's waist, and the delivery of a charter granting, or confirming, the earldom. Richard never honoured him with such a ceremony, so he never became earl in his reign according to the royal view of things, and was careful to describe himself simply as 'William Marshal' in his charters before 1199. He was a courtier and knew when not to press claims too far. However, whatever was claimed for the king, society's thinking was less clear cut, and there is plenty of evidence that it was thought generally that a man might automatically succeed to the dignity of earl on his father's death, whether the king belted him or not. There are a number of examples of sons of earls taking up the title on their own initiative. William seems to have thought about this too, and decided that even if he was not an earl, his wife, nonetheless, could be considered a countess. In one of his charters between 1189 and 1199 he had her carefully described as such, though he did not claim in it to be earl.[13] But although, as I have said, he never claimed to be earl, that did not stop other people calling him one. Seeing that he was enjoying the lands and daughter of Earl Richard of Striguil, a royal clerk in October 1189 unthinkingly described him as 'William Marshal, Earl of Striguil'.[14] Roger of Howden, another royal clerk, usually punctilious in his use of titles, was equally loose in this case, and William is 'Earl of Striguil' in his writings too.[15]

The crowning act of this fortunate year was for William to found a religious house to commemorate, amongst other things, God's grace to him in raising him to such a height. There were other reasons. The patronage of a house of regular clergy who looked to a magnate as its founder and protector had been since the early eleventh century a mark of the prestige of the greater aristocrats. By the mid-twelfth century many men with pretensions to weight in society had an abbey or priory as a mausoleum and as a means of intercession between himself and a God who men were well aware was not impressed with great wealth alone. The Marshal's father had adopted the Salisbury family's house of Bradenstoke in which to be buried, and had patronized it as far as his limited

13 Westminster Abbey Muniments no. 3137.

14 *Calendar of Charter Rolls* II 164: *Willelmo Marescallo comite de Strugull'*. This was not an isolated instance. When William appeared as witness to a charter of the king's brother, Count John, in London at some time between 1189 and 1193, he appeared as '*comite Willelmo Marescallo*' BL ms Egerton 3047 fo. 4r.

15 On the titles of earl and count in general see my forthcoming book *The Image of Aristocracy in Britain in the High Middle Ages* (Routledge).

resources allowed. However, by 1190 it was beginning to be *nouveau riche* to advertise power by setting up a monastery; there was a surplus of religious houses and men of quite low station, mere county knights, were scraping together resources to found tiny and often short-lived priories on corners of their estates. But for a parvenu, like William Marshal, the gesture still had meaning. So he devoted his estate of Cartmel in Lancashire to the foundation of a house of Augustinian canons. Two more things are significant about this gesture. He drew the initial colony of canons from the Augustinian house in which his father had been buried, Bradenstoke: a sign, perhaps, of lingering local and filial feeling. The other was the commemoration in the foundation charter of the two late kings he had served: Henry II and the Young Henry 'my lord'. Note which of the two kings he called his lord. This last gesture is not without its poignancy, he was willing to repay some of his first great patron's generosity to him by expending his own resources on masses for his soul. We can like the Marshal for that.[16]

. . .

## KING RICHARD ON CRUSADE, 1190–94

In the meantime, in July 1189, Richard had the ducal sword of Normandy belted to him in Rouen cathedral, and in August arrived in England, where William was one of the first to greet him. He stayed at the king's side for the next three months. These were great days for him. He had a leading part to play in the coronation at Westminster on 13 September, where he bore the royal sceptre before the king. Also at the coronation was a member of his family of whom he had seen little for many years, his elder brother, John. John too had his part to play in the ceremony, carrying before the king a massive pair of golden spurs. We do not know whether this duty was a customary one for the royal marshal at the coronation, for Richard's is the first time we have a detailed glimpse of what the ceremonial procession involved. But carrying spurs was a rather suitable coronation office for a marshal, so it is likely that John was doing no more than his father had at previous coronations. But for William to have a coronation office allotted to

16 The foundation charter of Cartmel is lost but copies of it exist in BL Harley charters 51 H 2, 83 B 38. It mentions William's wife so it has to have been made after the marriage, and the presence in it of John Marshal indicates a time when the two brothers were closest, before July 1190.

him too meant that Richard was deliberately increasing the Marshal family's dignity.

John Marshal had got nowhere at court in the reign of Henry II, but we do at least know that he was a man eager for court advancement. Failing the king, he had become an intimate of the young Count John before 1189, following him on one occasion as far as Maine in France. As proof of the count's attachment and trust he was made his seneschal.[17] So when John Marshal appeared at the court of Richard it was not as a forgotten backwoodsman, blinking in the light of the royal majesty. Like his younger brother, John Marshal wanted to be a creature of the court and reap all the rewards that might bring him. Nonetheless, there was a certain irony that he owed his breakthrough to William. He had had so few contacts with him until Richard was king that there must be some justice in suggesting a long estrangement, or at least indifference between the brothers. John had allotted his brother no lands from the paternal estate (as elder brothers often did), and the *Histoire* records no unequivocal contacts between the two. The *Histoire* does not reserve for John any of the adjectives it bestows liberally on people of whom its author approved: 'the brave', 'prudent', 'hardy' or 'loyal'.

William's family was much honoured in these last months of 1189. The king seemed to be willing to go quite out of his way to build them up at court and in the country. In September John Marshal was appointed the king's chief escheator in England; that is, the man who supervised the taking into royal hands of the lands of men who died without heirs, or at least without adult ones. Although he was later removed from the office, he seems to have had in compensation the office of sheriff of Yorkshire, a county available since the disgrace of the previous sheriff and royal justiciar, Ranulf de Glanville. In November John had perpetual grants of the private hundreds of Bedwyn in Wiltshire and Bosham in Sussex, which his father and himself had only held from year to year until then. William's younger brother, Henry,

17 In 1185 at Wexford John's seneschal was Bertram de Verdun, and his household seneschal was William de Wenneval, see Kent Record Office, U1475 (Delisle Deeds) T321/1; *Calendar of the Ormond Deeds* i *1172–1350 AD* ed. E Curtis Dublin 1932 3–4. So it is likely that when John Marshal appeared as Count John's seneschal in a charter dated at Le Mans it was at some time after that but before 1189, see *The Irish Cartularies of Llanthony Prima and Secunda* ed. E St John Brooks Dublin 1953 79–80. John appears in at least five acts of Count John datable to 1185 x 89, and in another after 1189 at Cranbourne.

was elevated in September to the rich deanery of York.[18] John and William Marshal appear together side by side in court from September to December in 1189. In a rather nice touch, when they appear together in royal acts, it is John who usually appears first as the elder, although William had by now outstripped him in influence and lands. When William and many other English magnates were summoned to meet the king in Normandy in March 1190, John Marshal went too, and both stayed with the king until at least June. William went on with Richard to the great assembly of the crusaders at Vézelay in July, and must have taken leave of him as the great army began the slow trip south to Marseilles and the fleet.[19]

In the meantime the world had changed for him. His young wife was pregnant before they left for Normandy and presented him with his eldest son and heir, whom he named William, in Normandy in 1190, perhaps as early as April. William had, with his accustomed ease, achieved the feat which eluded his brother and so many others of his contemporaries; a son to carry on his surname. A second son called Richard, to recall Isabel's legendary father, appeared the next year to consolidate his lineage. Regularly, year by year, Isabel would add to their family until they had a total of five sons and five daughters.

But to return from domestic to political success. It is not easy to work out whether Richard was smiling on the Marshal family in 1189–90 entirely for William's sake, or in an attempt to encourage the growth of a Marshal party at court, or even both. That there was such a party, however, can be seen in the reaction of other powerful men to the Marshals at this time. Geoffrey, the archbishop-elect of York, resisted vigorously the installation of Henry Marshal as dean of his chief cathedral until December 1189, although the king favoured the Marshal side. A more dangerous enemy for the Marshals was Richard's chancellor, William de Longchamp. There is evidence of his contempt for

18 *Gesta Henrici Secundi* II 85, 91. On 11 November 1189 King Richard I granted Wexcombe and Bedwyn in heredity *cum hundredo* to John Marshal (II) at a feefarm or perpetual rent of £30 p.a. PRO C52/21/9. The separate grant of Bosham with lestage (a port due) and its hundred for a feefarm of £42 p.a. is noted in *Rotuli Chartarum* ed. TD Hardy (Record Commission, 1837), in a confirmation to his brother, William by King John.

19 For William's and John's appearances at court in the reign of Richard, see L Landon, *The Itinerary of Richard I* (Pipe Roll Society 1935). I have added to this certain references generously made available to me by Professor J C Holt and his Angevin Acta project.

both William and John. It was he who removed John Marshal from office as sheriff of Yorkshire in the spring of 1190 after a serious anti-Semitic riot. The king had left for France leaving Longchamp with a free hand. He used it to swat those he saw as his enemies. There is some remarkable evidence that he attempted in person to seize Gloucester castle, the base of William Marshal's under-sheriff and retainer, Nicholas Avenel, at about the same time, while the Marshal was with the king in France.[20] There might have been some justification for this outrage if, as I have already suggested, the Marshals were perceived as auxiliaries of Count John at this time. But Longchamp failed in his attempt, and an oblique answer by the king to his peremptory actions in England was to include William Marshal amongst the four 'co-justiciars' who were to monitor Longchamp's rule in England.

So it was, in July 1190, when King Richard departed with Philip of France for the Holy Lands, that William commenced the role that the king had begun to fit him for as early as the meeting at Fontevrault, before King Henry's funeral. William became one of four 'co-justiciars', assistants to William de Longchamp. It was for this reason that the king had elevated William and his family as far as he had done. William had to have enough land to give him dignity before the other magnates, whom it was his duty now to help to control. Richard has been criticized for the arrangements he left behind him for governing his lands: for leaving William de Longchamp, an arrogant and tactless man, as chief justiciar; for attempting to buy his brother John's complacency with huge grants of lands and revenues in England, and then expecting to get him to stay on the Continent and not take advantage of the opportunities he had been left with. This is more than a little unjust. He was sufficiently aware of the problems to construct carefully a team of four experienced courtiers and magnates to supervise Longchamp: William Marshal himself, the talented Geoffrey fitz Peter (who now had the lands of the earldom of Essex), Hugh Bardolf and William Briwerre. William Marshal was very much one with fitz Peter and Briwerre; all three were from families who had spent more than one generation in royal service (the other two came from families of royal foresters); all three men were from the south-west of England. In the event, when things began to go wrong, Richard's precautions were to have some success. Over and above them, it is difficult to see what

20 Richard of Devizes *Chronicle of the Time of Richard I* ed. J T Appleby London 1963 12–13.

more he could have done, unless he had taken a reluctant John along with him, and risked his only viable adult heir alongside himself. The fact was that although Richard's arrangements were imperfect, he did at least find his kingdom intact when he returned after a much longer absence than he had anticipated.[21]

William Marshal's elevation to the higher circles of power in England carried its own problems. Chief of them would have been relations with the chancellor and justiciar, William de Longchamp, with whom he had already clashed before the king's departure. Almost as difficult was the problem of John, the king's brother, who was in England in defiance of his oath within months of Richard's departure. Both were impossible men to manage and were plainly going to tussle for control of England as soon as Richard was gone. With John there was a longer-term problem in that for years he would be the most obvious successor to Richard (despite the claims of Richard's nephew, the child, Arthur of Brittany). Now the Marshal was a great magnate, he could not afford to thwart John too openly; his interests demanded that he tread a careful line between his present and future lords. There was also the not unimportant point that John was his overlord for his lordship in Ireland. The Marshal may have had hopes that his own brother, still John's intimate friend, might ease him over this difficult patch. Both John and William Marshal appear together in the witness list of an act of the count's before June 1190, which tells us of at least one cosy tête-à-tête the brothers had with him before Richard departed.[22] He had already by 1190 obtained Count John's confirmation of his foundation of Cartmel priory.

In the event it was Longchamp who was the easier to deal with. His arrogance so alienated the barons, that he had no party to support him in England. Representations were made to King Richard early in 1191, then wintering in Sicily, about the problems Longchamp was causing. William Marshal was deeply implicated in these moves, and the result was a secret royal mandate authorizing the four co-justiciars to remove Longchamp when the time was right, and replace him with the archbishop of Rouen, Walter de Coutances, a man who had grown old and wealthy in the household of Henry II, a man indeed very much like

21 These arguments are rehearsed by J Gillingham in *Richard the Lionheart* London 1978 134–7, 218–21.

22 *Historical and Municipal Documents of Ireland, AD 1172–1320* ed. J T Gilbert Rolls Series 1870 50–1, another leading witness of this act was Bertram de Verdun, who left with Richard on Crusade and died in the Holy Land.

the co-justiciars themselves. William Marshal is known to have had recent and friendly dealings with him over the lordship of Kendal, which he had courteously conceded to the archbishop's nephew (see above).

A protracted political duel between Count John and Longchamp over control of England was ended in October 1191 when, with John besieging Longchamp in the Tower of London, the co-justiciars produced the royal mandate and replaced Longchamp with Archbishop Walter. Longchamp was bundled out of the country. The *Histoire* regards this move with satisfaction. Its author sees the Marshal as a moving spirit in the business, and there are other indications to support his view of William's antagonism to Longchamp. But the *Histoire* is less to be believed on how the *coup d'état* left the Marshal's relations with Count John. It gleefully describes the put-down given John's hopes of power by Archbishop Walter, who is said to have brushed him aside 'seeing to what end he would come'. In fact John's position after Longchamp's departure remained a powerful one. He had, after all, been recognized by the magnates of England as Richard's heir in 1191 at the time of Longchamp's removal, and John was not obliged to retract this claim. Over the next year we find him in a position powerful enough to be consulted over the election of a new archbishop of Canterbury; leading a campaign against the Welsh; and attempting to mediate between the committee of justiciars and Longchamp (for a bribe, we are told by Howden). It would be good to know precisely what the Marshal's relations with the count were in 1191 and 1192, but hindsight persuades the *Histoire's* author that they were already at daggers drawn. The one real indication is a reference that we have to William's part in mediating between John and Longchamp over possession of the castle of Nottingham, which is perhaps ambiguous.[23] But overall one cannot resist the impression that the Marshal must have found John by far the lesser of two evils, and a settlement that removed Longchamp and benefited John was not one that would have harmed or upset him. Richard of Devizes, no friend of the archbishop of Rouen, reports Walter's careful temporizing with Count John at this time, but chooses to see it as stabbing Longchamp in the back rather than searching for peace and future security. The Marshal may well have adopted a similar ambivalence. It is significant in this respect that in 1194, after Richard's return,

23 *Memoriale Walteri de Coventria* ed. W Stubbs (2 vols) Rolls Series 1872–3 I 462; an episode wrongly dated by the *Histoire* to 1193.

the Marshal refused to do homage to Richard directly for his Irish lands, but reserved his homage for John. The *Histoire* had to record this business, it seems, for it was too notorious an incident in the Marshal's career to gloss over. Longchamp, his enemy, remarked at the Marshal's refusal: 'Planting vines, Marshal?'. That is, he accused him of insinuating himself into the good graces of the future king, sowing the seeds of favour. The *Histoire* puts a huffy and legalistic reply in the Marshal's mouth, but even as the biographer records the exchange it sounds to me that Longchamp had the best of it.

News of Richard's capture and imprisonment in Germany on his return home, which reached England in December 1192, ruined what seems to have been a very satisfactory year for Count John and the justiciars. John was drawn into a conspiracy with Philip II of France and, after a trip to Paris, returned to England in March 1193 with a company of mercenaries and ambitions to confront the justiciars with his claims to the crown. In the event he did not secure much support and was besieged at Windsor by the reluctant justiciars. They seem to have been less than happy with developments. One of them, Hugh Bardolf, refused to fight John, saying that he was the count's sworn man and could not fight his lord. William Marshal might have used the same excuse, for he too was John's man for his Irish lands. He must have been heartily relieved when John agreed to a truce till November on hearing news of the ransom terms for Richard's release. Peace was once more re-established. With John discredited and Richard's return assured (once the money was forthcoming) the justiciars returned to their duties and John disappeared to France. But only in February 1194, with Richard's return imminent, did the Marshal and his colleagues finally move against John. William Marshal played his part, seizing John's main English stronghold of Bristol and other properties of the count in the south west: the area, as we will see, in which his political power base lay.

. . .

## KING RICHARD'S CAPTAIN AND COURTIER, 1194–99

One of the most revealing episodes in the history of the Marshal's political development occurred in March 1194, when Richard returned to England. It was not Richard's return that I refer to, so much as an event that took place at the same time, John Marshal's death. John Marshal had mixed fortunes during the years of King

Richard's absence. Although he lost the shrievalty of Yorkshire in 1190, he was compensated after Longchamp's fall with the shrievalty of Sussex, where he had lands at Bosham, and he retained Sussex till he died. He had married Aline du Port, the daughter of a Hampshire baron, but no issue had come from the marriage. This sterile union seems to sum up a career destined to have no continuing success. For his brother Henry Marshal, dean of York, things were different. Early in 1194 Richard, in Germany nominated him for the vacant bishopric of Exeter, apparently as a token of his appreciation of William Marshal's services. John Marshal's death occurred early in March 1194, just after his younger brother's election, and just before Richard landed in England. William Marshal was at Chepstow when the king arrived, and from the account of the *Histoire* seems to have heard the news of the landing at the same time as the news of his elder brother's death. Here was a pretty quandary for a professional courtier. What should he do? Go first to the king his lord, or attend the head of his own family to his grave? The *Histoire* carefully weighs up his predicament:

> He was in such grief for his brother when he knew of it that his heart all but broke! But so that his dilemma was not so evil, he had other news, thank God, that was fairer for him. A messenger appeared speaking well, courteously and wisely, who said that the king of England had come to his own land, safe, sound and happy. If he had been given £10,000 the grief which oppressed him could not have been so well assuaged. 'God help me!' he exclaimed, 'Although I have never been so afflicted as by the death of my brother, the coming of my lord has brought the best of consolations. I thank God as much for the adversity as for the prosperity which has come on me so fast, because such joy have I in the king's coming that I can stand against the grief I did not believe I could face.'.[24]

The Marshal's actions were as judicious as ever. His brother had died at Marlborough and he sent knights from his retinue to escort the body to Cirencester. There the Marshal met the corpse on his way to the king and viewed it, comforting his brother's widow. A mass was heard at Cirencester abbey but, we are told, messengers reached him at this point urging him on to meet the king. What could a courtier and magnate do? He sent his brother's corpse and widow on to Bradenstoke priory and the interment under his

24 *Histoire* I ll. 10023–48.

knights' escort, keeping three by him on the road to meet the king at Huntingdon, on the way to reduce the rebel garrison of Nottingham.

This episode tells us more perhaps than anything else about the sort of man William Marshal had become. We may discount the messengers who came to Cirencester urging on the Marshal to the king's side. They are a touch too opportune in their appearance to be credible. Their introduction is, however, significant. They are there to excuse the Marshal, because an excuse is necessary. No king could have cavilled at a day or two's delay in appearing if a courtier had to bury his brother, but William Marshal had chosen not to delay. He came direct to the king after the minimum of a ceremonial adieu to the head of his family. He could have been criticized in his own day for such self-serving, and the tone of the *Histoire's* apologetic leads one to suspect that he was. The Marshal was such a courtier that he was as happy in the royal presence as nowhere else, unless it were behind the king's banner in the field. John Marshal was not such a brother to him that his death could have distracted William too long from his natural habitat. Let us believe that William felt grief for his brother, but there are degrees of grief. That which William felt for John Marshal might rate as something a little beyond regret, with some guilt mingled in perhaps; a twist in the soul sapped by years of mutual diffidence and earlier tension. Not enough to keep William from the man who wore the crown, the true object of his affection, the man who could give him what his family had not.

For the rest of Richard's reign William Marshal was deeply engaged in the business of the court, and for the most part he spent the five years in France. The witness lists to Richard's charters seem to show a pattern to William's attendance between 1195 and 1198. He is with the king from spring to autumn, but is absent in winter. It is tempting to see him wintering in domestic content in his Norman castles, busy on his own affairs and begetting children in the least congenial season for campaigning. There is some evidence during this period that he paid attention to his English estates and interests, which he would have had managed for him by his stewards and bailiffs. He was in England briefly in the spring of 1196 and in the autumn of 1198, when he appears on the bench of the royal justices in Westminster Hall.[25] He might have used these opportunities to attend to his own interests and discuss

25 *Pedes Finium, 1195–1214* (2 vols) Record Commission 1835 I 176; *Feet of Fines, 1182–96* Pipe Roll Society XVII 1894 110.

his officers' actions. There is some evidence that these men were busy in his absence. In spring 1198, when William was in fact in Normandy, he recovered a property in Southampton from his brother's inheritance.[26] Although (like the other co-justiciars) he lost his shrievalty in 1194, he was allowed to keep charge of the royal forest of Dean, and his English interests were extended elsewhere by his inheritance of his brother's lands in Berkshire, Wiltshire and elsewhere, and by his brother's shrievalty of Sussex. But as far as England and Wales were concerned, the rival attractions of the royal court drew him away from them, to France where he had spent most of his adult life.

There is a certain evenness about these years which makes me think that the Marshal was happy enough during them. He was in high favour with the king who was scoring continuing victories over Philip of France; he had a congenial life and growing family in Normandy; his military prowess continued. Such was his influence with Richard that he was able to exert himself on occasions to mitigate the effects of the king's touchy temper. The *Histoire* gives us the example of William's ability to soften the fit of royal choler against the papal legate, Peter of Capua, when no-one else dared approach him. But another source confirms this, the Life of St Hugh of Lincoln tells of an incident where William Marshal and his friend, Baldwin de Béthune, saved the bishop from the king's anger over money he was owed.[27] The campaign of 1197 was a particularly happy time for William. By the end of that year he would have been fifty-years-old, greyer and slower, but still well able to take part in the assault on the French castle of Milly-sur-Thérain, a little to the north west of the French city of Beauvais on the northern Marches of Normandy. He clambered up a scaling ladder and defended a section of the wall till assistance came, flattening the constable of the castle with a blow to the helmet while he was waiting. The genuine Marshal shines through in this little anecdote. Feeling a little weary after his exertions, he sat on the body of the unconscious constable while the battle swept on past him and the castle was taken. After the fight Richard chastised him mildly for pushing himself forward in

26 *Curia Regis Rolls* i 50. The property would seem to have been the large tenement on Westgate Street, near the quayside that was later called 'Ronceval', from being given by the Marshal's son to Roncesvalles priory in France, C. Platt, *Medieval Southampton* London 1973 269.

27 *Magna Vita sancti Hugonis* ed. D L Douie and H Farmer (2 vols) London 1961–2 ii 107–9.

such a way at his age, but we can well imagine the smugness with which the Marshal must have regarded the incident at Milly, and the pleasure of his numerous followers at their ageing lord's exploit. Following Sidney Painter's chronology, Milly was followed by a prestigious and expensive embassy along with the Norman baron, Peter des Préaux, late in the year, to Count Baldwin of Flanders and Count Reginald of Boulogne, to persuade them to ally with Richard against Philip of France.[28] Being a vassal of the Count of Flanders for possessions in St-Omer made the Marshal a fitting emissary. During the course of the visit the Marshal took the field with Count Baldwin against the King of France, and although a battle did not in the end take place, the strategy he had advised was thought to have contributed to Philip's retreat.

This happy state of affairs came to an abrupt and unexpected end in April 1199. Early in March, King Richard had marched south from Anjou on a minor campaign into the Limousin. William Marshal took his leave of him and returned to Normandy on royal business. On 26 March the king received a crossbow bolt in his shoulder while reconnoitering the defences of a small castle he was besieging. Eleven days later, on 6 April, he died. There were two potential heirs: Count John, now aged thirty-one, who had led a blameless and useful life since the troubles of 1194, and Arthur of Brittany, son of Geoffrey, John's elder brother, a young man still under age. Richard, on his death-bed, left the kingdom to John, overriding whatever rights might have been thought to have come to Arthur through his father. There were two schools of thought on this question at the time: whether a younger brother could exclude a dead elder brother's son from the succession. William Marshal had, however, long committed himself to John's side of the question, which seems indeed to have been the traditional view of succession amongst the Norman aristocracy. The day of strict primogeniture had yet to come. The day after Richard's death, news of his illness finally reached the ducal castle of Vaudreuil by courier, where William and others were sitting as justices. It was not until three days later that news of Richard's death finally came to Normandy. When the news eventually reached Rouen, to which William and the archbishop of Canterbury had moved to secure the city, it was late at night after the

28 The *Histoire's* account of this is confirmed by a payment of 1,730 marks (£1, 153 6s. 8d.) made to Peter and William for their expenses by the Exchequer, *Pipe Roll of 10 Richard* 172.

Marshal had gone to bed. The *Histoire* tells us of a nocturnal debate between the hastily-dressed Marshal and the archbishop of Canterbury over the suitability of John to succeed. William stood out unequivocally for John, which simply confirms what his actions during the earlier part of the reign hint at. The *Histoire* mitigates what it obviously sees as a rare error of judgement by William in depicting him as gloomily listening to the archbishop's all too accurate warning that he would be sorry for his decision. But in fact, whatever the *Histoire* says, the Marshal must have calculated on John's initial weakness as a time when a discreet, ambitious and circumspect man could easily pick up gains and increase his power. Was that not the lesson he had learned in 1189? Did not every royal succession since the Normans first came to England prove it?

. . .

## LOSING NORMANDY AND ROYAL FAVOUR, 1199–1205

William and the archbishop were very soon dispatched into England by John and there they received an oath of loyalty to John from the barons and prelates, many of whom attempted to make their oath conditional on the king's respect for their claims. They grumbled, but accepted assurances that the new king would give them a hearing. With England passive, William returned to John in Normandy and escorted him back across the Channel to England.

One wonders if William did not bend the king's ear about what he considered his own claims on the return trip. Whether he did or not, if royal grants were what the Marshal was expecting in 1199, he was not to be disappointed. The author of the *Histoire* declares in a rather unhappy way that he had heard grants were made at this point, but he knew nothing of them, not being in England at the time. He seems to have been reluctant to credit John with any generosity to his lord and it is very odd indeed that he refused to describe the grants, which other sources tell us were great indeed. One wonders what sort of accusations he was trying to gloss over. The first, and perhaps the most gratifying grant, was the formal investiture with the title of earl, which William received just before John's coronation in London on 27 May 1199. Howden records that William was invested earl under the name of Striguil, but he was wrong. As early as June 1199 William Marshal appears in royal documents as 'Earl of Pembroke', a title he uses consistently for the rest of his life and the title by which he was generally known by others.[29] There has to be some significance in the revival of this title, and an abundance of other evidence soon confirms that William had indeed received from John at least the promise of the Marcher lordship of Pembroke. He did not receive it immediately for John was at this time engaged in hostilities with Maelgwyn and Gruffudd, sons of the late Prince of West Wales, the great Rhys ap Gruffudd. During 1199 and 1200 Richard's sheriff of Cornwall, John of Torrington, was transferred to keep what were still the royal castles of Carmarthen and Pembroke, and it is clearly stated that 'Pembrokeshire' too was in his wardship. John was still issuing orders to the sheriff of Pembroke and to 'his' barons and knights of Rhos and Pembroke in October 1200.[30] But in April 1200 John had released some lands in West Wales to Earl William, the territories of Efelffre and Ystlwyf east of the lordship of Pembroke itself, until he should deliver to William his land of Emlyn (then occupied by Maelgwyn ap Rhys, along with its castle of Cilgerran, originally built by the earlier earls of Pembroke). It seems likely that Pembroke came into the hands of its new earl at some time between October 1200, when John came to a settlement with Maelgwyn's brother Rhys, and May 1201, when William Marshal appears as the patron of the burgesses of Pembroke, securing trading privileges in London for them from the king.[31]

In reclaiming Pembroke, the lost possession of his wife's family, William Marshal had achieved what Earl Richard Strongbow, never a favourite at the Angevin court, had failed in. Pembroke brought him considerable prestige. In terms of land the area under the earl's jurisdiction was about twice that of his other Marcher lordship of Striguil, with much good arable land. This was 'Pembrokeshire' the area of jurisdiction of the earl's own sheriff, who presided over its central county court where criminal and civil justice was administered in the earl's name and by the county's own customary law. Beyond this lordship the earl had claims on

29 William is *comes Penbroc* in a charter of King John dated 20 June 1199 *Rotuli Chartarum* 79. His own charters have him either by that title, or *comes de Penbroc*, or some other spelling. The exception is in a charter of his to Bradenstoke priory, of which the original survives, Wiltshire Record Office Ailesbury/Savernake deeds 9/15/1 where he is *comes Penbrocsir[e]*, namely 'Earl of Pembrokeshire'.

30 *Pipe Roll of 1 John* 182; *Pipe Roll of 2 John* 226, 230; *Rotuli Chartarum* 98.

31 Ibid. 47, 95.

the allegiance of the lord of Cemaes to the north east, and it was obviously still remembered that the Marshal's wife's grandfather, Earl Gilbert, had included the castles of Cardigan and Cilgerran within his earldom. Pembroke was one of the most powerful Marcher lordships, thoroughly organized for war, which had been its natural state for a good part of the last century. It was a land of powerful castellans: at Roch, Wiston, Carew, Manorbier and Haverford. Perhaps most of all, it was the staging post for Ireland. The Marshal's new vassals at Roch, Carew and Manorbier were also some of the greatest men of Leinster. Possession of Pembroke was for him the first step to gaining effective control over his Irish lands. It is not surprising that he showed an immediate interest in its potential.

Although the *Histoire* has nothing to say about it, there is good reason to think that the Marshal visited both Pembroke and Ireland at some time towards the end of 1200 or early in 1201. We can imagine him meeting his new tenants, taking their homage and sizing up his new problems. We know of grants and concessions made by him on this visit to at least one of the great barons of Leinster, Adam of Hereford, probably on the occasion of his taking his homage; grants which also indicate that Countess Isabel had accompanied the Marshal to Leinster in 1200–1.[32]

32 Between September 1200 and March 1201 the Marshal drops out of the king's entourage. Since he appears in May 1201 as lord of Pembroke, we can reasonably suggest he must have gone to the place during this hiatus to take the homage of his men. From Pembroke it was a quick crossing, though stormy, to Waterford or Dublin. There is a reference in the Annals of Ireland, apparently quoting a foundation chronicle of Tintern Parva abbey, to the Marshal founding that house in Leinster in 1200 in fulfilment of a vow he made when caught 'for a day and a night' in a storm at sea, before safely making Wexford harbour. There is confirmatory evidence in the fact that in June 1203 the bishop of Ferns dedicated the cemetery of another new abbey, Duiske, for which William Marshal had already made some preliminary purchases of land at an unstated time. The Marshal could only have made plans for this other new abbey in 1200–1, as he could not have been in Ireland in the interim, see *Chartularies of St Mary's Abbey, Dublin* ed. J T Gilbert (2 vols) Rolls Series 1884 II 307–8; 'The charters of the Cistercian Abbey of Duiske' ed. J H Bernard *Proceedings of the Royal Irish Academy* XXXV 1918–20 14, 16, 24. The formal foundation charters of Tintern Parva and Duiske are all later than this, dating between 1207 and 1212, but such delays were by no means unusual. Further evidence of the Marshal's stay in Leinster and his contacts with his tenants there may be found in a charter of King John dated 1 March 1202 which confirms to the Leinster baron, Adam of Hereford, concessions in Ireland recently made to him by the Marshal, *Calendar of Ormond Deeds I 1172–1230 AD*, ed. E Curtis Dublin 1932 13–14.

The failure of the *Histoire* to mention the Marshal's first visit to Leinster is more than a little odd. It states boldly, on the occasion of the Marshal's crossing to Ireland in 1207, that its hero had never been there before; but this cannot be true. We know from several sources that he had been there six years before exerting himself in Ireland, taking the homage of at least some of his tenants, winning over at least one significant supporter, the bishop of Ossory; making grand plans to erect two new, Cistercian abbeys to commemorate his assumption of the lordship of Leinster; and leaving behind him as seneschal his knight, Geoffrey fitz Robert, whom he had married some years before to Basilia, sister of the late Earl Richard Strongbow. When the *Histoire* can be detected to have kept quiet about an incident there is a reason for it; it is seeking to protect its hero. There must be more to this than just the memory of the nausea of the rough and dangerous sea-crossing, which one source tells us that he had. Looking ahead to the problems he was to have in Ireland in 1207–8 it might be suggested that the Leinster expedition of 1200–1 did not go smoothly. As we will see in the next chapter, Leinster was a coherent political community, its greatest men closely related and frontier warriors all, with a strong sense of place and identity. They had proved in the past hostile to effeminate courtiers, as they seemed to regard them, from across the Irish Sea (they had handled roughly Henry II's steward, William fitz Adelin, in 1176, and had been less than impressed by John, the king's son, in 1185). Into this exclusive and hostile community sailed the Marshal. It may well be that they would not take him seriously and found cause to resent him. A hint of how he might have offended is to be found in his known doings on that expedition. His new monasteries were pious intrusions, acts of patronage directed back across the Irish Sea; colonies of his abbey of Tintern in Gwent, and the Wiltshire abbey of Stanley. The old colonials of Leinster might have had their hackles raised by this, especially if it was combined with grants to the knights who came to Ireland in the Marshal's entourage. The parting appointment of seneschal to Geoffrey fitz Robert, who had as wife the sister of the great Strongbow, might be seen as a soothing gesture to settle ruffled feathers.

Back at the court the Marshal had further grants from the king. He once again received the shrievalty of Gloucestershire and to this was added the keeping of Gloucester and Bristol castles. By 1201 he had the keeping of the lands and heir of the baronial family of Giffard of Brimpsfield, powerful in the south west. As in 1189,

William's relatives were not forgotten in his surge of good fortune. His nephew and household knight, the bastard John Marshal, was awarded by the king the heiress of the Ryes family, who brought him the Norfolk barony of Hockering and the small honor of Ryes in Normandy. In this way the bastard son of John Marshal found more than enough compensation for the diversion of his father's lands to his uncle.[33] Between John's coronation in May 1199 and the end of 1201, William Marshal was generally to be found in the king's company, whether in England, Normandy, Gascony or Poitou. In April 1200 at Westminster, in August of the same year at La Réole in Gascony, and in May 1201 at Cirencester, John

33 The question of the parentage of this John Marshal has for a long time been unnecessarily clouded. Meyer, followed by Painter and recently by Duby have concluded that John could not have been the son of John Marshal (II) because William Marshal was in fact his brother's heir. William's nephew John, they say, must therefore have been the son of a younger brother, perhaps that Anselm who briefly appears in the *Histoire*. The *Complete Peerage*, the bible of English aristocracy, dismisses this, saying that William's nephew, John, could very easily have been John Marshal's bastard. In fact there is conclusive proof that he was just that, firstly in a charter of William Marshal's dating to the 1190s in which John is called 'the younger John Marshal', and in another charter dating to a time after 1199 in which William confirms his deceased brother's grants to Bradenstoke priory, his nephew John appears in the witness list, where he is called, significantly and forlornly, 'John Marshal, *the son of John*', see, *The Cartulary of the Cistercian Abbey of Flaxley* ed. A W Crawley-Boevey Exeter 1887 175; Wiltshire Record Office, 9/15/1 Ailesbury-Savernake Deeds. Furthermore, a charter of *Johannes Marascallus filius Johannis Marascalli* (that is, William's brother) concerning Nettlecombe, Som, is attested by *Johanne Marascallo filio meo*, see *Collectanea Topographica et Genealogica* II London 1835 164. Lastly, in his old age John Marshal, the nephew of William, made grants to the Norfolk priory of Walsingham not just for his father, John, but also his mother, *Alice*. The fact that he commemorated his mother by name must mean that she was no casual prostitute, but a woman of good birth. This brings us to the identity of that Alice. In the early thirteenth century, Alice de Colleville, made a grant at Maidencourt, Berks, to Poughley priory, Berks, for the souls of the brothers John Marshal, and William Marshal Earl of Pembroke (putting John first). In this pious grant for the dead lover and his brother, her son's patron, we may have the evidence we need to pinpoint John Marshal's mother, see Cartulary of Walsingham BL ms Cotton E vii fo 95v; Westminster Abbey Muniments no. 7242. There are two known contemporary women called Alice de Colleville. One was an early-thirteenth-century Suffolk widow, alias Alice of Frostenden (who had married a Robert de Colleville), see *Blythborough Priory Cartulary* ed. C Harper-Bill (2 vols) Suffolk Record Society II, III, 1980–81) II 151–2. The other, and more likely candidate, was wife to a Sussex landowner, William de Colleville, around 1200 (John Marshal was a Sussex landowner and sheriff of Sussex from 1190–94) see *Curia Regis Rolls* I 200; III 93.

favoured the Marshal with numbers of charters of grants and confirmations; one, a grant of the advocacy of Notley abbey in Buckinghamshire, a Giffard foundation, was made 'out of the love we have for our beloved and faithful man, William Marshal, Earl of Pembroke, and because of the good and loyal service he has done us'.[34] There is no doubt that the Marshal, together with his colleagues Geoffrey fitz Peter, now Earl of Essex, and William Longespée, Earl of Salisbury, were seen by John at this stage in his reign as the main props of his rule, and lavish gifts followed. More established court magnates, such as the Earls of Leicester, Chester and Surrey, received rather less. Between 1199 and 1201 the Marshal reached the peak of his life as court favourite, raised by his lord to be the most powerful magnate in the southern Marches of Wales, or at least he would have been if he had ever stayed there long enough to exert himself.

There is little to say here about the Marshal's part in the loss of Normandy by King John. The *Histoire* is as usual reticent about the times in the Marshal's career when he was touched by failure. From late in 1201 John used him in a local capacity to defend the northern borders of Normandy and the Pays de Caux, where indeed most of his Norman estates were. Here he operated with some success until 1203 along with the Earl of Surrey, himself a great landowner of the region, and the king's half-brother, William Longspée, who had married the Marshal's first cousin, Ela of Salisbury, and received the earldom to which she was heir. This was the period when King John was alleged by several sources to have himself stabbed to death his nephew, Arthur, the boy whose rights to the throne had been argued against by the Marshal in 1199. This act was lamentable, both morally and politically; it undid all that John had managed to achieve since his succession. It alienated both the Bretons and William des Roches, John's chief support in Anjou, and destroyed his moral authority. The Marshal may have been in Normandy when the act probably took place, in April 1203. An attempt has recently been made to link William Marshal with this unsavoury event, but apart from a dubious passage in the *Histoire* which refers to an undatable dispute between the king and the Marshal, which might have been on a quite different subject, there is no evidence that he was anywhere near Rouen when the murder was said to have

34 *Rotuli Chartarum*, 74.

happened, he might even have been safe in England at the time.[35]

In 1203 John's continental domains began to fall apart and Philip of France was able to exploit the situation to the full. William remained with King John for much of that gloomy year, although at some time during it he was in residence at his castle of Hamstead Marshall in Berkshire, where he was visited by his friend, the bishop of Ossory, with whom he had struck up a relationship on his visit to Leinster two years before.[35] The *Histoire* has little to say of 1203; it has a distinct aversion to tales of failure and defeat. The Marshal still remained high in favour. The William le Gros who was made seneschal of Normandy early in 1203 would seem to have been his nephew of that name (see Chapter 5). The *Histoire* does not mention this, nor the failed expedition that the Marshal made to relieve the key fortress of Château Gaillard in the latter part of the year, which we learn of from French sources. William le Breton, Philip Augustus's chaplain, writes of the Marshal 'most faithful keeper of my counsels' being dispatched by King John with a considerable force to push the French back deep into the Vexin, but a delay to part of William's army led to the Marshal's repulse by the great French general William des Barres.[37] The omission is of a piece with what else we know of the *Histoire's* prejudices: William des Barres was another of those knightly characters whose reputation was exalted above his fellows: 'the flower of chivalry' as William le Breton called him.

In December 1203 the Marshal left Normandy for England with the king. The king would never return there, and when the Marshal returned six months later, the duchy was almost totally in Philip's hands. The loss of Normandy was a difficult time for the English magnates, many of whom held some land in the duchy which they would lose if they did not do homage to the new ruler. The English magnates of John's reign were well aware of earlier

35 M D Legge 'William the Marshal and Arthur of Brittany' *Bulletin of the Institute of Historical Research* IV 1982 18–24.

36 *Irish Monastic and Episcopal Deeds* ed. N B White Irish MSS Commission Dublin 1936 301–2.

37 William le Breton, *Philippidos* ll. 144–336 in *Recueil des Historiens de France* XVII 197–8. Painter refused to credit William le Breton's account on the rather specious grounds that he only introduced the Marshal's name in a poetic way to enhance the glamour of Des Barres' triumph, but the account is very particular on the identity of the leader, and names the Marshal on three occasions.

times when England and Normandy had separated, as in their fathers' days when the Count of Anjou conquered the duchy from King Stephen. Then most had had to give up either their Norman or English lands, following the ruler from whom they held most. The same happened in 1204, but unlike 1144 the position was to be permanent, and indeed there are indications that some Norman landholders anticipated the separation would be long-term. A number of Anglo-Normans divided their estates at this time, giving away the Norman portion to brothers or younger sons. The Marshal seems to have taken an optimistic view of the problem. It is undeniable that he loved Normandy, land of his youth and prime, and now as a man approaching his sixties would have been very reluctant to quit it. In 1200 he was still estate-building in Normandy, and by an exchange with Roger d'Abenon annexed to his castelry of Orbec in central Normandy Roger's considerable patrimony, in return for lands of his in England.[38]

The Marshal must have had abundant time to consider his response to the crisis. It would not be surprising if his urging of John to make peace, which we hear of as early as 1203, before they left Normandy, was not at least partly influenced by his desire for a stable situation in which he could reach some accommodation about his Norman lands. In May 1204 John sent him to Normandy as part of an embassy to Philip to seek terms. The other earl with him was Robert of Leicester, one of the greatest landholders in Normandy and a man with much more to lose than the Marshal. The mission was not a success, but both earls used it as an excuse to negotiate on their own account. King Philip, in return for a substantial sum of money, gave them both a year to meet his demand that all Norman landholders must do him liege homage or lose their lands.

The Earl of Leicester never had to face the decision. He was generously compensated by John with the keeping of the earldom of Richmond and, in any case, died before the end of 1204. No such generous a compensation was offered to the Marshal; or at least not directly. But there are some indications that John was trying to placate the Marshal with the possibility of gains in Wales. John made a direct grant to him in April 1204 of the lordship of Goodrich Castle in Herefordshire to add to his possessions in the southern March, and in August allowed him the privilege of a market in the town there.[39]

38 *Rotuli Chartarum*, 65.

39 Ibid. 124, *Rotuli Litterarum Clausarum* i 4.

This could by no means outweigh the loss of an honor the size of Longueville, but there was more in the balance than Goodrich. In November, or early in December 1204, William Marshal was in West Wales once again. With a 'mighty host' (probably at royal expense) he successfully recovered from the Welsh the castle of Cilgerran (an event we hear of only from the Welsh annals).[40] Cilgerran had been part of the earldom of Pembroke in the 1130s but had fallen into Welsh hands. In 1200 John had been unable to give it to the Marshal with the rest of the earldom because the princely house of Deheubarth would not give it up, so he compensated him with two lordships in Dyfed. John had now let the Marshal loose with a licence to take what he could by force. He had heard no doubt that Maelgwyn ap Rhys, the hitherto dominant prince of Deheubarth, had been defeated in war with his nephews in the course of the summer, and the Welsh of that region were now divided and weak. Again, we must ask why the *Histoire* does not mention this campaign, particularly because it was so obviously a success. The only answer that makes sense is that which applies also to the failure to mention the creation of William as earl in 1199 and the trip to the west in 1201: the author will not willingly recall anything that reflects well on King John. He therefore edits out all mention of the acquisition of the earldom of Pembroke and the king's subsequent grants. It is a remarkable fact that Pembroke does not feature at all in the *Histoire*, despite being the seat of William's earldom after 1199, except when King John embarked there for Ireland in 1210.

Before the year given to him by King Philip was up, in spring 1205, the Marshal was back in Normandy on another, more informal, embassy to King Philip. Before he had left England he

40 *Brut y Tywysogyon: Red Book of Hergest Version* ed. T Jones Cardiff 1955 186; *Annales Cambriae* ed. J W Ab Ithel Rolls Series 1860 63. These annals do not date the seizure of Cilgerran, and Painter calculated that it happened in summer 1204 (linking it with the Marshal's meeting with the princes of Gwynedd and Powys in July at Worcester, as the king's agent); but the subsequently discovered 'Chronicle of Wales' tells us that in fact the Marshal seized the castle 'at the turn of the year about Advent', see T Jones 'Cronica de Wallia', *Bulletin of the Board of Celtic Studies* xi 1946 32. The meeting at Worcester cannot therefore be linked directly to any campaign. The Marshal was with the king at Winchester on 6 October 1204, but there is no evidence of his being at court again until 16 December, at Clere, Hants. It is likely that the campaign in west Wales occupied a good part of the brief intervening period; the *Annales Cambriae* stress the Marshal's speed, appearing before the castle walls and taking it at the first onset, before the *teulu* (household guards) of Maelgwyn in garrison could even arm themselves.

discussed his plight with John, and he was generously allowed a licence to do homage to the King of France. The act was performed in March or April 1205, and the Marshal received back Longueville and his castelries of Orbec and Meullers. The one difficulty was that Philip would not be satisfied with less than the Marshal's exclusive liege homage for his Norman lands.

William returned to England to face the consequences. He may be forgiven for thinking that there would be no aftermath. His rise had been so effortless since 1186 that twenty years of continuing success had blinded him to the possibility of disgrace. His determination to hang on to his Norman lands went beyond reason. If it is a sample of the Marshal's capacity for independent political judgement then it is a sign that he had not yet become as good a magnate as he was a courtier. There were undeniable precedents for the position in which he chose to put himself. The best-known were the Counts of Meulan, who had been vassals both of the King of England and King of France since the eleventh century. In 1157 the then count came to a generally acceptable arrangement that he owed his liege, or principal, homage to the King of England. If the counts then followed the King of England in war against the King of France they did not lose their French lands, some of which were to send their normal quota of knights to the King of France for the campaign.[41] This was the position that the Marshal was attempting to secure for himself in 1204–5. It is the position that the legal treatise known as Bracton pictures him in while describing the situation of Anglo-French magnates in the thirteenth century.[42] But Philip was not so easily fobbed off and by the written terms of the 1204 settlement between him and William, which still survive in Paris, William was obliged to accept that he was Philip's liege man in Normandy.[43] This meant that he might not fight Philip in France without losing his lands. One cannot acquit the Marshal of wilful blindness here. He could not but be well aware of the plight of the then Count of Meulan, Robert, an old acquaintance of his from the days in Young Henry's household. He had in fact indulged in some sharp profiteering at the count's expense in the crisis of 1204. He took from Count Robert his Dorset manor of Sturminster when he was

41 D Crouch *The Beaumont Twins* Cambridge 1986 64–79.

42 *De Legibus et Consuetudinibus Anglie* ed. T Twiss (6 vols) Rolls Series 1878–83) VI 374–6.

43 Paris Archives Nationales J 399 no. 5.

in dire straits for money.[44] Count Robert had ended that year living as a pauper on royal charity in England, but this was a warning lost on the Marshal.

John's reproaches towards the Marshal were not long in coming. It is unlikely that John had seriously thought about the consequences of the Marshal's actions in Normandy, or at least had been persuaded that William had obtained preferential terms from Philip. When the Marshal returned he found that John had been acquainted with the exact terms of the oath, and the phrase that William was to be Philip's liege man in France had angered the king. The Marshal protested that this did not harm King John's interests, but John was not so easily reassured. It is not necessary to see the Marshal guilty here, as Painter did, of deliberate deception of the king, just over-optimism. But he was certainly being obtuse and rash in seeking his own advantage, and unjustified in hoping that he would muddle through unscathed in a conflict with the king. There is good evidence, indeed, that the Marshal was growing reckless in his behaviour to the king, and had already tried his patience. He had in fact indulged in at least one open dispute with John in the summer of 1204 which the *Histoire* does not notice. He had confronted the king privately with the demand that he override the proper process of law and award him the Meulan manor of Sturminster in Dorset over the heads of the two countesses who disputed its ownership with him. When John suggested mildly that the Marshal wait for a few weeks until the case could be brought before his full council, the Marshal had become stubborn, demanding a decision on the spot, and repeatedly refused to back down, until other courtiers intervened and mollified him. John had been annoyed enough to direct his clerks to file a report of the incident in the justice rolls.[45]

In June 1205 he came to an open breach with John. The king was determined on an expedition to recover his position in Poitou and William was summoned with the other magnates to go. He refused. A loud quarrel followed with both men appealing to the judgement of the barons. John accused William of conspiracy with the King of France, William said the king was inciting him to

44 *Curia Regis Rolls* III 124.

45 Ibid. The Marshal got his way. On 23 August 1204 Sturminster was committed to his household knight, Thomas of Rochford, and in the next month the sheriff of Dorset was directed to deliver the manor to him along with lands that had belonged to the Norman baron, William Martel, *Rotuli Litterarum Clausarum* I 6–8.

break the terms of his agreement with Philip. The barons preferred not to get involved, but the argument went on. Many of the younger household knights, who were a feature of John's personal following, were hot against the Marshal, but none were so confident that they would risk proving their case in battle against him. The barons, particularly Baldwin de Béthune, the Marshal's old friend whose daughter was now betrothed to the Marshal's son William, patched up a reconciliation, but there was no denying the fact that the Marshal had miscalculated and for the first time in his career as a magnate he was out of royal favour. A new political life had begun for him.

*Chapter 4*

# THE MAKING OF A REGENT

. . .

## HUMILIATION, 1205–1207

The Norman and Angevin kings of England had some obnoxious ways of dealing with courtiers who had offended them. The Angevins were the more sophisticated. With two sensational exceptions (the disposal of Arthur of Brittany and the starvation of the Briouze family), the time of King John was not notable for political murder. John was not given to political executions amongst his barons. Indeed, on one occasion he even expressed dissatisfaction with a baron who had (legally) executed a treacherous dependent. He was not a particularly bloody tyrant, however unpleasant and insecure a man he was. The Normans had fewer scruples. John's great-grandfather, Henry I, the Conqueror's son and, a man much praised of late for his sophistication as a ruler, had personally hurled a traitor to his death from a tower in Rouen. But as the ground approached, Henry's victim at least had the consolation that his learned executioner had disposed of him in the same way as the Ancient Romans dealt with treason to the Republic: precipitation, from the Tarpeian rock in the Capitol.[1]

The world of Henry II and his sons was less bloody; but this does not mean that it was a pleasant experience to be on the wrong side of the king. To offend the king, as several bishops and lay magnates did, was to court exile and financial ruin. Becket, of course, lost his life, although Henry II was not directly to blame for that. Becket's colleague and adversary, Bishop Arnulf of Lisieux, gives a better picture of how the Angevin method was meant to work. First, privileges were withdrawn, and the court became noticeably unfriendly. Royal bailiffs suddenly became harsher in their exactions, lands were occupied and lawsuits began to go

1 C W Hollister, 'Royal Acts of Mutilation: the case against Henry I' *Albion* x (1978), 330–40, cautions against regarding Henry I's brutality as psychotic: he regards it as necessary in the context of his times.

against him. His power drained away as men learned that the king had withdrawn his favour. Who would follow a man who could not further their careers? Therefore his canons, and even his nephews, turned against him. A stony silence met petitions. In the end Arnulf could cope no more and resigned his see after five years of humiliation. Harried out of Normandy he ended his days in the abbey of St-Victor in Paris, awaiting from the king a promised pension that was slow to come.[2] Even he was luckier than Robert Bloet, bishop of Lincoln under Henry I. His archdeacon, Henry of Huntingdon, records something of the same method employed against him and how, worn out at the end, he collapsed and died at the king's side.[3]

Barons too met the same method. But we know less of their roads to disgrace, for their problems were usually less well-documented. We do know that the Marshal's father, John, encountered royal disfavour from 1158 onwards. His part in the hounding of Becket was perhaps intended to buy him back some tranquillity. Now with William Marshal we see at last a baron under a cloud. It was not the deepest and darkest of clouds, but it was undoubtedly a chilly and uncomfortable place to be. The *Histoire* depicts the king retiring to his chamber after his encounter with the Marshal: 'He thought hard, after he had eaten, how he could get even with the Marshal, and how he could find a means to distress him'.[4] But if this was so the king was circumspect. The fact is that the breach between the two men in 1205 was not as severe as the *Histoire* wishes us to believe. After his death John was universally acknowledged to have been a bad thing, as indeed he still is. To be in opposition to John was to be on the side of the angels. So the author of the *Histoire* deliberately disguised the closeness between John and its hero in the first years of the reign. When the two men disagreed, it was an opportunity to persuade the reader that the Marshal was a hero of the moral resistance to the ogre-king. He was never that. He had made his fortune by loyalty to the king, and it was too late to change tack for him in 1205, even if it had been a practical course to take. Nor was there ever much danger of the Marshal sinking beneath the weight of the king's displeasure. He was only in a situation of real discomfort in

2 *The Letters of Arnulf of Lisieux'* lii–ix

3 Henry of Huntingdon, 'Epistola de contemptu mundi' in *Historia Anglorum* ed. T Arnold Rolls Series, 1879 299–300.

4 *Histoire* ll. 13249–52.

1208, and that was largely his own fault.

It may well be that John was more correct in feeling threatened by the Marshal, than the Marshal was to feel under threat from him. By 1205, once the great Earl of Leicester was dead and his estates dismembered, the Marshal sat at the head of one of the greatest political affinities in the king's realm. It may be for this reason that when the king challenged him, the barons around the Marshal kept their peace and would not take sides. When no-one would name the Marshal as a traitor, the king demanded the Marshal's eldest son, by then fifteen years old, as a hostage. The Marshal could only give the boy up, trusting in his own reputation for loyalty. John also began to whittle away at the Marshal's privileges, as well as his peace of mind. At Michaelmas 1205, just after the argument with the king, William lost the county of Sussex which he and his brother had enjoyed since 1190.

John was not yet prepared for an outright breach, if, that is, he ever intended one. Perhaps he may at this point have considered that he had warned the Marshal from further trifling with him. The Marshal remained at court for most of 1205, neither in favour, nor disgrace. Although the flow of grants to him ebbed considerably from what it had been in 1204, it did not wholly subside. In the summer of 1205, after his dispute with the king, he had the wardship of the land and heir of the baron, Warin fitz Gerold.[5] He was still in a position of trust. Indeed, in November he was detailed with three other earls to escort King William of Scotland south to a meeting with John at York.[6] He was probably at court for Christmas. He remained there in 1206 until the king departed from England into Poitou in June. The *Histoire* tells us that the king still had confidence enough in him to particularly charge the Marshal and his 'other best knights' to keep the realm in his absence. No insistence was made that he should go with John this year. We are told that the Marshal made sure to send many of his knights and sergeants with the king, so to that degree the *Histoire* admits that the Marshal had been chastened.

But, after April 1206, all trace of William Marshal disappears from royal acts. He did not appear again at court when the king returned to England at the end of September after a notably successful campaign. It is far from clear why he did not come back to the court. No source mentions a new breach in 1206 between

5 *Rotuli Litterarum Clausarum* I 39.

6 *Rotuli Litterarum Palentium* 56.

king and Marshal. Indeed before he left the Marshal obliged the king with a gift of wine and a loan of a hundred marks (£66 13s. 4d.) which the king promptly repaid.[7] On Boxing Day 1206 the king also obliged the Marshal by allowing him to resume the lands of one of his Norman tenants who had quit England for good.[8] There does not therefore seem to have been any obvious increase of tension between the men which would account for William's removal from court. But remove himself he did. For some of the time at least the Marshal was in his castle of Chepstow on the border. The only clue we have as to what was going on at this time is that the *Histoire* does say that William approached the king after he came back from France and sought his permission to go to his lands in Ireland; a request he made more than once, apparently, until the king graciously allowed 'our beloved William Marshal' such a licence in February 1207.[9] If affairs had come to a crisis, then there is little trace of it to be gleaned from the records, or even the *Histoire*. The crisis is more likely to have occurred in that rather impenetrable object, the Marshal's head.

. . .

## THE IRISH PROBLEM, 1207–13

The Marshal did not always bear up well under mental strain. He had departed the Young King rather quickly in 1182 after their breach, even though there was no question of any arrest or physical threat, and the Young King was still willing to employ him in the tournament field. We can therefore suggest that in 1207 the Marshal was running away, as he had run away in 1182. He was not a coward in any sense of the word. But the mesh of petty harassment in which he may have seen himself as caught was demeaning to him: an old lion snagged by a net of hemp. The *Histoire* is determined to picture the king and its hero as at loggerheads from 1205 to 1207, and that might indeed have been the Marshal's own view, if only with hindsight, because the two men were to fight out a savage political duel in 1207–8. But other indications tell us that the level of tension was low in 1205–6. However, we can still admit the possibility that the Marshal was jaundiced enough to want to be anywhere else but on the same

7 *Rotuli Litterarum Clausarum* I 72.

8 Ibid. 75.

9 Ibid. 81.

island as the king. Leinster was a convenient place to go: a lordship which was already a considerable worry to him. He might go there, knock heads together and feel better. A final consideration may well have been his wife's views on the matter. The *Histoire* suddenly brings Countess Isabel forward in the events of 1207–8 as a force in her own right. It is as if it cannot hold her part in her husband's affairs down any more, and she bobs to the surface of the narrative. It is perfectly possible that she worked on her husband at this time to do something about the principal part of the inheritance she had from her father, and which was on loan by marriage to the Marshal. When he died, and if she did not remarry, Leinster would one day be her own again.

The Leinster expedition of 1207–8 was a watershed in the political career of the Marshal. More so than the period of disgrace at the Young King's court in 1182–3, it put the Marshal in some real political danger. It is possible to overestimate the danger the Marshal was in from the king. In none of the subsequent events is there any hint that John once contemplated depriving the Marshal of any part of his own lands, or of his liberty. He did not even levy a fine on him to clear his ill-will. There is no doubt that the king was annoyed with him and suspicious of him, but clearly the suspicion never reached the level where the king felt he must break the Marshal or himself go down. Nor for that matter did the difficulties of 1207–8 shake the Marshal's public good-will towards the king. The real crisis was in the Marshal's ability to control events about him. He was a consummate lord to the men of his *mesnie*, and his charm and open face seduced many into his affinity. What had never been tested so far had been his ability to manage men who wanted nothing from him, and might be hostile. In Ireland in 1207 he went amongst men who had to be ruled by him, but were reluctant to be ruled. It cannot be said that he had much success at first; indeed in 1207 he experienced the ultimate humiliation for a well-intentioned lord: a rebellion against his authority. This is the importance of the Irish problem for William Marshal. It tested his capacity as no other episode of his life was to do. He had to fend off the king with one hand and preserve his lordship in Leinster with the other. He himself realized the nature of the crisis he had weathered, for after 1208 he single-mindedly devoted himself to the reconstruction and pacification of Leinster. Here we find the first signs that the man had some streak of greatness in him; that he was more than a simpering courtier. In the Leinster years we discover why the Marshal came in the end to rule England.

All went well for a short while in 1207. John of Earley and Henry Hose, two of the most intimate of his followers, were allowed protections by the king while they were with their lord in Ireland (for both were tenants-in-chief and, like their lord, needed the king's licence to go abroad). Then there was a sudden reverse. King John claimed to have had second thoughts about letting loose the Marshal in his lordship of Ireland. He sent to the Marshal demanding his second son as security for his behaviour when he was over the sea. We can perhaps see behind this a cheap scheme by the king to frustrate the Marshal. It may well be that he and his young friends had attempted to tease the importunate old earl. Doubtless the king expected the Marshal to refuse to give up his son. It was not in his interests to have William in Ireland then. John's limited capacity to judge men failed him again: the Marshal did as he was asked, yielded up the boy Richard and then promptly left. He had been assured in confidence by the royal envoy, who was a brother of one of his own knights, how much the king regretted giving him permission to sail. But he had the king's leave and for good or ill, as he said, he was going. Considerable evils did follow for him. As soon as the king heard he had gone, he relieved William of control over the castle and shire of Gloucester, the key to his influence in the west. The keeping of the forest of Dean and its castle of St Briavels was also taken back into royal hands. The king removed from the Marshal the keeping of the royal castle of Cardigan and gave it instead to the lesser Marcher baron, William de Londres.[10]

But whatever personal motive he had, there were practical reasons for the Marshal to go to Ireland: good enough for him to want to brave certain royal displeasure. Leinster was a problem of lordship he had only just touched on so far in his career. He doubtless went off to Ireland intending to wield a vigorous new broom. Unfortunately he may not have appreciated how much the king himself regarded Ireland as his own hobby; his oldest hobby, since his father gave Ireland to him in 1185. In 1205 John was in the midst of a sharp campaign to reduce the overweening power of the greatest lords of the island, one of whom, conveniently *in absentia*, was William Marshal. The king's instrument was Meilyr fitz Henry, his justiciar since *c.*1200, but also a tenant of the Marshal in Leinster. Meilyr had already annoyed the Marshal by laying claim to the region of Offaly in Leinster. In or around May

10 Ibid. 81; *Rotuli Litterarum Patentium* 70, 71, 74; *Pipe Roll of 9 John* 210.

1204, while he was still high in royal favour (perhaps following a meeting with his ally and middleman, the bishop of Ossory) the Marshal had sent his nephew and knight, John Marshal, as his seneschal of Leinster on purpose to combat the threat of Meilyr.[11] John was busy there for well over a year, although we do not know the degree of his success. He could not have done so well as to reassure his lord and uncle that he could leave Leinster to look after itself.

Late in February, or early in March 1207, the Marshal arrived in Ireland with his wife and all his *mesnie* to a mixed welcome. His arrival made something of a stir. A charter to Christchurch cathedral, Dublin, is dated by his coming.[12] The *Histoire* tells us that some of his men rejoiced to see him in Ireland; others, notably Meilyr fitz Henry, were less than enthusiastic. Meilyr wrote to the king urging him to call the Marshal back if he were to preserve his interests intact. The *Histoire* does not go deeper into this malevolence towards its hero,however. It assumes that Meilyr and his sympathizers, like all the Marshal's enemies, were motivated by simple malice. We, however, must try to look deeper.

Some reason may be found in the poem known as 'The Song of Dermot and the Earl'. It is a French work which describes the conquest of Leinster by Earl Richard and his men in the 1170s. The prominence nonetheless given in it to younger men like Philip of Prendergast (who had joined the Marshal's *mesnie* *c.*1189), Meilyr himself and the Cogan brothers, combined with the complete absence of any mention of Countess Isabel, the Marshal or the men he settled in Leinster points to a date of composition in the 1190s or early 1200s.[13] It was a poem composed for the

11 *Rotuli Litterarum Patentium* 40, 42, 50. We catch a brief glimpse of John Marshal's activities in Leinster in September 1205, acting on his uncle's behalf in a settlement between Cartmel priory and St Thomas's abbey, Dublin, *Register of the Abbey of St Thomas, Dublin* ed. J T Gilbert Rolls Series 1889 337–8. John is the leading witness to a settlement dated 6 September 1205 of which William Marshal and 'his canons of Cartmel' are one party. The composition of the witness list indicates that the document was drawn up in Dublin. Since William Marshal was on 9 September with the king at Bristol, having previously been with him in Essex on 10 August, the agreement is likely to have been made in his absence with John there in his capacity as seneschal of Leinster

12 *Crede Mihi* ed. J T Gilbert Dublin 1897 71. An agreement between William Marshal and the bishop of Glendalough made 'in the first year of the arrival of the earl in Ireland' (*anno primo adventus eiusdem comitis de* [rectius: in] *Hibernia*).

13 The dating of the work is admittedly difficult. Orpen, the editor, felt that part

edification of an embattled but self-confident community of aristocrats.[14] It was a statement of its difference and superiority as demonstrated by its heroic past achievements. The Anglo–Welsh of Leinster were pleased to hear themselves called the *Irreis* (the Irish) by their poet, not because they regarded themselves as part of the Celtic fringe, but because it described their identity as a group of warrior colonizers in the toughest and remotest outpost of Christendom.[15] The Welsh origins of many of them gave them further solidarity: St David was their particular patron (the dominant cult of Deheubarth), and kinship further linked them through intermarriages between the royal house of Deheubarth, the Geraldines and the Stephanides. They were men apart, and, naturally, they were superior to the soft *Engleis* across the sea. The existence of such a feeling could account for much of the animosity which Meilyr was at one point able to foment against the Marshal. Meilyr was in particular bound to see William Marshal as an intruder. He had fought his way across Leinster with the *mesnie* of Earl Richard, and rose after his death first in partnership with his kinsman Raymond le Gros, then on his own account under John's régime. He was the grandson of Henry I of England, son of a royal bastard engendered on Nest of Deheubarth. It is doubtful that he could ever have been impressed with the best knight in all the world, who now occupied the earldom of the already legendary Richard Strongbow, his sometime lord.

For his part, William Marshal soon realized that the arrogance of Meilyr and the unpopularity of the king's measures amongst the more powerful of the magnates of Ireland gave him some leverage. We know that some time early in May (only two months or so after his arrival) a body calling itself 'the barons of Leinster and Meath' addressed a letter to the king. We only know of it from the king's outraged answer. But this tells us that the Lacy family, who

of it at least had to have been written after 1225, because archbishop Lawrence O'Toole (died 1180) is referred to in it as a saint, and he was canonized that year. On the other hand there are numerous contemporary instances of the status of 'saint' being applied popularly to men not formally canonised, so this need not be so. To date it on the basis of the marriage and career of Philip of Prendergast, as Orpen otherwise did, is undoubtedly more satisfactory, and this produces a date of *c.* 1190 x 1227. *The Song of Dermot and the Earl* ed. G H Orpen Oxford 1892) xx–xxi. If we combine this with the lack of reference even to Countess Isabel, the heir of Earl Richard, then a date of 1190 x 1207 is likely.

14 M D Legge *Anglo–Norman Literature and its Background* Oxford 1963 303–4.

15 *Song of Dermot* 216.

dominated Meath and Ulster, and the greatest knights of Meath and Leinster (including the Marshal's retainer, Philip of Prendergast), had combined against Meilyr. The king's words alone give us the full savour of his reaction:

> I was astonished at the request you made of me in your letter. You seem to want to issue a new statute (*nova assisa*) in my land without me. In my days and the days of my forefathers it was unheard of that a new statute should be decreed in a country without the consent of its prince. What you ask is neither right nor has any precedent. You want my justiciar of Ireland to give something which I have ordered confiscated back to someone without my instructions! I tell you that you must withdraw the demand you made on my justiciar about Offaly. He is to reply to no man about what he has been ordered by me to confiscate, without my instructions.[16]

The Marshal is significantly absent from the letter. But his hand must have been deeply in it, for he was the greatest magnate of those parts, and most of the men named were his tenants. The land in dispute was Offaly, a region north west of his chief castle of Kilkenny, the marches of Leinster. It was an area he had to control, and the proxy petition to the king against Meilyr's holding Offaly can only have been a Marshal ploy. He was the 'someone' to whom the barons wanted Offaly returned.

The Marshal may have underestimated the petition's impact on the king, even though he knew that John was an insecure man, apt to suspect conspiracies. The king would have known who was behind the petition and his reply to it is laced with undisguised anger. He had not wanted William in Ireland; now he was there what he had feared might occur seemed to be happening. The result was an order to the Marshal to return to England, sent, the *Histoire* believed, at the prompting of Meilyr. We do not know the precise date of this order, for it does not survive in the royal records, but it must have been sent during the late summer, for the

16 *Rotuli Litterarum Patentium* 72. The concluding sentence of the letter (which I have not translated here) was interpreted by Painter as follows: 'The letter closed with the suggestion that the petitioners think less about the privileges of their lord, and more about the rights of the crown' (Painter p 155). The passage is difficult to translate, but to me it reads more along the lines that the king was unwilling to deny them justice when they asked for it, but would grant it when and where it suited him. Painter seems to have been unnecessarily determined that the king's letter should contain some scathing reference to the Marshal.

*Histoire* records that the Marshal landed back on the mainland at Michaelmas (29 September). With him came a large number of the barons of Leinster, including the justiciar himself. They had been summoned to the king, as seems probable, to discuss the petition concerning Offaly that had so upset the king, but which he had promised to consider in due course.

A little over a month later the whole crowd of them was attending King John at his palace of Woodstock. The king then proceeded to stage a convincing and damaging victory over the Marshal. The Irish barons who had come were heaped with gifts and promises. Meilyr was already in the king's pocket, but at Woodstock the king secured the public adherence of two prominent members of the Marshal's affinity: his nephew, John Marshal, and his wife's brother-in-law, Philip of Prendergast. The king bought Philip by substantial grants in Munster, near Cork. John Marshal accepted a week later a grant of the title 'marshal of Ireland' and the district of *Kylmien* for the service of five knights. Meilyr, Philip and John were lovingly and pointedly named by the king at this time as the three men in Ireland whom he held in the greatest trust. Others of the barons of Leinster who had supported the petition against Meilyr also turned their coats in return for grants or confirmations: William of Barry, Richard Latimer, David de la Roch, Eustace de la Roch, Adam of Hereford, Richard of Cogan, and Gilbert of Angle. Two Pembrokeshire barons who were present (Robert fitz Martin of Cemaes and Robert fitz Richard of Haverford) also had grants.[17] Again, the Marshal's absence from these dealings is significant. These were his barons and retainers who were being courted in front of his eyes. These men, there to support his dignity before the king, had metaphorically kicked the legs from under him and covered him in dust as they stampeded into the king's camp. The *Histoire*, of course, fails to mention these events.

What the *Histoire* does dwell on at this point is what the men of the Marshal's *mesnie* who had been left in Ireland were doing. Doubtless this was to point out to those in the know the contrast with the faithless men who followed the Marshal to England. The *Histoire* could not afford to be too specific on what the unfaithful did. Many of the men who deserted the Marshal before the king at Woodstock and Tewkesbury in November 1207 were still alive and powerful in the later 1220s. What was more, John Marshal was to return quickly enough to his uncle's affinity and serve him

17 *Rotuli Chartarum* 171–4.

well (it may even be that his delay of a week after the court at Woodstock before taking his grants from the king might have been caused by a pause to consult his uncle). It would have been unwise for the author to dwell on the doings of the Marshal's men and barons in November 1207 in England. Besides, what was happening in Ireland was a good story: a tale of valour and loyalty.

The Marshal and his men suspected that some attempt would be made against his lands when he left Ireland. For that reason he left most of his *mesnie* of knights behind him. At this point Countess Isabel came into the centre of events; a place in which she is not often seen. However, she was a key figure in Ireland; granddaughter of King Dermot and daughter of Earl Richard Strongbow. Her presence might rally to the Marshal side some of the sentiment that still clung to the name of Strongbow. The *Histoire* was written by a man who had little time for women, and who was writing for men who shared his apparent indifference, but there were times when his prejudices were overriden by reality. The *Histoire* gives the countess the chief place in the council of the Marshal's men held before his departure. It was her doubts as to King John's intentions that they debated. She had been prominent in an earlier council, held before they all left Chepstow for Ireland. She had not wanted her son Richard delivered to the king. We can fairly conclude from these fleeting but telling appearances, and from the charter evidence, that she was in reality no mere cipher in her husband's affairs. She was a great lady in a long tradition of powerful Norman aristocratic women; her advice and consent was both needed and sought.

The countess was left to defend her husband's (and her own) interests in Ireland, although she was once again pregnant. This abandonment may have been by her own insistence, rather than for health grounds. An advanced state of pregnancy had not stopped her travelling with her husband to Normandy in 1190. Two leading knights of the *mesnie* were detailed to serve as bailiffs under her in Leinster: Jordan de Sauqueville, and John of Earley. Earley was left in charge of Ossory and the southern half of Leinster, then known as *Okanceleie* (Ui Chennselaig); Jordan took the northern half up to the confines of the royal lands of Dublin. Earley was less than happy about the reponsibility, but took it at his lord's insistence, having as under-bailiff a fellow knight, Stephen d'Evreux. Stephen was the Marshal's cousin and we can see him as a key link at this time with the Lacy family. His family had been major tenants of the Lacys in Herefordshire since the eleventh century. The Marshal seems to have counted on him to steady and guide John of Earley. In all, another eight knights of his retinue, and the banner-bearer, William Mallard, were left with the bailiffs. According to the *Histoire*, only Henry Hose was detailed from the *mesnie* to escort the Marshal to England (John Marshal and Philip of Prendergast were Marshal followers but were at this time great men in their own right, and royal vassals).

The Marshal's last act before he departed was to summon an assembly of the barons and knights of Leinster to his chief fortress of Kilkenny. John of Earley urged him at this time to take hostages from amongst them for their good behaviour. Rather grandly the Marshal refused, though there is reason to think that he later changed his mind about being so mild to his men. Besides, many of the barons were travelling to the king with him, and he may have thought the measure superfluous, particularly since the greatest of them had put their names to the petition against Meilyr. Their turnabout at the meeting at Woodstock with the king must have come to him as something of a shock.

The terms of his final address to his men of Leinster at Kilkenny may or may not be what he actually said, although I am inclined to think them an honest attempt by his biographer to reconstruct the speech. However, they are most evocative of his situation in 1207. He made a dramatic entry, Isabel on his arm:

> 'Lords! See the countess, whom I here present to you; your lady by birth, the daughter of the earl who freely enfeoffed you all when he had conquered this land. She remains amongst you, pregnant. Until God permits me to return, I pray you to keep her well and faithfully, for she is your lady, and I have nothing but through her.'[18]

The accent is entirely on his wife; the lady of Leinster, then pregnant and in need of protection. He had nothing to say about his own claims on the men of Leinster whether on his own, or more particularly, his sons' account. He was declaring in clear terms that he felt that he had no hold on his Irish tenants; he could count only on his *mesnie*. The only force that could constrain the barons and knights of Leinster was that feeling of difference that we have already observed in the 'Song of Dermot and the Earl'. It had grown up in the 1170s under Earl Richard Strongbow, and the Marshal's wife, Earl Richard's daughter, was the only channel by

18 *Histoire* ll. 13532–44.

which he might tap it for his advantage.[19] The assembly mumbled the required responses of loyalty, but the jaundiced writer scoffs, 'the wicked will do or say anything'.[20]

Before he went, Meilyr 'the false' (as the *Histoire* takes care to call him, recalling that the Marshal was in fact his lord) planned a campaign against the Marshal to be carried out as soon as he and the old earl were gone: a proxy war in which neither of the principals was directly involved. Meilyr's kinsmen and retainers assembled and, a week after the departure of the Marshal and their lord, they descended on New Ross where the Marshal was developing a port and large borough.[21] They butchered a score of his men and burned down his granges, riding away with a haul of plunder: 'and so commenced in Leinster raids and open war'.[22] In the meantime, the Marshal received a cold welcome at court, and had to watch Meilyr and the defaulting Irish treated with pointed kindness and consequence. Meilyr followed up his advantage. He persuaded the king to allow his return to Ireland and to send letters recalling to England the three bailiffs the Marshal had left to protect his interests: John of Earley, Jordan de Sauqueville and Stephen d'Evreux.[23] They were sent around the beginning of

19 One must note at this point the bizarre comments of Duby on this speech (pp 157–8). In his interpretation, in leaving her behind the Marshal's chief fear was that Isabel would run off with someone else and leave him empty-handed; the knights of the *mesnie* and the men of Leinster were being enjoined to keep her under close guard. He is said to have feared that she would surrender herself to some public display of dalliance with another man that would force him to divorce her and render himself penniless (he would seem to have Louis VII and Eleanor in his mind here). One can only say that if this were his secret motivation in the speech then the events that subsequently came about must have surprised him: did the rebels of Leinster later fight to get into Kilkenny merely in order to seduce the poor, pregnant woman?

20 *Histoire* l. 13550.

21 The *Histoire* calls this place *la Novele vile* (i.e. 'Newtown'). Meyer thought it might be Newtown-Barry, co. Wexford, but that place cannot be linked to the demesne of the lord of Leinster. The Marshal's foundation of New Ross, co. Wexford, however, would be as likely to be called 'the New Town' in its early days and pillaging it would be a very good way to score a direct hit on the Marshal's prestige. New Ross was already in being when the foundation charter of Tintern Parva was issued (*Chartae, Privilegia et Immunitates* 80), and it is likely that the Marshal and his advisers had begun its construction during the visit of 1200–1.

22 *Histoire* ll. 13573–4.

23 Enrolments of these letters do not survive, unfortunately. We do know that

January 1208, carried by Thomas Bloet, one of the king's brightest young household knights; a man with Irish interests himself and younger brother of one of the Marshal's own knights, Ralph. Early in January Meilyr himself accompanied Thomas and the letters to Ireland.

Thus far things had gone remarkably well for Meilyr. Apparently his was one of the few boats that were able to brave the stormy crossing to Ireland in the four months after Michaelmas 1207. But on his arrival in Ireland, as the *Histoire* points out with a fine irony, uncomfortable reality caught up with him. Subsequent events prove the truth of W.L. Warren's observation that there was only a limited amount that the king could do to influence events in Ireland. His power there was more theoretical than real, unless he came himself with a large army. Because of the storms, the Marshal's men had not received the king's instructions, and so they had had several months to work uninterrupted at the defence of their master's interests. They had been able to make some resistance to Meilyr's men and had one of his favourite knights in prison.

When he arrived, Meilyr contrived a meeting with the opposition and with a triumphant flourish, he caused Thomas Bloet to hand over to the Marshal's men the letters recalling them. They drew aside to have them read out and pondered their significance, knowing their lands would be forfeit if they did not comply. John of Earley gave it as his opinion that they would be dishonoured if they gave up the position of trust in which their lord had left them. Stephen d'Evreux thought that the king might do as he pleased with their English lands, rather than they be shamed before God in giving up their charges. All agreed to stay put come what may, and Jordan de Sauqueville proposed outflanking Meilyr by negotiating assistance from Hugh de Lacy, Earl of Ulster, with whom the Marshal had established an understanding the previous year. They returned to Thomas Bloet and said firmly that they would not do that for which they would be scorned.

'Let us not complain of the game if we lose land and honour; better that than to lose land, honour *and* the love of our lord.'[24]

they were sent, however, for there is a reference in February 1208 to John of Earley's contumacy in ignoring them. They were said to have been dispatched 'two months and more' before 20 February. The *Histoire* also indicates that they were sent at some time in early January 1208. See *Rotuli Litterarum Clausarum* I 103.

24 *Histoire* ll. 13727–32.

This, according to the *Histoire*, was what Earley said, and indeed he may well have done so. They were brave sentiments, the sort that men of the age respected. The men stating them were remarkable men, and as knights of the *mesnie* in a position of particular closeness to their lord. However, it would not do to think that such warlike loyalty was typical of the age. Others were not so selfless. Philip of Prendergast, their former colleague, had returned with Meilyr to Ireland, and he was captured on the other side in the subsequent campaign.

The Marshal in the meantime was without news from Ireland, and closeted with an insecure king who feared him. From January to March 1208 he was in the most difficult position he was ever to know at court. We do not need the *Histoire* to tell us at this point that he behaved with a coolness that was remarkable. It was the sort of politic reticence that kept his men in awe of him. The Marshal was with the king at Guildford on 25 January 1208, a fortnight or so after Meilyr, Thomas Bloet and others had made the crossing back to Ireland. No news could filter back, for, as the *Histoire* tells us, the crossing was too stormy until early in February. Lack of real news did not hinder the king's malice against William, however. The *Histoire* gives a vivid portrayal of the harassment kept up by the king against his former favourite. In a fit of ill-natured petulance the king sidled up to him and asked whether he had news from Leinster. The Marshal said he had not. With a snigger the king announced to the Marshal that he had heard that there had been a siege of Kilkenny. The Marshal's *mesnie* had been caught in the open, and in attempting to relieve the place and free the countess Stephen d'Evreux and Ralph fitz Payn had been killed outright while John of Earley had been mortally wounded and had died later. The whole court was as astonished as the Marshal, for everyone must have known that there could have been no such news. The king, however, in his fevered desire to torment the impassive Marshal was willing to say anything to get a reaction. The reaction that he did get did not suit him. In the sudden silence which must have surrounded the men, the Marshal said, 'What a pity about the knights, sire, for they were your men too, which makes the business all the more regrettable.'[25] The king (blushing and ruffled perhaps) said 'I will think about it'.

The incident is one of those in the *Histoire* that has the ring of truth, despite what seems at first sight to be something of

25 *Histoire* ll. 13846–51.

contrivance in it. It opposes a most uncourtly king to its courtly hero and has the king ignominiously worsted by his own undisguised malice. But there is other evidence of such petty harassment. The king at this time had his officers take in hand all the lands of John of Earley and Stephen d'Evreux, whether held directly from him or others. He was, however, particular to confide such lands to the lords from whom they had been held. This was only proper, according to ideas of the time, but it also gave him an opportunity to boast of what he had done. A letter was duly sent to William on 20 February (which must have been before news of Meilyr's defeat had reached England) to inform him what had been done, particularly to John of Earley whom everyone knew to be as close to the Marshal as one of his sons:

> I want you to know that I have delivered to you the lands I confiscated from John of Earley, which he held from you [probably a reference to Earlytown, co. Kilkenny]. I took away his lands because more than two months ago I instructed him to come to me and he did not do so. I very much want you to produce both him and the others I summoned before me, as is right and proper. I need them here for my own business, and I will keep their lands until they surrender to me.'[26]

After the beginning of Lent (23 February in 1208), ships began to reach the mainland from Ireland. The news they brought was uncomfortable to the king. Meilyr had gone down before a coalition of the Lacy family and the Marshal's adherents in Ireland. Meilyr's lands and castles had been seized and the justiciar himself had been captured. He had submitted to Countess Isabel and given his son as a hostage for his good behaviour. Philip of Prendergast and the other rebel knights of Leinster had also come to terms, likewise surrendering their children, or younger brothers if they had no offspring, to the countess.

The king was very much afflicted by this news, according to the *Histoire*. Yet he managed to bring himself, nonetheless, to be philosophical about the defeat of his minister. King and Marshal met at Bristol some time in the first week of March. The Marshal kept up his front, giving no clue in his behaviour that he had heard the news and when the king asked him, pretended ignorance. The king had the dubious pleasure of breaking the good news to the Marshal, but seems to have carried it off with some nonchalance.

26 *Rotuli Litterarum Clausarum* I 103.

He had resumed the courtly pose whose shattering some weeks previously had so startled the court. The Marshal too was courtly in reply. He muffled his delight and replied temperately: 'Sire, I thank Our Lord. But I had no idea when I left Ireland that there was a man there who wanted to make war on me!'[27] The king smiled, he may even have taken the remark as a joke. The Marshal was happy to pretend ingenuous frankness, for in pretending he allowed the king enough face to be able to retrieve his position. The court scented the new mood and suddenly the Marshal was again the object of deference and respect. On 20 March the king and the Marshal came to formal agreement. The Marshal was to surrender Leinster to the king and receive it back on new terms, limiting his jurisdiction in some respects from what it had been: a strategic concession to allow the king to claim a victory of sorts.[28] On 21 March, Meilyr was briskly told to give Offaly back to the Marshal.[29] The Marshal's dangerous time had come to an end.

No difficulty was made about the Marshal's return to Ireland. In fact, it is likely that John now saw him as a better vehicle for his purposes there than the discredited Meilyr. That fact is a reminder that John was not wholly without judgement. Meilyr's subsequent disgrace was permanent, he was replaced in 1208 as justiciar first by Hugh de Lacy, then by the bishop of Norwich, and lived in obscurity on his estates till he died twelve years later. As for William Marshal, he seems to have wanted to do no more than retire for a period to Ireland. It may not have been a place of great tranquillity in the early-thirteenth century, but he had as good a cause to be as disenchanted with the court as such rarified spirits as John of Salisbury or Peter de Blois. Aged now over sixty, the Marshal needed a rest. So he returned to Kilkenny, a retirement plan of restructuring his Irish lordship seeming to be his main concern.

The Marshal lived in retirement in Ireland for the best part of the next four years. But it was by no means a quiet time for him. He made some reforms in Leinster. He made a point of settling many of his retainers in lands near Kilkenny: Mallardstown (from William Mallard, a prominent sergeant of his) and Earlytown (from John of Earley), co. Kilkenny, still recall some of his grants. Other grants came the way of his knights: Ralph Bloet, William le

27 *Histoire* ll. 13923–6.

28 *Rotuli Chartarum* 176.

29 *Rotuli Litterarum Patentium* 80.

Gros, Thomas of Rochford, Nicholas Avenel, Stephen d'Evreux, Jordan de Sauqueville, and Henry Hose. It was in Ireland that many of his political affinity became his tenants for the first time. The older colonists of Leinster who had previously opposed him had a thin time by contrast. The Marshal received them on his return to Leinster with withering coldness. David de la Roch, one of the rebels and one of the barons of Leinster who had sold out to John in November 1207, was made a butt of routine humiliation by the Marshal affinity for many years thereafter. Once Peter fitz Herbert, a Marshal ally in the south west, publicly snubbed him by refusing to sit next to him at a council in England. Meilyr fitz Henry had to give up for good his castle of Dunamase, one of the most powerful fortresses of the time in Ireland, and pledge the surrender of his lands after his death to the Marshal (the *Histoire* justifies the harshness of this persecution by pretending to have heard that Meilyr's son had not been born in wedlock). Philip of Prendergast's sons remained with third parties in England as hostages for his good behaviour until at least 1215.[30] If the Marshal could take punishment, he was also capable of giving it out, for he had learned well from his masters.

The Marshal had returned to Ireland pledged to conduct some punitary raids on the Irish as part of a reconciliation plan worked out with the king. He may well have done so; we know for certain of a bitter campaign in the west of the island in 1212.[31] In an epitaph composed on the Marshal, which was preserved by Matthew Paris, he was made to say, 'I am he who was a Saturn to Ireland, the sun to England, a Mercury to Normandy and a Mars to France.' Meaning, in the first case, that he had been 'a devastating conquistador' (as Matthew Paris put it) towards the Irish.[32] That the Marshal was none too keen on the Irish is evident enough. He was an accommodating enough patron to the English bishops in Leinster: the archbishop of Dublin, the bishop of Glendalough, and the bishop of Ossory. The latter in particular, had significant grants and concessions from him. If there were differences with the other bishops, they were at least allowed amicable settlements. On the other hand, the bishop of Ferns, a Cistercian by the name of Ailbe (or Albinus) O Maelmuidhe, got

30 *Rotuli Litterarum Patentium* 123, 144.

31 *Rotuli Litterarum Patentium* 80; *Annals of Loch Cé* ed. W M Hennessy (2 vols) Rolls Series 1871 I 247–8.

32 *Chronica Maiora* III 43: '*Fuit enim Hibernicis nocivus edomitor*'.

nothing from him but harassment and injustice. The Marshal's lands in Ireland were under interdict by the archbishops of Dublin and Tuam before the end of John's reign as a consequence. The case shuttled between the royal court and Rome until the Marshal contrived to evade Church jurisdiction early in 1218. Nonetheless, when he died, the Marshal was under excommunication by Bishop Ailbe for violently seizing and withholding two episcopal estates. Matthew Paris appears to have either met the bishop, or someone else who had, and felt a certain sympathy for him; he believed the excommunication to have been 'not undeserved'.[33]

In his Irish policies we can at last see the Marshal as ruler, rather than as courtier and soldier. He had commenced his lordship of Leinster in disastrous fashion; rebelled against by many of his vassals. There can be little doubt that this crisis disturbed him, for he acted with typical decision and, we may say, harshness once he had the upper hand. One cannot help recalling the way his father had dominated north Wiltshire in Stephen's reign. William chastised and terrorized those who came within his sphere and who opposed him. His men, monks and burgesses were settled on the land in order to secure it. Amicable agreements secured the goodwill of his powerful neighbours, Lacys and Briouze. Whatever naïvety he may have had at the outset of his career as a magnate, the Marshal had lost it by 1208.

. . .

## THE MARSHAL AND THE BARONS' WAR

The Marshal's most dangerous confrontation with King John ended with the reconciliation of March 1208. For much of the next four years he was out of sight – and probably mind too – in Ireland. There was a brief but bitter tussle between the two men in 1210. The particular problem in that year was the fate of John's former favourite, William de Briouze, a great baron of both the Welsh and Irish March. William Marshal chose to shelter Briouze for a short time when he and his family escaped to Ireland around the beginning of 1209. He may well have felt bound to do so because of what he owed to the Lacy family, into which Briouze had married.[34] However, he made no strong stand for Briouze. The Marshal joined the king's expedition against the Lacys in 1210,

33 Ibid. IV 492–3.

34 The Marshal's own excuses for his actions are hardly convincing: he claimed

even hastening from Leinster to Pembrokeshire to join the royal army *before* it embarked for Ireland. Although the king reserved some harsh words for what he considered the Marshal's lukewarm support, and took hostages and the castle of Dunamase, there was no major breach. The slight degree of his danger can be seen in the fact that other courtiers such as Geoffrey fitz Peter were not afraid to stand up and offer themselves as pledges for his conduct.

In 1212 circumstances, and the barons, conspired to bring the Marshal back into the centre of affairs. The king got wind of a plot amongst certain of the northern barons to assassinate him. In Ireland, William had helped in the crisis by assisting the justiciar in the suppression of a rising by the native Irish and, late in the summer of 1212, had bolstered the king's peace of mind by getting the Irish barons to write to the king pledging their support. William himself wrote, offering to come to England to help in person and volunteering advice on the king's problems with the pope. He chose his moment well, as the king's reply most feelingly tells us:

> I have thanked by letter my barons and men of Ireland for their good and faithful service and for the oath of fidelity they lately swore to me; but I do not doubt that it was by your counsel and motivation, as much as that of the carrier of the letters, that the assurance was made. By your good will I have all other men well-disposed in this business, so I am the readier to give you my thanks. I add to these thanks for your willingness to come to me in England, but I cannot allow you my permission at the moment. The bishop of Lincoln [the justiciar], who time and again by letter and messenger praised your loyal counsel and assistance, cannot spare your presence, so necessary to him in Ireland at the moment. I ask you to stay there, helping the bishop to maintain my interests, so that at a later time I might renew my eternal gratitude to you [sic]. I send you a copy of letters my English magnates made for me, and I ask you to seal a similar letter, along with my other barons of Ireland . . . You should better provide for your boy, who is with me and lacks horses and a robe. I will provide what he needs at my own cost, if you agree, and I will hand him over to one of your knights

not to know that Briouze was at odds with the king; he also claimed he had been obliged to shelter Briouze because Briouze was his lord – a claim no-one has successfully fathomed.

> (perhaps John of Earley, or one of his men). If you want it otherwise, let me know by letter that he is to stay with the court and that you will answer for what I pay in the boy's expenses. I will provide it in any case, and have the money from you when I can. Do not believe what was said to you about my wanting to send the boy into Poitou. I never had any such intention. I never even heard of such an idea until the justiciar told me about it.[35]

The letter is a rare insight into relations between John and one of his great magnates at a critical point. The fact that these sentiments were written at all tells how much store the king was suddenly willing to put by good relations with the Marshal. Normally at that time messages would have been by word of mouth, easily denied at a later stage; but here John was putting his need and gratitude for William's support on the record. He was giving the Marshal a stick with which he might be beaten later. He even carefully adds the little domestic details of young William Marshal, still a hostage at court (and now a knight and in need of horses and the requisite garments). The letter seeks to create, or at least project, a warm family atmosphere between king and magnate. The king denied rumours that he had meant to take the boy to Poitou without his father's permission in the campaign that had earlier been planned for that year: perhaps a last attempt to needle the Marshal, from which he now wanted to distance himself. We know that initially in August 1212 John had suspected the Marshal's complicity in the plot.[36] Harsh words may well have been said then around the court that must now be unsaid.

Everything was arranged as the letter suggested. One son (William) was delivered to John of Earley, although the king was eager to give him both in the end. John of Earley himself began to benefit from the Marshal's return to favour just as he had suffered when his lord was out of favour. He was entrusted with the county of Devon and named marshal of the royal household (according to the *Histoire*).[37] The other son (Richard) was given to Thomas of

35 *Rotuli Litterarum Clausarum* I 132.

36 *Rotuli Litterarum Clausarum* I 122: the king ordered a naval demonstration off north Wales to discourage Welsh adventurism at this point, but also warned that his commander 'must ever be vigilant that no harm be worked against you from the lands or jurisdiction of Earl William Marshal', see comments in J C Holt *The Northerners* Oxford 1961 83 and n.

37 In fact this episode may have been a confirmation of the royal chamberlainship which John's grandfather and father had held.

Sandford, brother of the Marshal's one-time knight, Hugh. The king's mood towards his barons softened considerably as a result of the shock of the conspiracy. The Marshal was one of many who was to benefit from the king's sudden need for friends. He did as he was asked in the king's letter and organized the petition from the barons of Ireland which the king wanted, in support of the king against the pope. Eventually, in May 1213, the king decided that he needed the Marshal more in England than in Ireland. He was especially needed because there was a widespread refusal amongst the English barons to turn out for military service. A summons brought the Marshal (and allegedly some 500 Irish knights) to Kent, now threatened with sea-borne invasion by King Philip. The *Histoire* remarks with approval, tinged with a little astonishment, on the judicious conduct of its hero: 'He took no heed of what had gone before with the king, nor his cruelty, because ever he loved loyalty'.[38] The good Marshal, the impassive and detached courtier, seems even to have been beyond the comprehension of his faithful knights at times.

After his return to England the Marshal was continually busy working at upholding the failing fortunes of his king. His support for John never faltered, and with the Earl of Chester he seems to have grown in importance to the king as others dropped away. The spate of rewards to him from the king increased in the same way as they had during the previous golden years of high favour between 1199 and 1204. The fortress and port of Haverford within Pembrokeshire was made over to him by a grateful king in October 1213. He was restored to his position of dominance in south Wales. The king gave him back the keeping of Cardigan, and added Carmarthen and Gower. This advanced the Marshal's fortunes in Wales beyond even what they had been in 1207. During the Marshal's period of disgrace, John had placed his loyal, and hated, officer, Faulkes de Breauté, in control of royal interests in the southern March. This position was now to be the Marshal's, in augmentation of his already considerable lands in the region. It is no exaggeration to say that he emerged from his period in the wilderness stronger than he had been at the peak of his influence with King John in 1204, virtually justiciar of the March.

For a while things went very well for the king. A naval victory by the English fleet at Damme in 1213 removed the threat of invasion. What was more, the king took the line with the pope that the Marshal (and many others) had advised in 1212. He submitted,

38 *Histoire* ll. 14588–90.

and as a result found himself the favoured son of Innocent III. There were general promises made of reform to the barons, which for a while placated them. For a while it seemed that John's fortunes had turned. He optimistically prepared for the reconquest of Normandy and his other lost lands. Unfortunately for him, the shattering defeat by King Philip of his ally and cousin, the Emperor Otto IV, at Bouvines in July 1214 crippled his ambitious plan. He returned to England discredited and morose, at the mercy of the barons whom he had for so long oppressed financially and politically. In the words of Professor Holt: 'the road from Bouvines to Runnymede was direct, short and unavoidable'.[39]

William Marshal was now, at the age of sixty-seven, a venerable figure, held in deep respect not just for what he was, but for the living link he represented with the great days of the Angevin hegemony of north western Europe. He made a prestigious and effective chief negotiator for the king. His impassive loyalty was a most necessary anchor for the party we can now call the royalists.[40] We are at a loss for his actual thoughts about the rights and wrongs of the situation (although John of Earley might well have known them). The *Histoire*, for good reason, refuses repeatedly to talk about the royalist and rebel barons' motives. It would have been difficult for its author to do so. One of his chief patrons, the second William Marshal, had fought against John in the war, while the elder William had been for the king. Far better for him to gloss over the whole question.[41]

The king and his officers and advisers were shaken by Bouvines, and two days after battle messages were already speeding out from John to his men, getting them prepared for the worst. Gradually disaffection spread south from the core of opposition in the north of England. Many barons, even loyal ones, did not meet payments they owed the king. Troops were recruited from Poitou and dispatched to England. Royal castles were hastily provisioned; siege machines constructed. England was a disturbed ant-hill of military activity in a way it had not been since the so-called 'Leicester war' of 1174, when the earls had risen and the Scots and Flemings invaded (the Marshal was by now one of the very few

39 *The Northerners* p 100.

40 The term 'royalists' (*regales*) was applied to Stephen's supporters in the civil war of his reign. *Realx* (king's men) was the name applied to men of the royal *mesnie* in the reign of Henry II, and it was the cry of the Marshal's men at the battle of Lincoln in 1217.

41 Painter p 180, makes this same point.

surviving magnates who had been an actor in the events of that year). There can be no doubt that John expected the worst in the autumn and winter of 1214, and was getting prepared for it, even though the barons' demands were not formally put to him until January 1215 at London.

William Marshal, alone amongst the lay magnates, stood surety in the London negotiations for the king's good intentions when John persuaded the meeting to postpone discussion until after Easter (19 April) 1215. William was delegated by the king (along with the archbishop of Canterbury and other bishops) to meet the northern barons at Oxford on 22 February. But the meeting was arranged at short notice, and might never have happened. On 27 April William and the archbishop were again deployed to meet with the barons who had finally lost patience and had gathered in arms at Brackley, Northamptonshire (the chief residence of the dissident Earl of Winchester). They were to receive the demands of the rebels, but when they brought them back, John would have none of them. When the barons heard this they marched from Brackley and began the war by besieging the royal castle of Northampton. At this point the Marshal ceased being a negotiator and was sent off to rally royalist support; perhaps, as Painter suggests, he was sent to raise his affinity in the south west. It is likely enough that the security the Marshal affinity offered him was at least part of the reason why the king operated from the southern March and the south west in the years of the war. In the meantime the barons unexpectedly turned south and with the connivance of the citizens, seized London. This was a severe stroke against the king, for London was already regarded as the capital of the kingdom, and some of the machinery of government rested in Westminster.

When the Marshal returned to the king, it was to resume the role of middleman once more. The king was already beaten, for the seizure of London had led to mass defections to the barons. William Marshal was prominent in the negotiations that led up to the sealing of Magna Carta at Runnymede on 15 June (although it is highly unlikely that he was the joint author of the charter, as Painter wished to believe). What is more, it was he who was sent to London to announce the king's surrender to the barons' terms. The *Histoire* again has nothing to say on this affair (other than to assure the reader that its hero took no part in the baronial seizure of London). Partly this may well be because the charter and the brief baronial victory of June–July 1215 did not have much significance when viewed from the author's standpoint in the mid-1220s. Partly also it may be because of the position of the younger William Marshal in June 1215. He was now in his mid-twenties, a baron in his own right; a man who now had raised his own banner. He was already a widower. His first wife, Alice, daughter of the elder Marshal's friend, Baldwin de Béthune, had died after only a few months of marriage. As a demonstration of his importance, some sources already attribute to him the style of 'earl' long before his father's death.[42]

The Young Marshal, for unknown reasons, took the baronial side at some time in May or June 1215, and was named by Matthew Paris as one of the twenty-five barons who were to monitor the king's performance of his obligations.[43] He was to be an adherent on the rebel side until after the king's death. The *Histoire* attempts to pass over the young Marshal's flirtation with rebellion. This can only indicate some later sensitivity and embarrassment about it in Marshal circles. We can only guess what his father thought about it, but some of the guesses that can be made are seductive. Might the old Marshal have been so devious as to actually encourage his son to go with the barons, to act as his informant and insurance in case the king went down beneath his troubles? The compiler of the Worcester annals certainly believed that the elder and younger Marshals were in collusive communication, even though on opposite sides, late in 1216.[44] It is an entertaining but unprovable, suggestion, though even Painter found it irresistible (however, he was sure it was never a conscious scheme on his hero's part). Bearing in mind the Marshal's other exploits in duality (particularly his tightrope

42 *Pipe Roll of 17 John* 40, 43; *Chronica Maiora* II 605. This was not by accident; contemporary society credited men as 'earls' more loosely than was done in subsequent centuries. Henry, the bastard son of Earl Reginald of Cornwall, calls himself earl in his charters at this time, although indeed he was never created earl by the king. Matthew Paris calls the same Henry earl, showing that the practice was general.

43 The young Marshal was named as one of the rebel barons in London early in June 1215, see J C Holt *Magna Carta* Cambridge 1965 app. VII no. 1 pp. 342–3.

44 *Annales de Wigornia* in *Annales Monastici* IV 406. The Patent Rolls record a protection for the young Marshal to visit his father in April 1216 under the escort of the Master of the Temple in England (the Marshal's particular friend). *Rotuli Litterarum Patentium* 175. Whatever the ostensible reason given to John for the meeting, it could not have been other than a family strategy conference in the light of news from France.

walk between John and Philip in 1205), I would not have put it past him at all, indeed there is reason to believe that he was repeating a strategem he had used many years earlier. If the elder and younger Marshals were in clandestine concert in 1215, then the situation was very like that between the two Marshal brothers, John and William, in 1190–94: one Count John's man, the other Richard's.

Magna Carta, as a means of averting open war between royalists and rebels, was an unfortunate failure. The northern party of barons simply rejected it soon after Runnymede. War against the king was already in progress in the north in August, while the barons in the south were still talking to the king. But by September mutual lack of trust between the parties had caused the settlement to crumble into warfare. The Marshal remained with the king until the end of July, attending a make-or-break conference at Oxford, to which the barons had come armed to indicate their impatience. It was at this time that the king abandoned the charter and secretly sent to the pope asking him to annul it. Thereafter the Marshal's military skills were what was needed and he moved, or was sent, to the southern Marches. The Welsh had perceived John's weakness. An opportunist alliance was forged between the Marshal's old adversary, Maelgwyn ap Rhys; Llywelyn ap Iorwerth, the dominant prince of Gwynedd; and the younger members of the Briouze family. From the summer of 1215 through into the winter of 1215–16, the Marshal had the difficult task of organizing resistance to Welsh incursions to the west, while monitoring rebel movements to his east. Indications are that there was not very much that he was able to achieve in the face of this war on two fronts. He could do little more than sit tight and try to hold what he could, while the Welsh overran the north of Pembrokeshire, Carmarthenshire and Gower. King John in the meantime had rather more success. He penned the rebels in London while he had considerable success in picking off outlying garrisons. He took the formidable castle of Rochester in a meticulous and brilliant siege.

The rebels did at least make one significant move. They appealed to King Philip of France for aid, and offered the crown of England to his son, Louis. Some reinforcements were sent to London, but Louis did not immediately appear. At this point, in the spring of 1216, John attempted to persuade Philip not to send his son to England. The Marshal was one of the ambassadors selected to reason with Philip and so, for the last time, he crossed to France. The embassy was a failure, and the Marshal and his colleagues returned early in April to report to the king. Within two months Louis himself appeared in England, to the consternation of the royalist party. With the aid of King Alexander of Scotland, the royalists were driven out of the north, down to the Trent and Humber. Apart from Dover and Windsor, the south east went over to the French. In many ways it was a situation not unlike what happened in 1066. The *Histoire*'s sentiments at this point would have done justice to one of Harold's defeated thegns.

> Many fine casks and barrels of wine were drunk by the rascals of France. They were so full of themselves that they said England was theirs, and the English had abandoned their lands to them, having no right to them.[45]

This seems to have been a sentiment stemming from the Francophobe element in the Marshal's English *mesnie*. Doubtless it was also a sentiment shared by a wider group within England. It was generally believed that French arrogance was the reason why the Young Marshal ultimately abandoned Louis's cause.[46] But this view of matters does not square with the Young Marshal's determination to make the best of his position at Louis's court. He had his right to be Louis's marshal in England recognized by the prince, and attempted to get Louis to restore to him the castle of Marlborough which his grandfather had lost in 1158. His failure to do so might well have been the true reason for his disenchantment with the French.

The king slowly retreated into the west, basing himself at Corfe castle and abandoning much of the east coast. The Marshal too was back in the southern March in June, waiting on events and watching. The royal party in England had shrunk. Even the king's half-brother, the powerful Earl of Salisbury, had gone over to Louis. Apart from the Marshal and the Earl of Chester, only the Earls of Derby and Warwick remained attached to John's cause, and neither of them disposed of a political affinity of any great weight. Things remained dire in October 1215 when John suddenly decided on a sally into the north to reinforce the loyal garrisons of Lincoln and Newark and drive a wedge between Louis and the Scots. Although the campaign was a partial success (apart that is from difficulties in crossing the Wash), John fell ill at Kings

45 *Histoire* ll. 15102–8.

46 *Chronicon Thomae Wykes* in *Annales Monastici* III 47.

Lynn and it rapidly became clear that he was dying. A few barons, including the Marshal's nephew, John, were with the king when he reached the fortified palace of the bishops of Lincoln at Newark. The abbot of Croxton was called from his Leicestershire abbey to doctor the dying king, but in the end could do no more than confess and embalm him. The *Histoire* depicts an affecting scene as the king publicly apologized for all the ills he had done the Marshal, begged his forgiveness, and recognized at the end his worth and loyalty. What was more he entreated those present to entrust his young heir, Henry, to the Marshal's keeping. The Marshal alone could help the boy now.

Some such scene was doubtless acted out, even if in reality it was more likely that the king's departing words on the Marshal formed part of a longer deathbed confession of the king's past sins to various individuals; however, the declaration that the Marshal was to be the keeper of his son and the kingdom is a different matter. Another source, an anonymous French history of the Norman and Angevin houses, does mention the king on his deathbed entrusting his son and kingdom to the Marshal,[47] but it is likely that the author (in the same way as the author of the *Histoire*) was simply extrapolating from what happened later at Gloucester. The *Histoire* itself mentions that there was an expectation at Gloucester that the Earl of Chester would contend for the regency. The generally reliable Barnwell chronicler has the Marshal, Gualo (and the bishop of Winchester) entrusted with the king and kingdom 'by the common counsel' of the magnates.[48] If this were so, then at least one well-informed contemporary did not see the late king's provision as the source of the Marshal's regency. So it may well be that the king's deathbed provisions were vaguer than the *Histoire* describes. The king's brief deathbed testament – of which a text survives – says very little as to the future government of his realm, but entrusts the 'rendering assistance to my sons for the recovery and defence of their inheritance' to a council of thirteen executors and ordainers, of whom the Marshal was only one.[49]

47 *Histoire des ducs de Normandie et des rois d'Angleterre* ed. F Michel Societé de l'Histoire de France Paris 1840 180.

48 *Memoriale Fratris Walteri de Coventria* II 233.

49 Translated in W L Warren *King John* 2nd edn London 1978 255, from T Rymer *Foedera, Conventiones, Litterae et Acta Publica* ed. A Clarke and F Holbrooke (7 vols) London 1816–69 I pt I 144.

. . .

## PROTECTOR OF THE KING AND THE KINGDOM

The *Histoire* reports that the Marshal was deeply affected by news of the king's death. Whether or not his grief was more than conventional, he certainly acted promptly to take as much advantage from the new situation as he might. He was at Gloucester when the news reached him, and rode with the papal legate, Gualo, to meet the cortège for the funeral at Worcester, where the king had chosen to be buried. The funeral was carried out with some care and pomp, despite the circumstances. The dead king was even interred in the black cowl of a Benedictine, a token that he had been admitted into the spiritual benefits of the monastic order which ruled the cathedral.[50] The Marshal might well have stage-managed the funeral himself for we know that he sent his nephew, John, to appropriate cloths of brocade and silk from a royal storehouse in order to cover the royal tomb.[51]

There is other good evidence that the Marshal was pushing himself forward at this time. Following the funeral, he and the legate summoned a council of the royalist magnates at Gloucester to consider what was to be done next. The nine-year-old Henry III was brought from his refuge at Devizes to meet the magnates. The Marshal made a point of meeting the royal party on the road near Malmesbury, and greeted the boy-king, who was riding before the saddle of his chief attendant. Then there was a genuinely affecting scene. The new king was a bright and attractive boy. He apparently already knew the Marshal and liked him; the old man seems to have had a way with the young. He assumed that the Marshal was to be his guardian (perhaps there had already been talk around him as to what might be done) and he asked God to give the Marshal the power to protect him. 'Upon my soul, my lord,' said the Marshal, 'there is nothing I will not do to serve you in good faith while I have the strength.' Tears stood in the eyes of everyone present, not least the Marshal's, and they turned their horses towards Gloucester.

Once there the talk was all about the Earl of Chester, and what might be his attitude, and whether the council should proceed without him. Whatever the little king and his household might have thought, and however much the Marshal was assuming to

50 I must thank my wife for pointing this interesting detail out to me.

himself, the magnates in general were not as yet agreed on a regency, or a regent. But speed was their necessity at this point, and without waiting for Earl Ranulf a coronation was arranged for 28 October (John had been dead but ten days). Suitable royal garments were run up (or rather cut down) for the boy, and his mother contributed a gold circlet for the ceremony. First he must be knighted, and the Marshal obliged, thus knighting the second King Henry of his career; uncle and nephew. 'He was a fine little knight' says the *Histoire* in a much quoted phrase. Then the ceremony proceeded, the king borne by his future master-in-arms, the Leicestershire knight, Philip d'Aubigny and a colleague. A mass was said and the legate himself crowned the king (the archbishop of Canterbury was at Rome). A banquet followed the coronation, as was customary, the young king being clothed in more suitable garments. Now it was that serious manœuvres began to produce an effective government. As they were sitting down to the meal a messenger arrived and announced that the Marshal's castle of Goodrich was even then under siege (probably by his Welsh adversaries). The Marshal had to rise from the table to arrange the dispatch of a relieving force. It was all very dramatic and underlined the need for a quick decision from the magnates.

They opted in a body to ask the Marshal to assume the regency at once. But events were moving quicker than he liked. A courtier such as he was knew that he must first have the consent of Earl Ranulf. He refused to answer until he could consult with the Earl of Chester. Although he had been keen enough to take on the burden at Malmesbury a day or two earlier, the *Histoire* preserves a scene later in his rooms at Gloucester castle which tells of some new doubts. Closeted with John Marshal, John of Earley and Ralph Musard, the sheriff and castellan of Gloucester, he said he had misgivings and wanted their advice. John Marshal and Ralph Musard were eager that he should accept, the latter seeing great promise of future patronage for the Marshal's men. John of Earley, with more of an eye to his lord's age, advised him to refuse. The Marshal brooded on this advice and then promised to sleep on it.

The next day brought the Earl of Chester to Gloucester. As things fell out, he did not want to be regent and was happy to defer to the Marshal. When the council convened the Marshal once more brought forward his doubts (referring to himself for effect, and somewhat erroneously, as an octogenarian), but they were speedily overcome. If they were intended as a *nolo episcopari* they were treated as perfunctorily as he could have wished. He was to exercise joint power over England with the papal legate. In counsel later with the same three friends of the night before, he found John of Earley less discouraging now that the decision had been made. He was full of the honour of the deeds that needed to be done; the desperation of their situation; the need never to surrender. He proposed retreat to Ireland to carry on the fight there, if Louis took England: 'never will a man have earned such honour in the land!'. The Marshal caught his mood: 'Your advice is true and good. If everyone abandons the boy but me, do you know what I shall do? I will carry him on my back, and if I can hold him up, I will hop from island to island, from country to country, even if I have to beg for my bread!'.[52] We can never be wholly sure if the *Histoire* reports what were the actual words of the Marshal, but these somehow ring true.

The Marshal and his royal ward quitted Gloucester on 2 or 3 November and moved to King John's favourite residence at Tewkesbury, moving thence to a great council of royalist magnates and bishops at Bristol. The royal clerks began to work out precisely what official position the Marshal should occupy. At first they thought that he should be called 'justiciar of England',[53] but decided that that would not work. Hubert de Burgh, King John's loyal aide and then castellan of Dover, had been the late king's justiciar since 1214 and his importance meant that the new government wanted to keep him in the post. Besides, King John's former ministers were to argue that their appointments remained valid until Henry III came of age. So a new title was created for the Marshal. In the reissue of Magna Carta on 12 November 1216 at Bristol, he was called by the king's clerk *rector noster et regni nostri* 'our keeper and the keeper of our kingdom'. Perhaps 'keeper' or 'guardian' is a better translation of the word *rector* than 'regent', but 'regent' expresses better the power that the Marshal now wielded. His authority lay behind all royal acts. Within days of the coronation the majority of letters or grants issued in the king's name went out 'by the earl', and were attested either by him alone, or with the legate. Many administrative acts went out in his own name, although how many is uncertain, since they were not

52 *Histoire* ll. 15688–96.

53 See *Patent Rolls, 1216–25* 2: *iusticiarius noster Anglie* on 2 November at Gloucester.

registered by the Chancery.[54] The Marshal's seal was appended to royal letters, for the young king had none of his own until the end of 1218. Payments owed the king were often made to William Marshal in person, rather than to the exchequer. For nearly three years the Marshal was the mainspring of what government there was.

The Marshal's task was now to pacify England. In general he was lucky: Matthew Paris – and modern historians seem to be in agreement – expressed the sentiment that people were more well-disposed to Henry III 'for it seemed to all that it was not right to put the evil of the father upon the son.'[55] The Marshal and his colleagues assisted this feeling by offering easy terms to those willing to submit to the king, and by offering general restitution for ills. During the winter of 1216–17 the balance of power between the two sides hardly quivered. The greater men amongst the rebels did not show any sign of reconsidering; the Marshal did not have the resources to take much action. Louis on the other hand did not have any success against the great castles holding out for the king. In February 1217 he returned to France to consult with his royal father, but had small comfort from the visit. Philip was under great pressure from the Church and would not assist him in any useful way. When Louis returned to England late in April he found that the situation had worsened considerably. Before he had left the royalists had been able to make some headway in the Cinque Ports. The Young Marshal and the Earl of Salisbury had taken advantage of his absence to return to the royalist camp. If there had been any collusion between elder and younger Marshals, the need for it had now passed, perhaps. The *Histoire* says that the two men simply fell in with the Marshal's raid on the Sussex castle of Knepp (the centre of the confiscated Briouze lordship) then in the hands of Roland Bloet, brother of one of the Marshal's knights. It fails to mention the fact that they had been on the opposite side until then. These two were the most prominent of the *reversi* 'the returners' (as royal records call them).

54 A copy of one such Marshal precept, addressed to the sheriff of Lincoln instructing him to assist the younger Marshal in collecting a scutage from the men of the fees of Earl David and Gilbert de Gant, survives on an Exchequer Remembrancer's roll, PRO E368/3 m. 3d. Another, addressed to the barons of the Exchequer, is a receipt for 20 marks which the abbot of Tewkesbury had paid him in person and which he wanted the barons to note on their accounts, PRO, E368/1 m. 7d.

55 *Chronica Maiora* iii 2.

The rolls recording the king's correspondence register an ever-increasing number of protections and safe conducts to men who were returning to their allegiance.

But the kingdom would not be regained by the Marshal sitting still and waiting for Louis to go away. There must be some successful military demonstrations to regain the initiative and a measure of prestige. The *Histoire* records the subsequent campaign in great detail, its author occasionally stopping to tell us that he was reconstructing the complicated military manœuvres from written descriptions sent him by his informants. The course of the campaign has been reconstructed with great care by Dr David Carpenter, and there is no point in duplicating his work.[56] Let it suffice here that attempts were made to move along the Channel coast and hamper Louis's communications with France, and a number of important castles fell. In the north Midlands the Earl of Chester continued John's campaign of the previous autumn of harrying the rebels there, in order to stop the northern barons linking with Louis. Ranulf was not quite as strategically minded as the late king or the Marshal, however. He chose to combine business with his own personal concerns and attacked the Earl of Winchester's castle of Mountsorrel in the Soar valley in Leicestershire. It was a castle from which the earl of Winchester's predecessors had ousted Ranulf's grandfather.[57] In the circumstances this did not really matter. It was enough that the rebels were being pressed and kept off balance. In the event the siege of Mountsorrel set off a train of events leading to an outcome that was more than gratifying to the Marshal.

Louis was persuaded by the Earl of Winchester that a column should be sent to the relief of Mountsorrel. A substantial force was provided, the French in it captained by Thomas, the Count of Perche. When they arrived there, it was to discover that the royalists had already retreated. The rebel forces therefore moved eastwards, pillaging as they went. They headed for Lincoln castle; long under desultory siege by a mixed force of northerners and French, but hitherto defiant under its remarkable female castellan, Nicola de la Haie. They did not know that the Marshal had concentrated the main royalist army at Northampton, behind them and was in pursuit.

56 See D Carpenter *The Minority of Henry III* (forthcoming).

57 See E King 'Mountsorrel and its Region in King Stephen's reign' *Huntington Library Quarterly* XLIV 1980 8–9.

Taking what forces he had, and scraping together what he could from local garrisons, the Marshal assembled at Newark a force which the *Histoire* totals at 406 knights and 317 crossbowmen. These figures sound convincing, because they are not the large, round numbers which literary sources usually employ. It may well be that the author had access to the muster rolls of the army. It was the Marshal or his agents who were supposed to keep these rolls, so this is not unlikely. On 19 May 1217 this modest-sized column left Newark for the twenty-five-or-so mile march to Lincoln. Still ringing in their ears was the Marshal's pre-battle harangue. This was a custom beloved of Roman generals and still practised from time to time in the medieval world. As the *Histoire* records this speech it was short, simple and unaffected; well-adapted for the circumstances. His men were to remember their honour, families and lands. They were not to be backward in deeds that day; for they were fighting for the Holy Church. He stated their task and circumstances simply: to destroy the French who had come to take their lands, or be destroyed themselves. The French were God's enemies and they had foolishly divided their forces; now God had given the opportunity to finish them. It was a most effective piece of rhetoric mixing land, possession and peoples in a volatile, dangerous cocktail. Before they left, the legate had given them a plenary absolution for their sins to that day. Those who died fighting the excommunicate rebel force would go direct to heaven.

They spent the night at Torksey, having passed down the Trent. The Marshal did not choose to take the direct route to Lincoln along the Fosse Way. An approach from the south west would mean that he would first have to have fought his way through the city, which climbed up to the hill on which castle and minster stood. The French had stationed their siege machines and main force in the city, not being sure of the loyalty of the citizens. After a mass the troops were marshalled at dawn in companies before him. He made another address along the lines of that given at Newark. Then the army began to move, in very good heart, as if to a tournament (as the *Histoire* says). It was a march of about ten miles to Lincoln and the stiff pace tired their horses. According to Roger of Wendover, it was still early in the morning when they reached the city. They were seen some time before they reached it by beseiged and beseigers alike. The French forces retired within the city gates, deceived as to the inferior numbers of the royalists. The lady Nicola was able to send out her deputy through a postern gate to inform the Marshal of the state of her defence, and more importantly to tell him that a gate communicating to the country was open for the reception of the royal forces.

So it was that the Marshal was able to send royalist troops with ease into the castle while he covered the city gates, looking for a point of access. The account of the *Histoire* is more than a little confused here. It relied on the memoirs of several men for the events of that day, and more than one was willing to take credit for finding a way into the city: 'Those who gave me my matter don't agree, and I cannot follow all of them; I shall lose the right road and won't be believed.' At any rate it seems clear that Faulkes de Breauté was able to distract the French by deploying his crossbowmen on the broken walls of the castle to harass their engineers, but was unable to assault the French through the castle's main gate into the city. Both John Marshal and the bishop of Winchester claimed to have found an alternative and unguarded route into the city.

Whoever deserved the credit, the royalists were able to penetrate the city with great effect. The Marshal, who must have realized that this was to be his last battle, was rather too forward for the comfort of his colleagues and *mesnie*. Once the way was found he would not wait for scouts' reports, but rode forward until reminded that he had forgotten to put on his helmet. But then he was now perhaps seventy years of age and may have felt he had something to prove. He had the satisfaction during the battle of seeing off with several smart strokes Robert of Roppesley, one of King John's young *mesnie* who had turned traitor. He also had the strength to take scatheless several blows on his helm, which were strong enough to dent it. The royalists, though outnumbered, pressed in on the French and rebels with great success. In many ways the fight was like the first action in which the Marshal had participated in the streets of the suburbs of Neufchâtel-en-Bray: a constricted street fight with no possibilities for a decisive charge. Although having the advantages of numbers, the French were unable to rout the royalists: it may have been a matter of lack of morale, or it may have been dismay at the sudden inrush of the royalists and their quick seizure of their artillery. A stand before the minster (probably in the present Exchequer Gate) led by their commander, Count Thomas of Perche, failed when the young count was accidentally killed. The Marshal was present at his fall and was upset by it. He and the count were first cousins. After the count's fall, the French were pressed down the hill to the southern gate of the city: the royalists having the advantage of fighting downhill now. In the middle of the afternoon their resistance finally broke and they scattered out into the suburbs and countryside. There many of the foot-soldiers were slaughtered by the local peasantry. However, only three of the horsemen involved in the battle died (including the Count of Perche). Great numbers of rebels were captured however: forty-six barons and 300 knights, including the Earls of Winchester, Hereford and Lincoln. John, the Marshal's nephew, took prisoner himself seven bannerets and their followers.

Great victory though Lincoln was, it was not enough to persuade Louis to leave England immediately; he wanted terms by which he could decamp to France with a minimum loss of face. Early in June he opened negotiations with William Marshal, settled with his army at Chertsey on the Thames below Staines. A subsequent meeting between plenipotentiaries of both parties actually managed to reach a settlement. Great men were present: four elder abbots of the Cistercian order and the archbishop of Tyre; probably dispatched by King Philip to assist in extricating his son from an increasingly sticky situation. Unfortunately Louis balked at the failure to include his chief clerical adherents in the amnesty promised to the barons. Negotiations broke down and Louis chose to sit tight in London until he heard news of his wife's efforts to send reinforcements to him across the Channel. The Marshal moved to prevent this, assembling his army at Sandwich late in August. The Cinque Ports, which had frequently opposed John, were willing to accommodate the Marshal and the young Henry III.

The subsequent sea-battle off Sandwich was a conclusive victory for the royalists. The Marshal had not taken ship, his men had persuaded him that he was too valuable to risk to the uncertainties of a shipboard battle; and he had gone along with them (not unwillingly according to Matthew Paris).[58] We may well believe him: such a battle would have been a new experience for the Marshal, and he had reason not to be fond of maritime travel. The victorious admirals in this case were the justiciar, Hubert de Burgh, and Richard of Chilham, the bastard son of King John; the Marshal and the boy-king watched the distant fight from the clifftops. There could be no argument with such a judgement of God. Louis began negotiations for his withdrawal at once.

58 *Chronica Maiora* III 28.

There was at the time a view that the Marshal should have closed in on London and worked for the capitulation of the remaining French force. That he did not do so opened him in later days to accusations of double-dealing from which it was difficult to exculpate him. Since the Marshal's policy from the assumption of the regency had been to deal gently with the rebel party as long as it was willing to talk, it is hard to see what else he could have done. Temporizing had been successful to date and a change of tactic would have seemed unnecessary. Besides this, it really would have been as embarrassing as his later detractors suggested had he taken prisoner the son and heir of King Philip, his lord for his Norman lands. The fact that he had a fleet move to block the Thames estuary hardly indicates (as Painter suggested) that he was torn between two courses of action: the militant and the pacific. It was simply a means to improve his bargaining position, for bargaining was what he intended doing. The terms he was willing to accept were very easy, in fact they were much the same as the two sides had agreed in June.[59] Prisoners were to be released free of further ransom payments, and lands restored to Louis's English followers. The Scots and Welsh allies of Louis were to give up their gains. An indemnity of 10,000 marks (£6,667 6s. 8d.) was to be paid against Louis's expenses in England. All that Louis had to do was to leave with his men, and undertake to assist in the future restoration to Henry III of the lands in France his father had lost. Needless to say, the last condition was never fulfilled, despite the Marshal's particular care that the indemnity was paid in full.

Such easy terms towards Louis (although not to the repentant rebels) did not endear the Marshal to future generations. Matthew Paris records that Henry III in later days peevishly berated the Marshal's son, Walter, for what he was pleased to call the old Marshal's treachery. From the same source comes the story that Philip Augustus announced with relief, after hearing of the disaster of Lincoln but that the Marshal still lived, that he had no fears for his son.[60] It is likely that Matthew was recording a genuine feeling of disenchantment later current in royal circles about the Marshal's doings at this time. Matthew Paris is also a little uncharitable to the Marshal's memory at other times, recalling with disgust his treatment of the bishop of Ferns. Such a

59 The terms agreed in June still survive in a draft copy, as does the eventual treaty of September 1217. The textual problems are considered by F M Powicke *King Henry III and the Lord Edward* (2 vols) Oxford 1947 I 25–9.

60 *Chronica Maiora* III 25–6, IV 157.

courtier as the Marshal was could hardly have expected a completely favourable verdict from posterity once he was no longer available personally to harry his accuser with offers of a duel. Indeed he hardly deserves complete absolution; there remains too much that was ambiguous in his political career for that.

. . .

## THE MARSHAL'S GOVERNMENT

The Marshal enjoyed nineteen months of power after the departure of Louis from England. In those months his government achieved some degree of success in settling the kingdom. Before the Marshal resigned, the exchequer was restored (although the sheriffs were reluctant to account to it), and some old debts began to be reclaimed; taxes were levied and collected (although not at the high rates of John's reign); and the justices in eyre began their circuits once more. The government had at least regained the appearance of being in control; although it is clear that the regent and his council had not been able to restore the strength of the Angevin monarchy which John had inherited. The sheriffs and castellans of the civil war were not easily displaced and had learned to think of themselves as supreme in their localities. At the centre moreover, it was government by the magnates for the magnates. The full restoration of government was not the Marshal's achievement; it belonged to Hubert de Burgh after the Marshal's death. The Marshal's regency served its purpose in winning the war; the rest of its story is of amiable drift. Nonetheless, after all the qualifications have been made, the Marshal provided a prestigious figurehead and a politic and affable presence at the head of affairs. In the period of slow recovery from civil warfare his charm and (by now) venerable presence was invaluable.

Where we get closer to the Marshal at this time is in those affairs which touched his *mesnie* and estates. He did not neglect to promote the interests of both himself and his affinity while he was regent. This remark is not meant as a criticism of his conduct; what he did was no more than any other man would have done in his circumstances. He was neither rapacious nor impolitic in his use of the greatly amplified powers of patronage that his position gave him. No doubt he was quite sensitive to the necessity of restraint when his power depended on the consent of the barons who had raised him to the regency. He was still one of them; no degree of royal charisma touched him at all. He was not such a regent as England had ever had before: no royal sibling or consort.

The Marshal certainly served himself, although he did not take a greedy share of the pie. Perhaps the most satisfactory acquisition he made was the castle and town of Marlborough, recovered from the rebels in 1217. This was quite likely where he had been born and he had certainly spent much of his childhood there, for it had been the centre of his father's activities until Henry II had taken it back into royal hands in 1158. He might well have reflected that he deserved some compensation for the losses he had to suffer in west Wales, where Cardigan, Cilgerran and Carmarthen had to be abandoned to the Welsh. Nearer home his lands had been much battered by the Welsh prince Morgan ap Hywel (or Morgan of Caerleon, as he frequently called himself in Anglo-French fashion). The house of Caerleon was a curious survival of native lordship in south east-Wales. The lords of Caerleon were descended from Caradog ap Gruffudd, who had been client king of Glamorgan allied to the Conqueror until his death in 1081. His kingdom had then disappeared and his son been impoverished, but in 1136–7 under his grandson, Morgan ab Owain, it had been restored. King Morgan had dominated Gwent under both Stephen and Henry II until his death in 1158; his power based on the castles of Caerleon and Usk.[61] The family had great prestige in Wales and played up their connection with the Roman fortress in which their castle was built: feeding on the Arthurian legend associations invented by their neighbour, Geoffrey of Monmouth.

Subsequent princes of the line had not fared so well. Earl Richard Strongbow had reduced and taken Usk in the 1160s and later had dispossessed them temporarily of Caerleon. Nonetheless the lords of Caerleon remained a power, fitfully allied with the king and Marcher interests. Morgan of Caerleon's father had been a major prop of Henry II's power in the southern March. Hywel had died in 1211 and Morgan had gravitated into the political orbit of Llywelyn ab Iorwerth, Prince of Gwynedd. He had fought with Llywelyn for Louis's interests in the civil war, but unlike Llywelyn did not lay down his sword after the departure of the French. He was hot to recover land which he claimed the Marshal had occupied. This may be a reference to lost Usk or some part of the Welsh portion of Netherwent. A damaging war ravaged the

61 D Crouch 'The Slow Death of Kingship in Glamorgan, 1067–1158' *Morgannwg* XXIX 1985 20–41.

Marshal lordships in Gwent. Two members of the Bloet family, Roland and Walter, fell in the hostilities along with several other knights. Even the capture of Caerleon by the Marshal's bailiff (probably John of Earley) around the end of September 1217 did not end the hostilities. The Marshal soon afterwards had the Countess of Gloucester's castle of Newport and the lordship of Gwynllŵg committed to him.[62] The reason for this was that Morgan's last fortress was the castle of Machen in upland Gwynllŵg. If he controlled Gwynllŵg he could pursue Morgan into the hills legally, rather than trespass into another Marcher lordship. In the end, under pressure from Llywelyn, Morgan reluctantly submitted to the adjudication of a council at Worcester in March 1218. This took Caerleon from him, and he did not recover it in the elder Marshal's lifetime, although it was later restored.

The Marshal was also able to secure for himself half of the English lands of the Count of Perche, who had been slain at Lincoln. The counts of Perche, great magnates on the French side of the southern Norman March, had accepted lands in the south-west of England to seal an alliance with King Henry I, and had remained one of the small number of French counts with English interests ever since. Following the fall of Count Thomas of Perche at Lincoln, his several demesne manors were given to the Earl of Salisbury. This earl would not part with them after the settlement with Louis. The Marshal did not insist, and by a quiet arrangement allowed Longespée to keep two, while he took two for himself (including, oddly enough, Newbury, Berkshire, where his father had abandoned him as hostage to King Stephen over sixty years before).[63] The Marshal and Longespée may well have cloaked their seizure under the tenuous claim of kinship to Count Thomas, for the Marshal was the count's first cousin and Longespée's wife was also a relation. Geoffrey II of Perche had married the Marshal's mother's sister (who was sister also of Patrick, Earl of Salisbury). The two earls were also successful in filching the royal manor of Shrivenham, Berkshire, which had been held by the counts of Perche at the king's pleasure. They bought out Count Thomas's heir, the bishop of Chalons, in December 1217.

62 *Rotuli Litterarum Clausarum* I 330.

63 This interesting sidelight on the Marshal's activities is described fully by David Carpenter in his forthcoming book.

The Marshal was reluctant to use royal manors in his patronage of other men. The royal estates had been too badly enfeebled by the war. Some short-term patronage was available in the confiscated lands of rebels, but by the settlement of 1217 these had to be given back. For a while his son enjoyed the lands of two earls Winchester and Huntingdon, and those of the baron, Gilbert de Gant, but their submission deprived him of this princely estate. He was compensated by several large cash payments 'for his support in the king's service'. By this time the younger Marshal was supporting a sizeable *mesnie* of knights in his own right, and some enlargement of his income was very desirable to him. In February 1218 this was provided in a grant of the profits of the royal exchanges in the greatest cities in the kingdom. John Marshal also did very well out of confiscations. He had a grant of the master forestership of the kingdom (apart from the forests that had been appropriated by several magnates); he also had the keeping of Devizes castle. The Marshal otherwise provided for his men in grants of wardships, escheats, fairs and markets; such as those granted to John of Earley, Jordan de Sauqueville, Ralph Musard and Ralph Bloet (as well as himself, his son, and his nephew).

. . .

## RESIGNATION, DEATH AND AFTERWARDS

In Westminster, around the end of January 1219, the Marshal suddenly became ill. A severe bout of internal pain seems to have rendered him entirely unfit for business until the second week of February. He was now, or was approaching, the age of seventy-two. Until this sickness he had been a hale old man; a stranger to illness. It may not have been at once apparent that he was dying, for he was able to resume business. The doctors were allowed some scope to practise their arts on him. On 7 March he was strong enough to ride to the Tower, attended by Countess Isabel. Here he must have come to the bitter realization that he was dying. In the middle of the month he was placed in a boat and rowed upstream to his manor of Caversham on the Thames opposite Reading. Caversham, and his family's ancestral castle and centre at Hamstead Marshall, were his two favoured English homes. It is not surprising that he wished to be taken to one of them to die. It was an easy journey and he had made it in less than a day when he had used the manor as a staging post in his journeys about the kingdom over the past three years. This time the journey was made rather more gently, and spread over three days in easy stages.

The Marshal continued to transact business from what he might not yet have finally decided was his deathbed at Caversham. For nearly three weeks after his arrival a steady output of letters left Caversham, mostly under his name rather than those of his fellows in government. The king was settled across the river at Reading with his tutor, the bishop of Winchester. Nevertheless the pain continued and his appetite was quite gone. To an untutored historian, the description of his illness sounds like a wasting form of bowel disease, perhaps a cancer, since it was not associated with any flux. The reader may treat the observation for what it is worth.

It was not until the week before Easter (7 April) that the Marshal resolved to pass on the reins of government. A council summoned by the Marshal sat around his bed for two consecutive days (8–9 April) and deliberated what was to be done. Brushing aside the claims of the bishop of Winchester, the Marshal commended the eleven-year-old king to the legate's care. Suppressing the acute pain by which he was racked, the Marshal took the boy by the hand. He earnestly, and pointedly, prayed God to cut short the king's life if he followed the example of any criminal royal predecessor (*alcun felon ancestre*): it seems that he was uncourtly enough at the end as to (almost) criticize King John openly. The king and the court left him then and moved away to Wallingford.

The Marshal had yet another month of life before him after taking leave of the king. The story of those days has been often told and well; a tribute to the quality of the *Histoire*'s verse at this point; I will have more to say about it in a later chapter. There is only need to refer here to the steadfast attendance of his son and his knights; the tearful farewells to his wife and daughters; and his reception into the order of Knights Templar. But to the end he remained Earl of Pembroke, distributing robes to his knights just before he died. He deliberated his last testament in council with his men the day after he laid down the regency, and before he became a Templar. Few texts of baronial testaments survive from before the late thirteenth century, so the description of the Marshal's will is particularly valuable. The Marshal firstly provided for the division of his lands. Until her death all the lands he had by marriage would return to his wife alone, but he could determine their future division. Like his father he meant to provide for his two eldest sons; there was no hint here that the practice of primogeniture had as yet any hold on the aristocracy of England. The *Histoire* does not say precisely how this was done, but we know from the later history of his family that Leinster, Pembroke, Striguil and the ancestral Marshal lands in England went to the eldest son, William. Richard, the second son had the Marshal's Norman lordship of Longueville, but also the Giffard honor of Crendon in England. The Marshal chose to continue the integrity of the Giffard lands in Richard, and did not intend to use his testament to remove for ever the problem of his divided allegiance by splitting his lands at the Channel. Gilbert was to be a clerk and so there was no problem in providing for him. Some provision was made for Walter who was still a boy in 1219. He had his father's acquisition of Goodrich and other manors. The youngest of them, carrying the ill-fated Marshal name of Anselm, was initially to be ignored. However, the intervention of John of Earley with the Marshal secured Anselm lands in Ireland worth £140. Only one daughter, Joan was unmarried at this time, and she was temporarily provided for by £30 of land and a cash sum of 200 marks (£133 6s. 8d.). There were also legacies to his monasteries: fifty marks (£33 6s. 8d.) to Notley abbey and each of his foundations in Ireland, and 10 marks (£6 13s. 4d.) to the cathedrals of Leinster (did he include Ferns, one wonders). He left his body to be buried at the church of the New Temple in London, and the manor of Upleden, Herefordshire, was his gift to the order. A few days later his almoner, Geoffrey the Templar, drew up the testament in written form and it was sealed by the Marshal, his wife and son. It named as executors Abbot David of Bristol, John of Earley and Henry fitz Gerold. It was then carried off to the legate, the archbishop of Canterbury and the bishops of Winchester and Salisbury, who were to be the supervisors of the testament, and who confirmed its contents. It seems that they also nominated the archbishop's steward, Elias of Dereham, to assist the executors named in the testament.[64]

The Marshal died about midday on 14 May 1219; the windows and doors of his chamber flung open; his silent men and several prelates about his bed; supported by his son, his eyes fixed on the cross. So ended in the fullest of medieval pomp his remarkable story. He was buried in great splendour. His body was embalmed

64 For Walter Marshal's share of his father's lands at Goodrich, Sturminster Marshall and Bere Regis, see *Close Rolls, 1227–31*, 527, 539, 552. For Elias of Dereham as co-executor see his statement in the exchequer in 1244, PRO E368/15

at Reading abbey – not particularly well as it later turned out – where he was laid in state in a side chapel which he had earlier financed. His wife and *mesnie* were at the abbey, and his men no doubt stood vigil that night, as he had in his day watched at the corpses of his masters. His wife – who enjoyed the relative freedom of widowhood for less than a year before she herself died – courteously made a grant of rents to the abbey that had welcomed his corpse. After mass the next day the bier was borne to Staines, where several earls and barons met it to escort the body to London. Thence it was taken to Westminster abbey where another solemn mass was said before it. It was laid to rest the next day in the Temple church, the burial service performed by the archbishop of Canterbury and the bishop of London. Some relics of the tomb are still to be seen there. The earliest of the Temple's knightly effigy tombs, damaged by idle tourists and a German incendiary bomb which landed in the church, is traditionally said to have been the elder Marshal's. This cannot be proved for certain, for the tomb has no inscription, but its style of carving makes it likely.[65]

The *Histoire* records several posthumous tributes said of the Marshal, all laudatory. He died certain of his salvation, for he had planned for it as carefully as he planned any of his military campaigns. If treasure invested in the fabric of churches and the prayers of monks and priests could bring him everlasting life, then indeed he had cause to be optimistic. His men at least believed that he rejoiced with the elect of Heaven: 'we believe that his soul is in the company of God, because he was good in this life and his death'. Such indeed was their partisan view. Matthew Paris and others were less sure. The Marshal had died excommunicate by the Bishop of Ferns, who was obdurate in refusing to lift the ban, even at Henry III's insistence. When, many years later, building work at the Temple necessitated the opening of the elder Marshal's tomb, the corpse was found to be in a very poor state; its remains nauseatingly decayed despite the attempts at embalming and its being stiched into a bull's hide packed with salt. Men saw this as the result of the Irish Bishop's curse. Matthew Paris was less sure where the Marshal's soul resided than was John of Earley.

65 I must thank Sandy Heslop for his advice on this.

*Chapter 5*

# THE MARSHAL'S MEN

One particular side of William Marshal's career has never had the attention that it deserves: his relations with the men who looked to him as lord. The subject is an important one: it touches on the very nature of aristocratic and royal power in the Marshal's lifetime. Historians have only recently begun to look at the general nature of the power wielded by the aristocracy in the period 1150–1250. The neglect of this aspect of the Marshal's career is consequently the more understandable. My own work indicates that the Marshal's career occupied a time of change in aristocratic society.[1] A brief sketch of the developments runs as follows. For three generations after the Conquest of England the magnates had based their followings on the tenants of their lands, bound to them by a miscellany of links conjured up by the phrase 'knight service'. From 1066 through to the reign of Henry II, magnates either relied on families endowed in the first great surge of landed patronage in the reign of the Conqueror, or they raised up new families by further land grants. But during Stephen's reign the flow of land grants began to dry up: magnates no longer had the spare land available to endow new men. As the flow dried up, so relations between magnates and their traditional followers became brittle, and often snapped. The 1180s and 1190s, the very time when the Marshal was promoted into the baronage, was a time when the knights of England were becoming more mobile in their allegiance. New magnates with access to court patronage could exploit this, and attract men to them who were looking for the rewards that their traditional lords could no longer offer. The Marshal (who inherited little in the way of a landed following) was one of the

1 This will be set out in my book *Aristocratic Power in England in the High Middle Ages* Yale University Press (forthcoming).

first great magnates in England to create a political connection not based on landed links and traditional allegiance, but on political interest and more subtle forms of reward; an 'affinity' as the Marshal's contemporaries were already calling it. He laid the foundations of his power in society on the rubble of an older society (though it is unlikely that he realized it). In the study of the Marshal's following, which is the basis of the next two chapters, we can find much to explain this change. The exercise of re-creating the Marshal affinity is no small step towards finding a new view of medieval England.

We are not short of evidence. The *Histoire* has a lot to say on the subject, although, as you might expect, what it says needs to be treated with care. Methodical as he was, Sidney Painter stopped short of the work necessary to balance and complement what the *Histoire* says. This would have involved tracking down and analysing the surviving originals and copies of the Marshal's writs and charters. True, this is a tedious task, but it is not unrewarding. I have found sixty-seven of them, with several charters more that were drawn up in the earl's presence. Most are charters of grant or confirmation to individuals or to religious houses, a few are letters of various sorts. Forty-nine of the charters have that important appendage, a witness list. This was a list of men present when the Marshal gave his instruction that a charter should be made by his clerk; the men who could later stand up in court and swear to the facts of the matter should anyone question the charter's authenticity. The men who are in the witness lists of the Marshal's charters between the years 1189 and 1219 should theoretically be the men who were his trusted companions, the members of his *mesnie*. Comparing the evidence of the charters with the people who are named as members of his *mesnie* in the *Histoire*, we can say (thankfully) that the charter witness lists mirror what the *Histoire* has to say: the same people appear in both. One of the incidental benefits of studying the Marshal and his men, is that the comparison of evidence involved vindicates the use of witness lists to recreate baronial followings.

Between the charters and the biography therefore we have a unique insight into the composition of the Marshal's following. But there are some odd omissions in the *Histoire* which the charters make good. The *Histoire* tells us little about the Marshal's non-military followers: the minor estate officers, the lesser household members and, with but one exception, the clerks who surrounded the Marshal. But these men are to be found in the witness lists of his charters. Their absence from the *Histoire* tells us a lot about the prejudices of its author and his patrons. They had no time for clerks, not even those who served the Marshal loyally for two decades. The only one of these who is ever mentioned is the clerk, Philip, who is pilloried by the author for suggesting to the Marshal in the days before he died that he sell the robes that the Marshal had in stock to distribute to his knights, and use the money for the good of his soul. Here again we find that streak of anticlericalism and antagonism between the household clerk and knight that was so marked in the following of the Young King decades before. The *Histoire* in its omissions and sly prejudices preserves this malign spirit for us to examine. Yet oddly it preserves it by the means that clerks used, and in a way that tells us that this divided world was decaying. The *Histoire* was composed and written by a layman, perhaps one of those literate knights who became increasingly common as the twelfth century progressed. The Marshal, bred for the battlefield and the court, never really needed to know the skills of reading and writing. Other young aristocrats, particularly those destined to succeed to lands and a place in local or national life, had different needs. They needed to cast accounts, or at least be able to understand the accounts their servants made for them; they needed to be able to read the stream of writs successive English kings, particularly after Henry II, poured out from their chanceries. Some indeed learned to enjoy a book for its own sake. A good example was the Marshal's wife's first cousin and his neighbour in the Wye valley, Gilbert fitz Baderon, who is said to have kept a library of French and Latin works in his castle of Monmouth. He is said to have lent one of these to the poet, Hugh of Roteland, in a literary conceit to explain the origin of one of Hugh's romances.[2] By the fourteenth century the word 'clerk' would have lost its restricted meaning and could be employed indifferently of any professional scribe, churchman or not.

. . .

## THE KNIGHTS

The chief part of the Marshal's immediate following, when it came into being after 1189, was his retinue of knights. Judging by the

2 Hugh of Roteland *Protheselaus: Ein Altfranzösischer Abenteuerroman* ed. F Kluckow Göttingen 1924 ll. 12707–14.

spirit in which the *Histoire* was written, his knights would have been the first to agree with that observation. They gave him much of his political weight in society, and their attendance at his side gave him dignity. His contemporary, Gerald of Wales, portrayed such medieval attitudes in the lame but evocative Latin word-play: 'Earls [*comites*] get their name from "accompanying" [*comitando*], for it is right that they be accompanied by many men.'

The Marshal had already had some experience of keeping his own following by 1189. In 1180 he had been lent by the Young King Henry, a sufficient following to form up under his own banner on the field of Lagny. These knights were not his to keep or support from his own resources; they were a temporary gift from his master to enhance his favourite servant's dignity. But the important thing was that after 1180 the Marshal might raise his banner as a baron and recruit what following he was able. Certainly we know that before the Young King's death at least two young men were attached to his banner rather than the king's. One was his squire, Eustace de Bertremont, a Norman first mentioned in 1183. He was a landless soldier who was to live all his life in the Marshal's household. He was never among the first ranks of his intimates, and his lack of weight in society might well explain this. The other was a certain Henry Norreis ('the Northerner'), from his name an Englishman. This man, by his unwise trumpeting of the Marshal's fame, roused a good deal of animosity against the Marshal in the court of the Young King. It is not necessary to see him as the Marshal's herald, as Duby did, merely as an ill-judging sycophant.

Henry II's favour added new members to the Marshal's household. In about 1187 the young John of Earley came into his household where he then filled the part of the Marshal's squire. He was a wholly new addition to the Marshal's growing dignity; an aristocratic ward. John was born about 1172 and his father, William of Earley, had died at the end of 1180. William of Earley had been a titular royal chamberlain and had considerable estates in Berkshire and Somerset, enough to be considered a lesser baron rather than a knight. On his deathbed he had devoted certain estates and churches for the foundation of a priory at Buckland, which he committed to John's great-uncle, Thomas of Earley, archdeacon of Wells, for Thomas to set up the new monastery. The other Earley lands remained in royal keeping until 1194. It seems very likely that the boy John of Earley came into Thomas's care until the aged archdeacon died in around 1186. When

Thomas of Earley eventually died, John, as an under-age tenant-in-chief of the Crown, would have come into the king's hands; by then he was a young man of about fourteen years, just the right age for fostering into a noble household. The king gave him, but not his lands, to William Marshal until he came of age. As we have seen, the Marshal had another ward in Heloise, the heiress of Kendal, around this time. From these arrangements William had an access of dignity from the keeping of young aristocrats and future tenants-in-chief, but there were more practical benefits. According to the usual arrangement, the Marshal should also have had the right to marry off his wards. He could have given John of Earley to one of his family, or sold his marriage for a suitable sum. We might know a lot more about the Marshal-Earley relationship if we knew what he did with the marriage, but all we know of John of Earley's wife is that she was called Sybil. Her name suggests a Marshal family connection, but we cannot prove it.[3]

After 1189 the appearance of the Marshal's charters in some numbers gives us a much better picture of the size of his household. Careful winnowing and comparison of evidence gives us a total of eighteen knights who can be linked to the Marshal for long periods of time. (To make the nature of the Marshal's following clearer, a break-down of its lay members can be found on p. 138 in Fig. 1, a detailed analysis of it is to be found in an appendix). From this group would be drawn his riding retinue: the *Histoire* tells us that ten knights accompanied him to Ireland in 1207; charters suggest a group of seven knights around him was not unusual. The 'pool' of eighteen knights does not include certain others who appear no more than once or twice in his charters, or not at all (Ralph Musard and Thomas Basset, for instance), but who were clearly linked to the Marshal. Both Ralph and Thomas joined the Marshal in John's reign.

3 Sybil was a Marshal and Salisbury family name, as borne by the Marshal's mother and daughter. It is interesting to speculate that he somehow married John of Earley to a Marshal before 1194. The only Marshal who had produced children by then was William's brother, John, and he had only one known bastard. But what if Sybil, wife of John of Earley, had been another of John Marshal's bastards? This would go a long way to accounting for the remarkable attachment of John to William Marshal throughout his life. For William Marshal would have been his wife's uncle.

| | | |
|---|---|---|
| John of Earley | c. 1187–1219 | Berks, Som. |
| William Waleran | c. 1189–1202 | Glos, Wilts. |
| Geoffrey Fitz Robert | c. 1189–1210 (died 1210) | Wilts. |
| William Jardin | c. 1196–1219 | Beds, Suss, Bucks. |
| Jordan de Sauqueville | c. 1200–1219 | Bucks. |
| Ralph Bloet (III or IV) | c. 1189–1219 | Glos, Hants, Som, Wilts, Gwent |
| John Marshal | c. 1194–1219 | Norf, Wilts. |
| Hugh of Sandford | c. 1196–1205 | Berks, Bucks. |
| Henry Hose | c. 1199–1213 | Berks, Hants, Suss. |
| Henry Fitz Gerold | c. 1199–1219 | Berks, Oxon, Wilts. |
| Alan de St-Georges | c. 1189–1204 | Suss. |
| Roger d'Abenon | c. 1189–1200 | Surr, Hants. |
| Philip of Prendergast | c. 1189–1207 | Pembs. |
| Thomas of Rochford | c. 1189–1206 (died 1206) | Glos, Herts. |
| Thomas de Colleville | c. 1189–1200 | Yorks, Lincs. |
| Nicholas Avenel | c. 1189–1204 | Devon, Glos, Som. |
| Stephen d'Evreux | c. 1199–1219 | Glos, Herts, Worcs. |
| Eustace de Bertremont | c. 1183–1214 | – |

Fig. 1
The Marshal's Knights

Certain clear patterns emerge when we look at these knights as a group. Firstly, a majority of them had no 'feudal' connection with the Marshal. Twelve out of the eighteen (that is, two-thirds) were not his tenants. As I have said already, this is not a particularly surprising fact for the day and age we are dealing with. By the end of the twelfth century the bonds formed by land grants between lords and their followers back in the post-Conquest period had loosened. In some areas they loosened sooner than others. In Leinster, as I have already said, the Marshal could still count – and indeed insist – on the attendance of his tenants at his court. In England too there is evidence that he expected his men at least to come to his court when summoned. But it is equally clear that very few men indeed from his honors of Striguil and Crendon in Wales and England sought out places, or were given places, in his retinue. Only one of his Crendon tenants joined his circle, Jordan de Sauqueville, but according to his son's version of events, Jordan did not find his way into the Marshal's graces because he was his tenant. Jordan had besieged the Marshal with petitions because the king's officers had made encroachments on his manor of Fawsley while Crendon was in royal wardship.[4] Jordan was an opportunist who was allowed to leap on the Marshal bandwagon when Crendon came into his hands. Either the Marshal had just liked Jordan's face, or has restored Fawsley as an act of policy to give him a friend in Buckinghamshire at no great expense to himself.

The tenants who do appear in the Marshal's entourage on a regular basis were all very significant men. The most important was Ralph Bloet. The Bloets could not be ignored by any lord of Striguil. It was not just that they were the principal tenants of the honor of Striguil in Wales and England. Ralph Bloet's brother William had married a sister of the late Earl Richard Strongbow, and Ralph and William both had acted as keepers of the honor and the castle of Chepstow before William Marshal obtained Earl Richard's heiress. It was Ralph who would have formally delivered Chepstow castle to the Marshal or his attorneys in the summer of 1189. The extensive English lands of the Bloets were a useful piece in the jigsaw of influence he was building up in the south-west of England. Their manors lay in Gloucestershire, northern Hampshire, Wiltshire and Somerset, precisely the areas in which the Marshal was developing ambitions to raise an affinity. Ralph's other brother, Walter, was castellan of Raglan and a great man in northern Gwent. Ralph too was an important character in the Marches of Wales. He had married Nest, a sister of Iorwerth ap Owain, the Welsh ruler of Caerleon and the hereditary enemy of the lords of Chepstow.

Nest Bloet was a woman whose importance was more than local. She had been Henry II's mistress at some time in her adventurous career and produced a son by him, Morgan, named after her uncle, the last Welsh king of Glamorgan. She remained remarkably influential in royal circles, especially with King John. She placed several of her legitimate sons in his household, and had a number of grants and favours from him. The co-operation of the Bloet family was an absolute necessity for the Marshal, and it is likely he sought them out rather than they seeking him. Ralph appears in his entourage as early as his Cartmel charter of 1189 x 90. He died around 1199 but his son Ralph took his place in the

4 J H Round 'Tales of the Conquest' in *Peerage and Pedigree* (2 vols) London 1910 I 285–6.

Marshal's entourage, and another son, William, entered the household of the Marshal's eldest son; he was the Young Marshal's banner-bearer at the battle of Lincoln in 1217.

Even before he inherited his brother's honor in 1194, the Marshal's entourage had begun to reflect a geographical bias. From his father, William Marshal must have learned the importance of controlling a distinct area, for John Marshal had been spectacularly successful in accumulating lands and followers on the north Wiltshire Downs and in the Kennet valley in Stephen's reign. The need for a magnate to have a country of his own was not necessarily for security's sake. In the 1190s it was not possible for the Marshal to accumulate the sort of lordship that his father had pieced together in the Anarchy of half a century before: a discrete castellanry designed for military security. Nor did he have the spare land to raise up new men in an area he wished to control. But what he could do was to define an area for his ambitions and work on existing landholders there, overawing and cajoling them with his influence at court. They in turn might seek him out for protection and advancement. The *Histoire* preserves a naked and unashamed statement of this political necessity. At Gloucester castle in 1216, Ralph Musard, a Gloucestershire knight who had long been in the Marshal's political sphere, advised the Marshal to accept the regency: 'You will be able then to advance your men, and others besides.' Ralph's advice was preserved to act as a foil to the more modest and less mercenary sentiments of John of Earley; but nonetheless lords must reward, and Ralph Musard was not offering advice that household knights and political adherents would have found in any way unethical or shameful.

What more natural for William Marshal than to pick on the land of his childhood for his country. In 1189, when he arrived in England, he already had some of the basic blocks to hand. His wife brought him lands scattered throughout the south-west counties. His brother joined up with him, and he was the first cousin of the Earl of Salisbury; both were men powerful in the same area. He obtained Gloucester castle and the keeping of the county; he had the promise of the substantial support of John of Earley when he came of age; and he acquired the support of the Bloets. Add to this the magnate alliance of the Berkeleys, which he made during the 1190s, and you have a decided geographical bias to the Marshal affinity. Right from the beginning, his recruitment of knights reinforced this West Country trend. Stephen d'Evreux had a castle in Herefordshire and estates in Gloucestershire, William le Gros, the Marshal's nephew and lord of Sodbury, and Ralph Musard were also Gloucestershire knights; William Waleran, Geoffrey fitz Robert and Ralph Bloet were from the Wiltshire area; Henry Hose and Alan de St-Georges came from Sussex; Hugh of Sandford, Thomas Basset, John of Earley, Jordan de Sauqueville and William Jardin were all from the Thames valley; and Nicholas Avenel from Devon or Somerset. No wonder that in founding Cartmel priory in the far north he used canons of the family mausoleum of Bradenstoke, or that in founding the abbey of Duiske in Leinster he solicited Cistercians from the Wiltshire abbey of Stanley; from Chepstow to the Thames valley everyone would soon have realized that William Marshal had come to England determined to make a political mark in the one corner of the kingdom he might call home. In a way he was the typical home-town boy made good, come back to dazzle the folks with his wealth, a species not otherwise unknown in the twelfth century.[5]

Apart from the insignificant Eustace de Bertremont, there was not a Frenchman amongst the Marshal's followers. No wonder the *Histoire* introduces a sour anti-French note now and again. The household on which the author drew for his sources was wholly English. When they recalled for his biographer what had happened in 1183, those of his household who contributed their views were quick to blame the Norman knights of the Young King's household for their master's disgrace: he was overthrown, they were convinced, because he was an Englishman raised to high favour by the king over Frenchmen. There is defensive antagonism in this; the Marshal's knights resented the French, maybe they were fed up with being told how superior the French were in military capacity to the English. There is a smug delight in the tales of the Marshal's tournament days that it was an Englishman who had created for the Young King a *mesnie* that bore down all others in competition. In the description of the campaigns of 1217 there is great outrage at the 'pride' and 'bravado' of the 'French rascals' who presumed to invade England and despoil the English of their lands. A century and a half earlier the followers of Harold Godwinson could not have been more outraged at the arrival of William of Normandy. Whether the Marshal had shared their prejudice is another matter. The bare facts of his itinerary in the

5 Compare Orderic Vitalis's story of the English royal justice of Henry I's reign, Ralph Basset, who came back to Normandy and expended his new wealth on a luxurious castle on his small ancestral estate, to the disgust of his neighbours.

1190s demonstrate that he loved Normandy. At Lincoln he treated with great respect the claims of the Normans in his army to have what they contended was the traditional honour of the first blows of the battle, even though he then awarded the privilege to the Earl of Chester's men. The mocking jibe put in the mouth of his old master, the Chamberlain of Tancarville, about England being a poor place for a military man, might well have been the Marshal's own, made palatable by being put into the mouth of the quirky and disagreeable old chamberlain.

. . .

## THE CLERKS

Most great magnates tended to acquire particular friends in the Church. The Marshal was no exception. This sort of man was occasionally part of his clerical household; the way the Berkeleys and the Béthunes occasionally came into the orbit of his lay household. They added a certain tone to the Marshal's reputation in the world, a respectability and profundity of counsel. He opened a long and profitable relationship with Hugh le Rous, bishop of Ossory, on his visit to Leinster in 1200–1. Bishop Hugh returned the visit in 1203, staying with the Marshal at his Berkshire seat of Hamstead Marshall. He assisted the Marshal with his Cistercian foundations of Tintern Parva and Duiske. Later he exchanged the ancient seat of his diocese at Aghaboe for a new cathedral in the Marshal's chief city of Kilkenny, all in aid of the Marshal's comprehensive plans to reorganize Leinster.[6] This was quite a contrast to the Marshal's venomous relations with another episcopal neighbour, Ailbe, bishop of Ferns, a man less amenable and courtly, and worst of all, Irish. The Marshal was particular friends besides with two English abbots, Edward of Notley and David of St Augustine's, Bristol. Notley was a Giffard foundation within what was called the 'advocacy' of the Marshal, and Bristol abbey was within his political sphere. Edward of Notley was involved at one point with the Marshal's plans to reorganize the church in Leinster,[7] and was at his deathbed,

6 J Graves and J G A Prim, 'The History, Archaeology and Antiquities of the City of Kilkenny' *Kilkenny and S.E. Ireland Archaeological Society Proceedings and Transactions* new ser. II pt 2 1859 328–9; *Irish Monastic and Episcopal Deeds*, 217–18.

7 Edward of Notley formed one of a commission in Leinster to investigate the possession of the church of Wicklow, Cartulary of Llanthony, fo. 287r–v.

offering comfort. Abbot David was a late comer to the Marshal's circle, probably during the time after he became regent, but he was particularly trusted. In February 1218 he was said to be in Ireland, specifically on the Marshal's business, not his abbey's.[8] He was to be one of the executors of the Marshal's last testament.

We do not know much, in fact we know almost nothing, about relations between William and his clerical brother, Henry. Since Henry Marshal owed all his promotions in the Church to his brother's fortunes at court, we can hope that relations were good between them, but there is little evidence of any relationship at all. Doubtless this was because Henry died more than a dozen years before his brother. If he had survived him, he might have made a significant contribution to the *Histoire*; we might perhaps have had his memories of the Marshal family history and William's early days. But he did not, and so as a result, the work is fuller of inaccuracies than it might probably otherwise have been. The one known point of contact between the two brothers was their joint patronage of their nephew, Anselm le Gros. William had him in his household for a while and Bishop Henry, before he died, promoted Anselm to the treasurership of Exeter cathedral.

From the beginning of his career as a magnate, the Marshal had a large clerical staff. Some of these were called 'chaplains', the others 'clerks'. Since the chaplains always precede the clerks in witness lists it is likely that they were in priestly orders and the clerks in the less restricting and burdensome orders of deacon. Details are lacking, but it is probable that the chaplains of the Marshal's household were there to say mass and take confessions for the itinerant retinue, as ministering priests. They formed the Marshal's 'chapel': not a building, but his travelling entourage of spiritual advisers, with their vestments, portable altars and sacred vessels, and whatever collection of missals, psalters and relics the Marshal kept. The clerks, on the other hand, doubtless did the job of keeping central accounts and conducting correspondence; although in orders and capable of holding church preferment, they were men who were 'clerical' in a modern, as well as a medieval, sense. In general, throughout the twelfth century, an earl or great baron would employ as many as a dozen clerics of whatever description at any one time, sometimes more. They did not follow him continuously. We are told of Waleran, Count of Meulan (who died in 1166) that he always had four working chaplains in his employ, two of whom he would keep by him in his travelling

8 *Rotuli Litterarum Clausarum* i 377.

household. The other two would be left by the count to go about their own affairs or be detached on other missions.[9] Doubtless the Meulan clerks would have alternated at their master's court on a sort of rota. Some clerical households had formal chiefs, chancellors, to oversee the lesser clerks just as the seneschal d'hôtel controlled the lay household. A number of great French potentates, and in England the Marshal's contemporaries, Earl Ranulf III of Chester and Count John of Mortain, employed such officers, and so did the Marshal's son after 1219, but not the Marshal himself so far as we can tell.

None of the Marshal's household clerks were as important to him as the great prelates who might have called themselves his friends. But that is not to say that his clerks were not trusted or intimate with him. A few of them served him for quite as many years as his longest-serving household knights. It would not be reasonable to think that (whatever the tensions within his household) the Marshal, seasoned practitioner of courtliness and amiability, slighted one section of his entourage for another, indeed we will see how he furthered some of his clerks in much the same way as he furthered his knights. Two charters, dated at either end of the Marshal's career as a magnate, tell us most about the size of the Marshal's travelling clerical household. In 1189 x 90 a charter shows him accompanied by three clerks and a chaplain. In 1214 he was at his house at Caversham, Berkshire, with, again, three clerks (one of whom, Philip, named himself as scribe of the charter) and this time two chaplains (on another occasion one of these same two, Nicholas, was called 'the earl's chaplain', the other, Walter, 'the countess's chaplain').[10]

Throughout the Marshal's career there were nine clerks who can be closely associated with him. In terms of attestations, the clerk Michael of London witnessed fifteen charters, more than anyone else apart from John of Earley – and was in his service from at least the first year of King Richard to the crisis of King John's reign: nearly twenty-five years. He followed him through England, Normandy and Ireland. On one occasion Michael is named

9 *The Beaumont Twins* 153–4.

10 BL Harley Ch. 51 H 2 (charter of 1189 x 90) Oxford, Christchurch muns. DY 13 (a) m. 4 (charter of 1214). For the earl and countess's individual chaplains see 'The Charters of the Cistercian Abbey of Duiske' 28. The countess also had her own clerk, Robert, who was murdered in Gloucestershire in or soon before 1219 *Excerpta e Rotulis Finium* I 34.

as the scribe of one of the Marshal's charters. He performed a range of services for his master besides draughtmanship. He represented him as his attorney at Westminster in 1199 and 1201, whether before the barons of the exchequer or the royal justices.[11] It can be proved that others of his clerks were in the Marshal's following for long periods: William de Lisle, Master Joscelin and Michael of Kendal all appear in his acts in the reigns of both Richard and John. The clerk Philip attested with the Marshal eight times, but only in John's reign. It is interesting to speculate on the reason the *Histoire* singles him alone out of the clerical entourage of its hero for criticism. It may be that because he was a relative newcomer, his intervention at the Marshal's deathbed rankled more with the knights of the household.

There are less chaplains than clerks evident in the Marshal's household. Two appear with him in Richard's reign, Eustace and Roger. The one who served him longest was Eustace de St-Georges who was in his entourage from the mid-1190s to the time of the Marshal's long residence in Ireland from 1207–12. At the end of that period he seems to have transferred his function to that of clerk. In his later years, the Marshal and his wife still relied on two chaplains, Walter and Nicholas, who we find in his entourage from the time of the Irish expedition.

A certain Roger appears as the Marshal's almoner on one occasion. The post may have been an additional hat for Roger the chaplain. Much later the Marshal had as his almoner Brother Geoffrey, a Templar knight. He was following a fashion of the times. Hugh of Avalon, bishop of Lincoln (died 1200) and John, as count and king also had Templar almoners. The almoner gave out, from day to day, food from his lord's table to the poor at his door, and perhaps also small sums of money; the fiscal expertise of the Templars might account for their appointments to great households in this capacity. Brother Geoffrey was not above clerical tasks, however, and was the man who wrote out the Marshal's last testament in April 1219. All magnates saw the giving of alms as a pious duty in the twelfth century, and a chaplain-almoner was to be found in the household of the Marshal's colleague, Robert, the last Count of Meulan, who we are told had the needy fed outside his gates at the same time as he ate in his various halls.[12]

11 *Memoranda Roll of 1 John*, 6; *Curia Regis Rolls* I 421.

12 *Chartes de l'abbaye de Jumièges* ed. J J Vernier (2 vols) Rouen 1916 II 207–9.

We know next to nothing about the backgrounds of the Marshal's clerks. His chaplain, Eustace de St-Georges, might well have been some connection of his knight Alan de St-Georges, but that is about all we can say. Three of them, at least, had had a good education in one of the more significant schools of England and France, for the clerks Joscelin, Michael and Pentecost took the title 'Master' (*magister*). We know a little more of the way the Marshal rewarded his clerks' service. Master Joscelin (son of Hugh), for instance, was in 1196 (doubtless because of his lord's influence) given by the priory of Longueville the lease of its lands in the Marshal's manor of Caversham for a term of fifteen years, in return for paying an annual rent of five marks (£3 6s. 8d.). The Marshal himself, one of his knights, and the seneschal of Crendon stood as sureties for Joscelin's good behaviour.[13] Joscelin was also given by his lord, before 1199, some of his houses in the Earl of Pembroke's estate at Charing, at the end of the Strand where it met what was then called King Street (now Whitehall) between the city of London and the palace of Westminster. The Marshal reserved for himself his right to lodge in these houses with his men when he was attending on the king. Since Joscelin for many years before and after 1201 deputized for his lord at the exchequer, carrying out his duties as marshal, the grant of houses just up the road from Westminster was a great advantage for him.[14] There is some evidence besides that Master Joscelin was rector of the church of St Matthew Friday Street in the city of London, which he had served for him by his own chaplain.[15] We know for certain that he was also rector of the Marshal's church of Tidenham in Gloucestershire, just across the river Wye from Chepstow.[16]

The Marshal's clerk, Michael, was another of his clerks with

13 *Newington Longeville Charters* ed. H E Salter Oxford Records Society III, 1921 54.

14 *Pipe Roll of 3 John* 42, 243, 265. This shows Master Joscelin as a member of the Exchequer in 1201, present amongst the barons when an important letter was opened before the Justiciar, it also tells us that Joscelin had acquired the name 'Joscelin Marshal' from his long occupation of the office. By 1211 Joscelin had been succeeded in the deputy-marshalship by one William Toke, see *Curia Regis Rolls* VI 188 He was dead by 1216, see H G Richardson, 'William of Ely, the King's Treasurer' *TRHS*, 4th Ser, xv (1932), 85–6.

15 *The Cartulary of the Cistercian Abbey of Flaxley*, 174–5. Some time later Joscelin chose to settle his rights there on the abbey of Flaxley (alias Kingswood) in the forest of Dean, where he wished to be buried.

16 *Curia Regis Rolls* VI 29.

London connections. Indeed in 1216 he was called 'Master Michael of London'. In 1204 he was acknowledged as the owner of some land in the north of the city in the parish of St Stephen, Coleman Street. Since he had it by inheritance it is very likely that he was a Londoner himself.[17] It is an intriguing thought that the Marshal might have enlisted his services when he came to London in July 1189 to be married, and had to fill up a number of vacancies in his new household in a hurry. In 1216 Master Michael was said to have been the owner of certain houses in Bristol which he had bought from Margam abbey.[18] Another of the Marshal's clerks, Philip, was given preferment by his lord in the Marches. He had a half share of the rectory of the wealthy church of Llantrisant in the lordship of Netherwent. The Marshal paid a substantial annual sum to the canons of Llanthony for them to withdraw the claim they made on Philip's church.[19] The curiously named Marshal clerk, Master Pentecost (of Inglesham), had the rectory of the Marshal church of Easton Royal in Wiltshire at the time when his lord decided to concede the church to Bradenstoke priory. The Marshal had Pentecost's life interest in the church assured by the bishop of Salisbury.[20]

There were other members of the household apart from chaplains, almoners and clerks, who might be considered to be 'clerical' in the loosest sense. These were the chamberlains. The most prominent of them was the chamberlain, Walter Cut, from his name an Englishman and from his position in witness lists probably also a clerk, although not a high-ranking one. He seems to have been in the Marshal's service only in Richard's reign. But his colleagues and successors might be found amongst the four men also called chamberlain in his entourage at one time or another: William, Geoffrey, Osbert and Gilbert. By this date chamberlains had tended to assume a specialized function in the households of the great as keepers and receivers of their lord's money. It is sometimes found that chamberlains were also clerks, for literacy was a desirable quality in the job. The chamberlain would have kept the Marshal's financial office, his 'chamber'. It is interesting how, like 'chapel', the various early offices of the great household took on the names of rooms in the contemporary

17 *Pipe Roll of 6 John* 98; *Rotuli de Finibus et Oblatis* 198.

18 *Rotuli Litterarum Clausarum* I 294.

19 Cartulary of Llanthony fo. 287r.

20 Cartulary of Bradenstoke, BL ms Cotton Vitellius A XI fo. 104v.

mansion complex. The chamber (*camera*) was the private room of the lord, the furnishings of which the chamberlain (*camerarius*) once kept. The specialized subject of the Marshal's chamber and wardrobe, and the wider subject of his finances, are ones which will be dealt with fully in the next chapter. For the purposes of this chapter it only needs to be observed how promptly the Marshal recruited such a man as Walter Cut to his side. This hardly betrays the attitude of the ingenuous knight and single-minded devotee of the tournament field, that Painter would have us believe he was in 1189.

. . .

## THE HIDDEN HOUSEHOLD

A puzzling absence from the Marshal's retinue is that of falconers and hunters. The master hunter or master forester, always of knightly rank, was a figure that several great magnates began to employ on a regular basis in their households in the Marshal's generation (notably the Earl of Chester and the Count of Meulan). The Marshal certainly possessed enough parks and forests on his estates in England, Wales and Ireland to be able reasonably to employ such a prestigious figure, but he did not as far as we can tell. Odder still is the utter lack of any mention of his hunting or hawking; the most ancient of aristocratic enthusiasms. Can we suspect him here of unconventionality? Did his preoccupation with the hunting of men on the tournament field spoil him for these scientific pursuits?

There were others of whom we are never likely to hear anything; the porters who packed and carried the boxes and satchels that bounced up and down on the sumpter horses that made up the Marshal's train. There must also have been waggoners or carters employed by the Marshal. We do hear on at least two occasions of Humphrey the Marshal who must have supervised the mechanics of William's itinerant household. We hear nothing of the workers in his hall; his cooks, ushers and menial attendants; only, as the Marshal neared death, of the knights, squires (*valet*), servants (*servant*) and all the others of his household (*maison*) who wept as he prepared for death. Absent also is much mention of the messengers who carried his letters about the country, keeping in fitful touch with the various components of his great estates. We only hear of one, Richard, who was murdered on his master's service near London by a group of highwaymen for the sake of his purse and robe just before 1219.[21] Nonetheless we know from studying other households that such men existed, and would have swollen his touring retinue to the number of maybe forty or fifty. By such numbers, as well as by the glitter of gold and the sheen of silk and fur, the Marshal was known to be a great man.

21 *Curia Regis Rolls* VIII 142.

*Chapter 6*

# LOVE AND LORDSHIP

. . .

## LOVE AND LOYALTY

The sources are such that we can learn a little of what went on in the heads of those long-gone men, the Marshal's knights, and something of the tensions in their mobile, shifting community. First, as we saw in the last chapter, there was the schism between the lay and clerical households. No doubt both sides being cordial and courtly under the eye of their lord and employer, but both feeling the superiority of its own order, each distinct in its rites of passage and education. The knights feeling all the force of their trained hands and horses; the long cloak – the *chlamys* – of aristocracy and the gold spurs on their heels telling of society's recognition of their superior standing. The clerks in their sober garb and shaven scalps confident in quite a different source of power, the power evoked by Gregory VII, St Anselm, Becket and, latterly, Innocent III. Both groups competed in self-importance, both expected by this date to be respectfully addressed as *messire*, *dan* or *dominus*.

This was the natural schism within the household, but there were other tensions brought on by outside pressures. Some of the Marshal's men had acquired lands, wives and responsibilities. True, they owed everything to him, but they had responsibilities too towards others, their own followers and their families. For some the rival attractions of the royal household, the ultimate source of favour and good things, was too much. John Marshal, William Waleran, Hugh of Sandford, Philip of Prendergast and Alan de St-Georges were some of the Marshal's knights who at a moment of crisis, or over several years, left him for the king's entourage. They became king's men first and the Marshal's men second. Even kinship could not prevent this, as John Marshal proved. Henry Hose simply left him when his father died in 1213 in order to take over his family responsibilities in Sussex. Such things happened in the twelfth and thirteenth centuries. It might have been an age when loyalty was prized, but there were many men even then who respected pragmatism and material ambition rather more than ideals. Loyalty was not absolute at that time, except in theory and in romances. The Marshal himself was perfectly aware of that fact; for that reason he was willing to tolerate a certain amount of backsliding from his men. There was no permanent breach between him and his nephew John, after John favoured the king in 1207 rather than his uncle. The Marshal had high standards of loyalty, as did others in his circle, such as the three bailiffs of Leinster in 1208, but he was a realist too.

However there remained a core of faithful friends in the Marshal's household who acted up to the ideal of fidelity. On them the Marshal had cast such a spell that they were willing to lose everything for him. It is for them that the *Histoire* makes its hero say: 'The man is not a friend who gives no help at great need'.[1] The debate amongst the knights of his *mesnie* left in Ireland in 1208, which was recalled for his biographer by some of them years later, is a classic exposition on loyalty between lord and man. The leaders of his *mesnie* were threatened by the king with the loss of their English lands if they did not abandon Ireland and appear before the king. These were men who at that time held little or no land from the Marshal. Yet John of Earley nonetheless said that if he lost his lands and even his honour by opposing the king, he would at least still keep the love (*amor*) of his lord. Love too was the word for what these men returned to their lord. By their love and honour, as he was to say after the crisis of 1208, they had saved his lands, and he blessed them for it. Long ago as it is, we can still feel something of the warmth that linked the Marshal to some of his men, a bond which was in those days in England often expressed physically by embracing and kissing. If the kiss of peace was denied by the Marshal to erring followers, as it was to Philip of Prendergast and David de la Roch, then it was a matter for bitter tears and lament: a public rejection, like a slap or a father's curse.

Maybe for some of them it was not so much the need to honour the personal bond, perhaps it was the strictures of their fellows they feared, unwilling to risk the ridicule that went with overt materialism. This ridicule was a fearsome and unforgiving thing, as the *Histoire* itself shows. David de la Roch, one of the Irish

1 '*Quer cil n'est pas amis entiers, qui a grant besoing faut d'aie*' ll. 6904–5.

barons who opposed the Marshal in 1208, is said to have found it difficult to make friends afterwards. The influential West Country baron, Peter fitz Herbert, publicly snubbed him by refusing a seat next to his at a council. Such social delights, chuckled over by the loyal core of the Marshal's household, awaited the unsubtle opportunist.

The Marshal's household knights were young men, much younger than the Marshal. John of Earley was his junior by a full generation, still in his thirties during the crisis in Leinster which so deeply tested the quality of the Marshal's household knights. The same seems true of all the others; only Alan de St-Georges was near in age to the Marshal, and even he must still have been a good decade younger than his lord. Henry fitz Gerold was literally what the men of that day would have called 'young': a landless, unmarried younger son. Likewise, the young Nicholas Avenel served the Marshal as under-sheriff of Gloucestershire while his father was still alive and he had a career to make for himself.

Some lingering expressions of devotion from his men to the Marshal reach us from the dry folios of monastic registers. John Marshal, the Marshal's nephew, remembered his uncle William, and his aunt Isabel too, in his own old age and commemorated them in a gift to Walsingham priory in Norfolk, seeking the canons' prayers for his late lord's soul.[2] Geoffrey fitz Robert also made a point of commemorating the Marshal and Countess Isabel (then still alive) when he founded the priory of Kells in Leinster, although this was a more perfunctory gesture because the foundation was on the Marshal's land.[3] Rather more interesting in terms of assessing the extent of the *amor* which called forth such gestures is the grant by Alice de Colleville to the canons of Poughley in Berkshire. As has been explained, there is good reason to think that Alice was the lover of William Marshal's brother, John, and the mother of John Marshal his nephew. She commemorated both brothers' souls (naming the elder, John, first) in the grant.[4] It was a poignant gesture by what

2 Cartulary of Walsingham BL ms Cotton Nero E VII fo. 95v. John, although a bastard, remembered his father and also his father's lover, his mother, whose name he gives as Alice; from this it seems that whatever her morals, she had been a gentlewoman and makes the identification with Alice de Colleville the more likely (see above).

3 *Irish Monastic and Episcopal Deeds* 300–1.

4 Westminster Abbey Muniments no. 7242.

may by then have been a rather lonely old lady, living out her days in retirement in the Thames valley; a farewell to her youth and, maybe, lost love and young friendship.

But John of Earley is the man through whom we can get nearest to what these followers thought. When he first met the Marshal he was little more than a boy sent abroad to a foreign land by a mandate from a remote king, into the care of a stranger. The Marshal must have made him welcome and been pleasant to him. Why not? He too had had the same experience; dumped abroad for an education with strangers. The two were from the same part of the world, their fathers' chief seats within the same county, Berkshire. John was fatherless, William Marshal not yet a father but a man, we know, who thought much of fondness to the young, praising King Stephen, who had indulged him as a boy. The Marshal was indeed good with children and we can say with some certainty that he earned his own sons' love. He was besides a man that a boy could respect. We can guess that the Marshal and John might well have fallen into each others arms, their interlocking, emotional needs a strong bond between them. When in 1194 John of Earley had become a knight, and a man of considerable means in his own right, he did not quit the Marshal's household. He lived on, with no other desire apparently but to serve his one-time guardian, in political and emotional servitude. By following his lord to Ireland in 1207 he risked losing his patrimony, and lose it he did. In the fullness of his malice, King John actually wrote to the Marshal taunting him with the fact that Earley was now landless, and his service to the Marshal had made him so.[5] The king knew how to hurt most cruelly. On another occasion, to unbalance the Marshal, he pretended to have news that Earley and others of his men were dead in Ireland, defending the Marshal's interests. To this tormented king the bond between the Marshal and his men was a way to twist and torture the Marshal's composure; to undermine his courtly tranquillity, though it is to be doubted that he could have said to what constructive end he did it.

John of Earley took no reward for his service, other than a manor in Leinster, and that only because it may have been a convenient place near to his lord's chief castle of Kilkenny. It was all for the great love and honour (*de la grant amor e de l'onor*) between the men. When the Marshal was brooding over the

5 *Rotuli Litterarum Clausarum* I 103.

problems of accepting the regency in 1216, John of Earley advised him not to take it up, although others of the *mesnie* were keen that he should, seeing possibilities of great advancement. John saw his purpose in following the Marshal differently from some of his colleagues. At the Marshal's deathbed he was still there to attend his lord's needs. And after death he served him still, not just as the executor of the Marshal's testament (a task which was still engaging his energies several years later) but as one of the promoters of the project that produced the *Histoire*. He poured out his memories for the author to work into a fitting monument to his lost lord, and not just his memories, his money too supported the biographer as he worked. The *Histoire* may well be a distorted and partial work, but we should not forget that it is distorted by this almost incomprehensible love of a man for his lord and, we might properly say, father.

But this would not be the right point to leave the Marshal and the subject of his lordship over men. We must also consider the Marshal and people who were not his men, or at least men who were outside the charmed circle of his household and affinity. Enough has been said about his relations with the barons of Leinster to realize that there was another side to his lordship, the sharp edge of his sword. Philip of Prendergast found he had only the Marshal's formal forgiveness after his unsuccessful conspiracy in 1208. His son David was still a hostage for his good behaviour to the Marshal seven years later.[6] Once he had Meilyr fitz Henry at his mercy, the Marshal made sure that neither he nor his family would bother him again. He took his castles and ensured that Meilyr would have no more than a life interest in his lands. This is symptomatic of the other side of the coin of lordship to that represented by the Marshal's *amor* towards his true men. William Marshal knew, as his stories of his father demonstrate, that the world was a hard place, and that a lord's duty was to be a welcoming fortress to the men who were loyal to him but turn a flinty face to the others. The *Histoire* is full of evidence of this. It sorrows over the rebel plundering of New Ross in 1207 and the Welsh devastation of the Marshal's lordship of Netherwent in 1217, but is indifferent to the wasting and burning carried out by the Marshal himself on his many campaigns. The duties of a lord were nicely framed by Geoffrey of Monmouth who wrote in the heyday of the Marshal's father's career in the late 1130s. A good lord must be a great oak to his

6 *Rotuli Litterarum Patentium* 144.

men, spreading his sheltering branches over them. But to others he must be a name of such terror that the fear of him keeps off ill-will from the men under his protection.

The Marshal as a lord was therefore a harsh man, except to the intimates of his household and his political friends, the very people who had the *Histoire* written as a monument to him. The *Histoire* therefore tells only half the story. The Marshal's ideas of justice add to this picture. Eustace de Bertremont, his longest-serving retainer, contributed to the *Histoire* his memories of an incident in 1183, on the Marshal's return to the Young King's household. While resting by the road the Marshal and his friends were passed by a couple riding hard, a man and a woman. The woman's complaints of her weariness attracted the Marshal's attention. He stopped the pair and interrogated the man. It transpired that he had eloped with the woman, the sister of a prominent Flemish castellan; what was more, he was a runaway monk. This shocked the Marshal, but he was willing to let the pair continue since the woman did not appear to be under any constraint. But an idle inquiry about how the two were to live changed his mind about intervening. It turned out that the man had a sum of money which he intended to put out at interest. The Marshal, under threat of violence, promptly confiscated the money and sent the couple packing into poverty and degradation, as we must imagine. The audience of the *Histoire* was expected to approve of this. Knights must applaud the confounding of a lecherous clerk who corrupted a noblewoman; clerks must approve of the frustration of the scandalous scheme by a colleague, already compromised by sexual incontinence, of living on the profits of illegal usury. What *we* notice is that the money thus acquired went straight into the Marshal's pocket, to be used for his own purposes of patronage; that some years later the Marshal himself was exploiting the Jewish debt market in Normandy; and that the roadside justice he did to this couple was summary and merciless and had no warrant. Another man as outraged would have apprehended the pair and delivered them to the agents of the local archdeacon, the officer with the approved power to try and to punish them.

We know very little about the Marshal as judge in his own court. When he sat as a royal justice it was always with other, more experienced men, which does not encourage any faith in his reputation. But there is one example of what went on in his own court which gives some hints as to the measure of the man's justice. Soon after he married Countess Isabel, the Marshal made a particular point of holding a court of his honor of Striguil, as any new lord would, to receive the homage of his new tenants and, just as important, what they must pay him on his entry into possession for charters of confirmation of their lands. He was, as we know, short of money. One tenant, Payn of London, did not turn up to do homage for the land he held in Barrow, Suffolk, nor did he send an agent to represent him. The Marshal had him summoned in court the proper three times, and on his non-appearance, sent his men to take possession of the land. So far he was completely within his rights and was indeed acting wisely. No lord could safely allow tenants to evade their obligations. However, when Payn's son William appeared before him to reclaim the land by a payment and to begin a dispute in the Marshal's court with the man who he said should have done the homage instead of his father, the Marshal refused him a hearing. This was outrageous behaviour, it was refusing a tenant justice, and in 1194 Payn and his son went to the king to complain and commence a suit against the Marshal himself.[7] We do not know the result of this suit, which probably means that it was settled by a compromise in due course. But it does not show the Marshal's ideas of lordship in a good light. His only motive in refusing justice to Payn of London was to keep the land he had taken back for his own purposes.

The essential hypocrisy of the Marshal is not something that we can avoid. It was as a courtly dissembler that Matthew Paris remembered him after his death. William de Longchamp (a man who never mastered the skills of the court and therefore may well have prided himself on being blunt and plain-speaking) accused the Marshal in the presence of the king of being two-faced: a difficult accusation for any courtier to avoid. The Marshal, as we have seen, happily elevated his own interests into justice. Time and again in his differences with the king his justifications of his position are merely paper masks for his self-interest. But to be two-faced was something that his own society and background forced on him. He grew up in the household of a father who served his own interest in a particularly brutal way in a chaotic and dangerous period. This father, whose memory he apparently respected in later life, used William's infant life as a bargaining counter with the king. At the courts of his various lords he had to smile and simper amongst men, some of whom were his deadly

7 *Rotuli Curiae Regis* I 62–3.

enemies and who plotted his downfall. His composure is a matter of record. He rarely revealed his innermost feelings, however chatty he might have been to his young knights about the amusing exploits of his own youth. It was proverbial in the twelfth century that a man who talked too much was storing up trouble for himself, and it was by such proverbs that the Marshal had been educated in court-craft.[8] It was not until he was on his deathbed that he spoke to his son, John of Earley his *carissimus*, and others of his intimates, of the spiritual awakening that he had undergone in the Holy Lands, and only then did he produce the grave cloths he had bought over thirty years before. We can only guess in these circumstances how important were his relations with his family and his intimate followers. But to me they were all important. Courtly tranquillity and composure must have taken its toll of his peace of mind as much as the unrelenting pursuit of his own advantage. Family and friends must have seemed the one stable, warm part of his life. No wonder he was so little inclined to forgive the likes of Philip of Prendergast, whose treachery had compromised not just his dignity and affections, but the security of his lands. Lucky for Philip that ideas of propriety had advanced to the point where the Marshal would not execute him, as his wife and *mesnie* wanted.[9] Instead Philip was excluded from the Marshal's inner circle, which to the Marshal and his men might have seemed a satisfyingly cruel form of emotional extinction.

. . .

## LORDSHIP AND AFFINITY

Around the fringes of the Marshal's retinue was a penumbra of men whom it would be difficult to call 'followers' because they did not follow him on any regular basis. But they were of great importance to his exercise of power in society. Some (the Irish barons) were his dependents, holding land in his lordship and technically owing him knight service, but others were in a more

8 Such a saying appears in the 1170s in Chrétien de Troyes *Le Conte de Graal* ed. F Lecoy (2 vols) CFMA 1972–5 I l. 1652.

9 Such things did still happen, however. Roger de Lacy had executed in 1193 the constables of Tickhill castle, his sworn men who delivered the castle to Count John against his orders. His action was not illegal but called down great opprobrium on his head, *Gesta Henrici Secundi* ed. W Stubbs (2 vols) Rolls Series 1867 II 233.

hazy relationship to him, you might call them 'friends' or 'allies' depending on the degree of emotion or pragmatism that you could detect in their relations. The Marshal did have an enviable capacity for making friends; something that stood him in good stead in his political career. He was a courtly man in a courtly age. Great magnates in the twelfth century ideally conducted themselves with affability and humour at court. The most politic amongst them massaged each other's egos with care and consideration. A fair sample is the speech of the Earl of Chester in 1216 at Gloucester when men were split as to whether he or the Marshal should assume the regency. The Earl of Chester did not want the job, although no doubt he was flattered to be considered. The Marshal, who did want the job, deferred to the younger earl; he was old and feeble and could not do it. A younger man like Earl Ranulf perhaps . . .? But no, said Earl Ranulf, that cannot be, 'You are so good a knight, so fine a man, so feared, so loved, and so wise that you are considered one of the first knights in the world. I say to you in all loyalty that you must be chosen. I will serve you, and I will carry out to the best of my power all the tasks that you may assign to me'.[10] Here is as good a specimen of the dance of the courtly magnates as you are likely to meet with. No naked ambition, no disagreeable and aggressive moves. All is arranged by gentle nudges and affectionate phrases. Powerful men have to defer to each other, to disagree and offend unnecessarily would be dangerous, it would commit them to expensive and damaging hatreds.

But there were warmer and more sincere relationships, even at court, just as there were more openly hostile ones (such as the acid relations with William de Longchamp in Richard's reign). Perhaps chief among these was Baldwin de Béthune, the younger brother of the Picard magnate, Robert, advocate of Arras. The two were intimate when they were both landless young hopefuls in the riotous household of the Young King. It was Baldwin who organized William's reinstatement into the household after his disgrace in 1183, and who corresponded with him while in exile. His career paralleled William's. Like William he achieved a county through marriage, in his case Aumale on the Norman frontier, with other lands in Yorkshire. In 1205 he stood up for William fearlessly at Southampton before the enraged King John. To seal their long friendship, William and Baldwin betrothed, and eventually married, William's eldest son to

10 The translation is by Sidney Painter.

Baldwin's eldest daughter. The *Histoire*, naturally, has much to say about Baldwin's valour and loyalty to its hero; he is all but the second hero of the work.

There were other magnates who were close to William Marshal. The most potent of all was Geoffrey fitz Peter. Geoffrey, like William, was the son of a royal official in the West Country, in his case Peter, the royal forester of Ludgershall in Wiltshire. It is not unlikely that William and Geoffrey's fathers were connected in some way, for John Marshal had held Ludgershall throughout Stephen's reign. William and Geoffrey had entered Henry II's household at much the same time and risen together in royal service, though by different means. Both were given great heiresses in 1189 by King Richard, and were created earls within minutes of each other by King John in 1199. Geoffrey attests several of William's early acts; perhaps those transacted within the precincts of the royal palace or when they were co-justiciars in King Richard's absence. A later charter still exists by which William gave to Geoffrey his share of the profits of the market of Aylesbury, Buckinghamshire, which they had divided between them.[11] Their relationship was doubtless less warm than that between William and Baldwin de Béthune; one tends to imagine Geoffrey – whether justly or not – as an obsessive businessman with not much time for personal relations. But to have his passive goodwill was no small thing in early Angevin England. King John is said to have confessed his fear of Geoffrey on hearing of his death in 1213: 'Now at last I am king!'. When such a fearful man stood beside the Marshal in his difficulties with the king in 1210–11 and put his name forward as guarantor for him, the Marshal might be easy in his mind.[12] Because he had such friends the Marshal might, on occasion, stand up to the king in a way that few others dared. The watching presence of his powerful friends at court could make the king tractable and cautious.

The Marshal's attachment to other, lesser, magnates has a more local political direction to it. From the Marshal's powerful

11 For the agreement between William and Geoffrey fitz Peter, see Birmingham Central Reference Library Archives Ch. 486019 (Hampton Deeds); it dates to the period after 1199. Geoffrey attests the following charters of William: Cartulary of Hungerford, Somerset Record Office DD/SAS/H/438 fo. 150v; B L Harley Ch. 51 H 2; Salisbury Chapter Muniments Press IV Box OE 1; all three date to the 1190s.

12 *Rotuli Litterarum Patentium* 98.

friends at court he wanted general goodwill and support. From the Berkeley family, on the other hand, he wanted acquiescence and collusion in his local ambitions. The relationship between him and the family of Berkeley had nothing to do with any land they held from him; the bonds were much stronger since they were rooted in local power and mutual security.[13] The Marshal and the Berkeleys were partners in the informal business of power-mongering. There is a record of the strength of the links between them. A year or two after the great Marshal's death, his son William wrote to the justiciar of England saying of Thomas of Berkeley, the brother and heir of Robert, who had married his niece, that '. . . for many years [Thomas] has been so bound and allied (*obligatus et confoederatus*) to me, that he could not leave my council'.[14] The Berkeleys were by far the greatest barons in Gloucestershire, the county which William controlled as sheriff for long periods in Richard and John's reign. They were patrons of the abbey of Bristol, and Bristol was a town in which they retained a considerable interest. Since William Marshal controlled Bristol castle between 1199 and 1205, the Berkeleys had to come to terms with him. Indeed, the brothers Robert and Oliver of Berkeley had the keeping of the town between 1201 and 1203, an impossible task unless they were already in the Marshal's camp. The Berkeleys were a very necessary political accessory for the Marshal: they controlled large numbers of manors and a hundred; they had a powerful stone castle dominating the road from Gloucester to Bristol; and what was more, a large following of their own knights. Their support was the keystone to the Marshal's structure of power in the West Country.

The Berkeley family, and also the earls of Salisbury – linked by kinship – were the more obvious and noticeable members of the Marshal's affinity. There were others who are less obvious, but whose behaviour in the period of 1214–17 indicates that they too were local allies of the Marshal: John of Monmouth, Countess Isabel's cousin and lord of the town from which he took his name; Walter of Clifford, another baron of the southern March; and Walter de Lacy, a great man in Herefordshire and Ireland.

13 Robert of Berkeley attests the Marshal's solemn foundation charter of Cartmel priory in 1189 x 90. Many of the Berkeleys of Berkeley, and Roger Berkeley of Dursley appear with the Marshal's following in a charter of 1200 x 5, Berkeley Castle Muniments, Select Ch. 85.

14 *Royal and other Historical Letters illustrative of the Reign of Henry III* ed. W W Shirley (2 vols) Rolls Series 1862–6 I 178–9.

They were all men of local power in their own right. Their affability to the Marshal, a more important man than they were, is the evidence that we must look to the West Country of England and the southern March if we are to begin to understand the Marshal's power. For it was here that the pattern of his own possessions dictates that he would have needed to form a local political connection, his 'country', as magnates were already calling their spheres of interest.[15]

The knights in the Marshal's retinue, for the most part, were also bound to him by local interest. The analysis in the previous chapter of the Marshal's following of knights revealed that two-thirds of them had no traditional ties with him based on homage, faith and service between landlord and military tenant. There was therefore little of the automatic and hereditary demand on his followers for their support. It was a personal loyalty, depending only on the shifting needs of the two men involved. When the relationship had served its purpose it ended and the men parted, often amicably, like Henry Hose and Nicholas Avenel, who disappeared from the Marshal *mesnie* to look after their own family interests, without a backward glance.

What we see in the Marshal's household is one of the first demonstrable examples of a great magnate's political connection based on different ties: self-interest, protection, place-seeking and the centripetal force of local domination. This sort of connection is the essence of what is called in a later period 'bastard feudalism'.[16] But in truth it is older than the later medieval period in which it is considered the political norm. Indeed as far back as Stephen's reign, we can see great magnates who responded to the troubles of the time in England and Normandy by widening their circle of followers beyond those with whom they had tenurial links. Waleran of Meulan in the Normandy of

15 Magnates of the twelfth and thirteenth centuries talked of their *terra* ('country') or *potestas* ('jurisdiction') when looking for words to express their local dominion. Later medieval historians occasionally treat the idea as a later development.

16 For the classic exposition of the idea of bastard feudalism, see K B McFarlane, 'Bastard feudalism' in, *England in the Fifteenth Century: Collected Essays* ed. G L Harriss London 1981 23–43. A very useful commentary is offered by G L Harriss ibid. pp. IX–XXVII; some further observations are offered in his review of the book by the late Charles Ross 'In the Pocket of the Aristocracy' *Times Literary Supplement* 25 November 1983 p. 1302. For some general and interesting comments drawn from more recent work, see also C Given-Wilson *The English Nobility in the Late Middle Ages* London, 1987 171–9.

the late 1130s fitted together an 'affinity' (the word was actually used by Robert de Torigny about his following) of lesser barons which dominated central Normandy until his disgrace in 1153. The same thing was done in the 1140s in the southern Marches and south-west Midlands by Earl Roger of Hereford (a political forerunner of the Marshal). Both Waleran and Roger used written compacts to attempt to secure their power; Waleran even contracted to pay one of his recruits a considerable annual money fee in return for his support. Such written instruments were refined by the fourteenth century into routine links between magnate and knight. Work is steadily revealing that the Marshal was not alone in exploiting such links in his time. Even an heir to five generations of local landed power, such as Henry, Earl of Warwick (who joined the beleaguered royalists in 1216), made efforts to widen his influence beyond his military tenants, who were too often going their own way, seeking the protection of others.

The strengths and weaknesses of the old and new social orders are seen to the full in the Leinster crisis of 1207–8. The Marshal brought his loyal *mesnie* with him to Ireland, but they were not enough to guarantee his success. In Ireland, as we have already seen, the Marshal's poor relationship with his tenants was nearly fatal for his successful lordship over Leinster. Since many of them were indifferent, or even hostile to him, he had to oppose to them such alliances as that made with Walter de Lacy, lord of neighbouring Meath, and his brother Earl Hugh of Ulster. In Ireland we see the conflict between the old feudal order and the new world of the affinity made corporeal. The Marshal needed the Lacys's non-feudal support because he could not trust his feudal tenants, and would not work at winning them into his affinity. The victory of the combination of retinue and affinity over the tenantry in Leinster was an allegory of the age; a Quixotic joust.

Other magnates in the Marshal's position in past days would have deployed grants of lands to assuage the hostility to the newcomer, but he could not do that, he did not have the resources for a free-for-all. It was the king who was able to give rich rewards, therefore it was to the king that many of these Irish tenants turned in 1207. They threw over the Marshal, setting the link of homage and service at nought. They were properly chastised for their mistake. After the crisis of 1207–8 it is heartening to see how many of the greater men of the province once more dutifully attest his Irish charters: Thomas fitz Anthony, Philip of Prendergast, William fitz David, Walter Purcel, Maurice of London, Ralph de Bendeville, Gilbert du Val, Richard of Cogan and William of Naas. It may be that after 1208 they were scared to stay away. They had learned that if lordship could not be bought, it might be imposed.

If there was not much land to grant, how did the Marshal appeal to the self-interest of the men he selected; how did he reward? We do not know if the Marshal paid money fees to knights of his *mesnie*, although we do know that his sons did settle life rents on some of their men. What evidence there is suggests that the Marshal did to his men what his lords had once done for him: supported them by grants of robes and, doubtless, other knightly accessories. The Marshal was also prepared to do a little to satisfy the more traditional expectations of his knights. Society had still not got over the expectations raised by the great binge of land patronage under the Norman kings. William held sufficient possessions (particularly in Ireland) to offer some of his followers perpetual grants of land; still the prime reward desired by such men. In this way what were originally 'bastard feudal' connections might be technically 'legitimized'. So it was that the young knight, Thomas Basset, son of the baron Alan Basset of High Wycombe, was given in heredity ten pounds' worth of land at Speen in Berkshire by the Marshal 'for that he might be retained, and of my *mesnie*'.[17] Speen was the sort of estate that the Marshal was able to give away; it was the Marshal's own acquisition and was not part of the ancestral estates he still reserved for himself, the demesne, as it is often called for brevity's sake. By this date demesne was sacrosanct to land-starved magnates; it must be husbanded and passed on to their sons and daughters.

One of the chief methods of rewarding the knights of the retinue is only mentioned in passing by the *Histoire*. This was the frequent delegation to the Marshal's followers of administrative duties. Yet, despite the silence of the *Histoire*, it is clear enough that the Marshal's knights were often to be found presiding over various portions of his widespread domains, or engaged in a

17 PRO E40/8006 . . . *et pro eo quod metum sit et de familia mea*. For Thomas Basset (died 1230) see the table of relationships compiled by S L Waugh *The Lordship of England* Princeton 1988 212. There is a possible confusion between the Thomas Basset of this grant and his uncle, the more famous Thomas Basset of Headington, but the younger Thomas is a more likely candidate for retaining in a household at this date. I must thank Dr David Carpenter for discussing this with me.

number of distinctly civilian duties as their master's agent. The *Histoire* only mentions the occasion in 1207–8 when the Marshal departed from a rebellious Leinster to an unknown fate at King John's court. Then he had divided responsibility for his great lordship between John of Earley and Jordan de Sauqueville as bailiffs, who were to be assisted by a council of the more loyal barons of the province: Geoffrey fitz Robert, Walter Purcel and Thomas fitz Anthony. Of those three men Geoffrey had already been a seneschal of Leinster and would one day be so again; Thomas fitz Anthony would also serve a turn as seneschal. Of the Marshal's household knights another two held that particular seneschalcy: John Marshal and William le Gros, his nephews. Leinster was a situation of considerable power and trust. The men who occupied its seneschalcy tell us as much; almost all were men close to the Marshal either in blood or in affection.

But seneschalcies and other such offices in the Marshal's gift, were also rewards as well as duties, and what was going on in contemporary households tells us that they were prized rewards circulated around the intimates of the household. In a way such positions were predecessors of the cash fees received by household knights of later centuries, an alternative method of reward to land grants. The Earl of Warwick, for instance, circulated his chief stewardship from one to another of his several household knights every year or two. To grant seneschalcies to one's intimate knights was part of the reward for their service in the Marshal's day, when it was less easy to come by land to give away. From descriptions of other, particularly ecclesiastical, seneschalcies we know that their holders might collect handsome fees. The lord would pay his seneschals an annual cash sum from the profits of the lordship. In 1189 the keeper of the honor of Striguil under the king was collecting £20 a year, enough money to keep two knights in their essential needs for a year. Sums of money might be demanded for holding the courts of the lordship and of its constituent manors; others for putting new tenants in formal possession of their lands, or for receiving homage to the lord. By this date also stewards would be expected to produce accounts for their period in office; revenue received and paid out.

So it is that Jordan de Sauqueville, joint-bailiff of Leinster in 1207–8, was to be found in 1216 as seneschal of Pembroke. John, son of John of Earley, was acting in 1219 as the seneschal of the Marshal's Marcher lordship of Netherwent, perhaps on his father's behalf. Stephen d'Evreux was the Marshal's seneschal in the ancestral Marshal lands in Wiltshire in 1199; in 1214 he was acting as attorney at Westminster for the Marshal's son.[18] Nicholas Avenel acted for the Marshal as his under-sheriff of Gloucestershire from 1192 to 1194 and 1199 to 1201, doing the routine work in the shire and travelling to Westminster to account for his master before the exchequer. He was succeeded by another Marshal knight, Thomas of Rochford, until 1204. One at least of the Marshal's knights, William Jardin, who first appears in the Marshal's service in England as his attorney at Westminster in 1194,[19] was allowed a particularly long term of office. He seems to have acted as seneschal of Crendon for the best part of its tenure by the Marshal. There were indeed other seneschals apart from these delegated household figures, more 'professional' figures, if the adjective can be applied in that day and age. Richard of Husseburn, a well-known clerk, occupied the seneschalcy of Netherwent at some time in John's reign.[20] In Normandy, William's seneschal in his honor of Longueville for many years was William d'Héricourt, not a knight, for he is listed separately from the knights when he appears in a charter of 1198. Such men would have been a necessary leaven to the delegated, household seneschal: administrative careerists to add their specialist knowledge to the Marshal's affairs. The two types of seneschal existed quite happily alongside each other, for all knights who were landholders were obliged to know the essentials of estate business and law, and indeed by this time many knights themselves employed such men on their own affairs.

Another notable fact about the Marshal affinity was the large part that kinship played in it, even though William Marshal had few surviving close male relatives after 1194 (other than his brother the bishop of Exeter, who died in 1206). Male kinsfolk were a ready way of enhancing the retinue. As far back as 1180 William had recruited his landless brother Anselm to his banner in France, once he was able to offer him a place.[21] His brother John had joined him in 1189 and with his brother came his

18 *Memoranda Roll 1 John* 62. The scribe seems to have garbled his name to . . . *smundus de Deuereals; Curia Regis Rolls* VI 51.

19 *Rotuli Curiae Regis* I 63.

20 Cartulary of Llanthony PRO C115/K2/6683 fo. 287r.

21 Anselm Marshal's total disappearance after 1180 must mean that he cannot have long survived Lagny.

nephew, the illegitimate John Marshal, his brother's son. The young John Marshal found a home in his uncle's *mesnie* when his father died in 1194, and in 1199 when King John was lavishing gifts on his uncle, John Marshal shared in the family's luck, securing an important heiress and a Norfolk barony of moderate size. Another nephew was that Anselm 'the earl's nephew' who appears with him in Ireland on one occasion amongst his clerks.[22] He was Anselm le Gros, made treasurer of Exeter by his other uncle, bishop Henry Marshal, before 1205, and later promoted to be bishop of St Davids. Anselm and his brothers derived from an otherwise unmentioned marriage of a sister of the Marshal to a Gloucestershire knight, William le Gros, sometime steward of Earl William of Gloucester.[23] Anselm's brother, William le Gros 'the eldest' (he had a younger brother of the same name) found a place in the Marshal's household. It seems likely that he is the William le Gros who was briefly seneschal of Normandy for King John in 1203–4, probably as a favour to the Marshal.[24] William le Gros, however, was later more prominent as a leading knight in the household of the younger Marshal, rather than that of the father.

In 1189 the Marshal was joined by Philip of Prendergast, an Irish and Pembrokeshire baron who was his new wife's brother-in-law (Philip had married Earl Richard Strongbow's illegitimate daughter, Mathilda). Another of Isabel's relatives by marriage was prominent in the Marshal's household: Geoffrey fitz Robert. Geoffrey was one of William Marshal's Wiltshire

22 *Register of the Abbey of St Thomas, Dublin* ed. J T Gilbert Rolls Series 1889 356–7.

23 For Anselm's career see J Le Neve *Fasti Ecclesiae Anglicanae* ed. T D Hardy (3 vols) Oxford 1854 I 291–2, 414. For William le Gros, steward of Earl William of Gloucester before 1160, see *Earldom of Gloucester Charters* ed. R B Patterson Oxford 1973 165. He is mentioned as the father of the two Williams, Anselm, Robert and Hamo le Gros in a Bradenstoke charter drawn up in the presence of Earl William, see Cartulary of Bradenstoke fo. 167r–v. He also seems to have been the father of a daughter, Margaret, whom he married to Ralph de Somery, another baron of the honor of Gloucester, before 1194. The marriage contract survives and was witnessed by William Marshal and his knights, see Brooksby cartulary, Bodl. Libr. ms Wood empt. 7 fo. 97r. The Le Gros family held a knight's fee from the earl at Old Sodbury, Gloucestershire, where William le Gros (II), Anselm's brother, erected a borough around 1218, now called Chipping Sodbury, with royal (that is, his uncle's) approval, see *Feudal Aids* II 249; *Book of Fees* II 1407; S Rudder *A New History of Gloucestershire* Cirencester 1779 673.

24 *Rotuli Litterarum Patentium* 33.

knights. Soon after 1189 the Marshal married him to Basilia, a matron in her late forties and the recently-widowed sister of Earl Richard Strongbow. Geoffrey was thus the uncle of Countess Isabel. Stephen d'Evreux was another of the Marshal's knights who was credited with kinship with him (the *Histoire* calls Stephen the 'cousin' of the Marshal), although the exact relationship between the two is impossible to work out.[25]

It is not unusual to find kinsfolk in some numbers in the households of the great: a family expected to share in the good fortune of its members. The same is as true in the household of a bishop or an abbot as in that of an earl. It was a great man's duty to promote his brothers, nephews and cousins, and suitably marry his nieces and female cousins as much as his daughters. William Marshal, a man fortunate in his relations, had benefited from this universal mechanism in society as a boy, and was to play patron to his relatives in his turn. This was not to say, however, that lords got more reliable service from their kinsfolk than from their other followers. Gerald of Wales and Arnulf of Lisieux both had cause to complain of what they had suffered from their ingrates of nephews, whom they had nurtured and promoted through the Church. William Marshal had to suffer the apparent treachery of his nephew, John, in the crisis of his fortunes in 1207–8, despite the fact that John owed everything to his uncle. But John would not risk his future by crossing the king in the matter of his uncle, so he temporized.[26] No doubt, if he had been in the same position, the elder Marshal would have found what he considered an appropriate justification for such an act. The *Histoire*'s silence on the defection, however, is eloquent testimony to what the Marshal and his more loyal followers thought about John Marshal's actions. Kinsfolk may well have been expected to be able to offer their lord more of the *amor* that a lord expected from his men, but society's expectations were not always fulfilled. In truth, family relationships were as far from

25 Stephen d'Evreux was the son of Walter d'Evreux and grandson of William d'Evreux, followers respectively of William de Briouze (II), lord of Brecon, and Walter de Lacy, lord of Weobley. One of these elder d'Evreuxs might conceivably have married a Marshal woman, although it is quite as likely that an earlier Marshal might have married a d'Evreux woman.

26 It is fair to point out here that Stephen d'Evreux, his cousin, was more loyal than the Marshal's nephew. Stephen, like John of Earley, had his lands confiscated. Stephen's castle of Lyonshall, Herefordshire, was taken over by the king's officers in 1208 and later entrusted to the men of Walter de Lacy, Stephen's overlord *Rotuli Litterarum Patentium* 91.

idyllic in the twelfth and thirteenth century as at any time in recorded human history. It was just that it was an age which had higher expectations of feeling and duty.

. . .

## THE MARSHAL AND MONEY

Money was important to the Marshal and his exercise of lordship and patronage. He, no less than other magnates, copied the king and operated a financial office. Some of his colleagues, like the Earls of Leicester, Chester and Gloucester, had long had elaborate annual sessions before their chief men and themselves sometimes called, like the king's, 'exchequers'. Here the seneschals and bailiffs of the various estates came to have their accounts audited. The Marshal probably had a less elaborate system. Like his brother John, and his cousin the Earl of Salisbury, William Marshal had a 'chamber' which took in money and issued receipts at some important castle or other centre.[27]

Since we know that the Marshal had close relations with London financiers, recruited London clerks, and based at least one of his clerks in the city, it is not unlikely that an office of some sort was kept up in the earl's houses at Charing (where we know Master Joscelin, his deputy-marshal, was based). Joscelin may well have administered there an institution later called a 'wardrobe', a storehouse and accounting office for the purchase and distribution of goods in the city for the Marshal's household. The 'wardrobe of Earl William Marshal' was specifically referred to by royal clerks in July 1217. Payments destined for the king had been made into it at Gloucester.[28] At that time the 'wardrobe' of the Marshal was itinerating with him (for London at that time was still in the hands of Louis of France), but some branch of it may well have been settled at London both before the French had arrived and after the city was recovered. It is very significant in this respect that in 1219 when the Marshal was contemplating his last distribution of livery robes to his knights, he ordered that if there were not enough that more should be sent for downriver to London. There, then, a small outpost of his

27 For the financial office kept by Osbert, chamberlain of John Marshal, see *Pipe Roll of 1 John* 226; for the chamber of Earl William of Salisbury see, Cartulary of St Augustine, Bristol, Berkeley Castle Muns. fo. 31v.

28 *Patent Rolls, 1216–25* 83.

household may well have worked, storing up the ultimate source of the Marshal's power; the silver pennies that paid his knights and servants, bought their robes, horses and arms, and the silks, furs, and precious vessels that displayed his dignity and grandeur to the world.[29]

The Marshal and money is an interesting subject. We tend to think of medieval barons as rather unworldly in that respect, urged on by a hungry class of dependents to profligate generosity. But the Marshal had been poor and knew the inconveniences of poverty. He had no great store of money in 1189 when he arrived in London to marry the heiress of Striguil. To Painter that made him a jolly knight errant, generous and profligate. The Marshal, like a pattern feckless aristocrat, found his way to the city magnates who were very willing to assist him. But at this point reality intrudes on the romance. His quickness and ruthlessness in levying a relief on his new tenants (that we hear of from sources other than the *Histoire*) demonstrates that he was not so foolish as to want to rely on the moneylenders for any long period. By the end of the century we find that he was the one who was exploiting the moneylenders. In Normandy in 1201 William Marshal had a grant from King John of a Jew, Vives de Chambay, and enjoyed the profits of his moneylending.[30] It seems likely that he was free enough with money in his earlier days, but like many men his hand grew closer as he had more to grasp. In London he and his sons enjoyed long and profitable dealings with the city magnate, and later sheriff and mayor, William Joinier.[31] His links with the city of St Omer in Flanders brought him into close relations with William son of Florent, a merchant of the city. He used William as his financial agent in raising the money to pay off the indemnity to Louis in 1217. Since Flanders had long been the destination of most of England's greatest export – wool – it may well be that the Marshal and this Flemish merchant were already engaged in mutually beneficial relations: disposing of the sacks of wool from his Welsh and Irish estates. The Marshal became a wealthy man. He himself advanced sums of money to King John in 1206

29 A gold cup belonging to the Marshal was mentioned in a schedule of debts drawn up for his executors *Roll of Divers Accounts* ed. F A Cazel Pipe Roll Society 1982 34.

30 *Rotuli Litterarum Patentium* 3.

31 *Cartulary of Waltham* BL ms Cotton Tiberius C IX fo. 91r; *Calendar of Charter Rolls* I 124.

and had been in a position to loan money to support a campaign against the Welsh in 1194.

Such indications of his canniness are intriguing reminders that the Marshal did not live in a heroic society, whatever the *Histoire* might try to persuade us. Earlier in the twelfth century the highest of Norman aristocrats, Waleran, count of Meulan, did not find it beneath him to take an active interest in the wine trade which passed through his lands on the way to England, and the herring fleets that used his ports.[32] Such great men did not market their own produce, but in forming close relations with the men who had the skills to do it for them they entered a world that some of them did not seem to find uncongenial. The world of commerce had its own excitements and dangers, and for the magnates with resources to exploit it was one way to accumulate the sacks of coins that made so much else possible. The Marshal was alert enough to his commercial interests to indulge in town development to improve his lordship of Leinster, with boroughs developed or improved at Kilkenny, Carlow and New Ross.

If nothing else, the Marshal's friendly relations with merchants, burgesses and his own household clerks should remind us, if we need reminding by now, how two-dimensional was the *Histoire* written to commemorate his life. Generations of romantically-inclined historians have long overstressed the military element in aristocratic life (for which the *Histoire* is in no small part to blame): it is as if we judged today's upper class only by their doings at Badminton, Klosters, Henley or on the golf-links. It is arrogant to assume that the twelfth-century aristocracy was less complex than ours, simply because it is so remote from us.

32 *The Beaumont Twins* 1986 185–9.

*Chapter 7*

# THE CHIVALRY OF THE MARSHAL

The Marshal was a paragon of the military virtues of his day. We do not just have to take the word of his biographer for that. He was tutor-in-arms to the heir of the kingdom of England for a dozen years; prized captain of three successive Angevin monarchs; and a (generally) successful commander in the field. These things we know from sources other than the *Histoire*, so we need not doubt what it says. The Marshal was a great practitioner of what his day and age called *chevalerie*; but what he meant by the word and what we read into it are two different things. Several writers have had much to say about the Marshal not just as a soldier, but as an example of what they see as an early pattern of 'chivalry' and knight-errantry. In a recent study John Gillingham has picked apart what modern historians have had to say about the Marshal's career as a soldier, and offered his own assessment.[1] He presents us with quite a different Marshal, one that I find rather more convincing than the Marshal of Sidney Painter and Georges Duby. The following chapter, therefore, is very much in Mr Gillingham's debt.

Sidney Painter had a vision of the Marshal as a warrior which seems at times to have owed more to Sir Walter Scott's *Ivanhoe* or *The Talisman* than the *Histoire*. He cast William in the role of the 'knight-errant', a man solely guided for much of his life by the pursuit of glory and honour, as he understood it. He saw a man who followed the classic career as described by the thirteenth-century statesman and writer, Philip de Navarre (or Novara); first acquiring renown, then settling down to lands, a wife and respectability. Honest man that he was, Painter admitted that his

1 J Gillingham 'War and Chivalry in the History of William the Marshal' in *Thirteenth Century England* II ed. P R Coss and S D Lloyd Woodbridge 1988 1–13.

category of knight-errant was 'somewhat arbitrary' but we were to understand that it should be taken to mean 'a knight imbued with chivalric ideals'. But what were those ideals? Painter was less than faithful to his text. Despite the delight of the *Histoire* in the Marshal's freebooting on the tournament and battlefield, which it regards as a perfectly respectable activity, Painter condemns the profit motive in warfare as 'unknightly'.[2]

He also depicts the Marshal as a pursuer – albeit an incompetent one – of the cult of courtly love. The *Histoire*, however, provides little evidence for this. It does not ignore women, it even (as Mr Gillingham points out) credits Countess Isabel with an important role in her husband's council (a role that the charters of herself and her husband go some way to confirm). But it does not venerate women particularly. William Marshal had a good deal of respect for his sisters; he made a point of visiting them on the rare occasions that he was in England in his early career. He was also deferential and polite to the noblewomen before whom he performed his deeds in the tournament. Women came within the bounds of his courtliness, for if they were not possible patrons themselves, they had husbands who were. He was, besides, a well-disposed man and on one occasion, at the firing of Le Mans, he had his squires assist an old lady whose house was burning down with all her goods inside. Perhaps he did not see the irony that it would not have been necessary at all if his colleagues had not set light to the city in the first place. But that is the extent of his 'chivalry' as Painter wanted to understand it. The Marshal saw nothing to admire in the woman he caught eloping with a clerk. He was as stringently moral on that occasion as the priggish Philip de Navarre would have wanted. There is nothing in the *Histoire* of the sensuality and playfulness of Andrew the Chaplain or Béroul, the Marshal's contemporaries. Their 'advanced' notions were far beyond the conventional morality of the Marshal and his men. The suggestion that the Marshal might have committed adultery with the Young King's wife is greeted with genuine horror and outrage. The Marshal prided himself on his sound principles.

To the author of the *Histoire*, therefore, women are (like the Marshal's own mother) assets and objects of material promotion; delightful, gentle and beautiful it is true, but still pieces in the game of ambition. The *Histoire* has a limited time to spare for women. Not one comes through as a developed character in her

2 Painter's particular blindness on this topic is just as apparent in his subsequent *French Chivalry* Baltimore 1940).

own right, unlike the women of Chrétien's romances. It paints a man's world, a world of violence, comradeship and high politics. The only traces of the world of romance are the adjectives borrowed to depict women from the vocabulary of the stock romance. Few women had any business in the real world of the Marshal's *mesnie*, and they were a positive menace to its emotional life. There men fed their need for security and companionship by fixing their affections on the iconic figure of the Marshal, their impassive lord and father, sinking their insecurities in the brotherhood of serving him. The chasm in their lives that his death opened up could not be filled, although the *Histoire* itself was an attempt by his bereft men to summon up a wraith of the Marshal, so that not all of what had once been was lost to them.

Romantic knight-errant the Marshal was not. He had a transparent horror of being without a patron in his landless, younger days. He needed a household in which to base himself; a master to follow, someone to pay for his horses, arms, the clothes on his back. The sort of knight that Painter described was a less than respectable character, the sort of knight who haunted the wastes and forests of the contemporary romances with a band of like-minded souls; ambushing respectable knights and their ladies in most unsporting packs, until they ended up at the wrong end of the lance of the hero, who unfailingly dispatched groups of up to a dozen of them at a time, as in a twentieth-century western or space opera.

Duby's view is even less in accord with what the text has to say, indeed at one point, as Mr Gillingham caustically but justly points out, Duby has to invent a more grandiose setting for the Marshal's knighting than the text actually provides, to support his views on the centrality of *l'adoubement* in aristocratic society. Duby, like Painter, sees William Marshal as essentially a simple knight. He goes further. He tries to maintain a view that William Marshal 'was blessed with a brain too small to impede the natural vigour of a big, powerful and tireless physique' (to employ Mr Gillingham's translation). We can concede Duby the physique, but he has misjudged the intellect that guided it. How could he describe one of the most successful courtiers of his age as a man of 'few thoughts and brief'? The Marshal had to have a vigilant sensitivity tuned to every tremble in the mood of the court, an ever-ready humour to help deflect envy and malice, and a certain deviousness if humour failed. Above all he had to have self-control; how otherwise could he have survived? No-one was likely in his own day to have rated the Marshal alongside a John of Salisbury, or even a Walter Map, but that is not to deny the man his due. He was no lucky bonehead. He was an astute, alert and cool-headed soldier and courtier, not a military genius or a Machiavelli, but a great proficient in the field and the council chamber, and no man's fool.

. . .

## THE TOURNAMENT

Let us look at the evidence. What is the chivalry the Marshal displayed in the tournament field? From around the age of twenty-one to the age of thirty-seven William Marshal was an habitué of the tournament. The *Histoire* lists sixteen tournaments in which its hero participated between 1167 and 1183. The rise of this sport to respectability was very much a feature of the Marshal's own lifetime. Meetings of knights for the purpose of military games are first mentioned in France in the early twelfth century, but little is known of these early tournaments. They were probably informal meetings of vigorous, military-minded free men, but not patronized by the higher aristocracy. They acquired a bad reputation as undisciplined riots. Kings and popes moved to ban them, in the latter case because they were a distraction of Christian energy from the Crusade. For a good century and more they occupied the same place in the view of the establishment as rock concerts or Stonehenge solstice-worship does now. Henry II of England would not allow them to be held in his kingdom, but as the *Histoire* indicates, permitted them in the Marches of Normandy and in Anjou.

It was during Henry II's reign that the tournament became a more respectable aristocratic pursuit. This was partly because the fact of being a knight had become more generally regarded, in northern France and England, as a social distinction rather than a military calling. But also, as Duby points out, the organization and sponsorship of great tournaments was a means for the great duke or count to pose as a leader of the nobility. In Stephen's reign in England we first hear of a magnate, Hugh de Mortemer, being killed at such a meeting. In Normandy in 1167, as the *Histoire* tells us, William de Tancarville thought it a desirable thing to lead his *mesnie* around local Norman tournaments. By the time William Marshal was the master of the Young King's *mesnie*, tourneying was all the rage and it occasionally found great patrons around northern France; Philip, Count of Flanders, being the chief of them.

Most of the tournaments were still small affairs, a score or two of knights divided for the purpose of the game into two informal teams. Such meetings were advertised by word of mouth and chiefly attended by local knights and people like the Marshal, professionals who drew much of their income from captures and ransoms. At the height of the season in France, in late autumn, a determined knight might get to one every two weeks. In such circumstances in the later 1170s William Marshal and a Flemish acquaintance, Roger de Gaugy, decided to milk the circuit for everything it was worth. They came to an agreement that they would team up and split the profits from the captures they made on their own account over the next two years. They were meticulous, they had to be, since the money they earned in this way made no small difference to the degree of aristocratic display they could flaunt. The Young King's kitchen clerk, Wigain, undertook to keep a tally of their captures (probably rather a relief for him to be doing something other than totalling the consumption of capons), which survived to be seen by the Marshal's biographer. In ten months Wigain's tally amounted to 103 knights. On his deathbed, the Marshal recalled with mingled regret and pride that he had taken as many as 500 knights prisoner on the field. If he was right one can only marvel at the obstinacy of the knights who were willing to place themselves in front of his lance; confirmation of the old belief that there is one born every minute.

But some meetings were different, great affairs and festivals, drawing hundreds of participants from all over France and England, some even came from Scotland. It is on these that the *Histoire* gives us the greatest detail. On such occasions great magnates from all over the Anglo-French world would converge on the chosen field, lords from the area comprehending Scotland, England and the Marches, Flanders, Anjou, Poitou, Normandy, Brittany, Champagne, Burgundy, Picardy and the area then called 'France', what we now call the Ile-de-France, the region ruled directly by the king. In the Marshal's day, this was as far as the tournament enthusiasm had spread. Few subjects of the emperor, no Italians, Navarrese or Spaniards are mentioned in connection with a tournament.

The patron of the great tournament would host and organize the gathering, feast his great guests and offer token prizes to the best knight on the day. In the case of Philip of Flanders, on one occasion he equipped with some generosity the Young King and his men who appeared at a tournament in the county of Clermont without the ironmongery of war. The tournament patron, whether Count of Flanders, Duke of Burgundy or the lesser Counts of Clermont, Beaumont-sur-Oise or Dreux, clearly expected to gain something from this considerable outlay. No doubt Duby is right to suggest that it was done as much to assert their dignity against the growing power of the French monarchy, by providing bread and circuses for the knights, as for pleasure. But one should not avoid the more simple cause of the patronage of tournaments: its usefulness in promoting the status of great magnates against each other, as much as the king.

The Marshal owed his position and favour with the Young King to his infection of the boy with the lust to tourney. Duby's description of the Marshal as the 'team manager' of the Young King's tourneying *mesnie* has a certain validity, although player-manager would be nearer the truth. The king's continuing favour to William depended on unbroken success, and the Marshal did his best to provide it. He exerted himself to attract into what was a basically Anglo–Norman *mesnie* the most distinguished knights of Flanders, France and Champagne. Such men could name their own price to enlist under English colours for the season. This was very much a transfer fee market. When in 1183 the Marshal had informally parted from the king, a number of dukes and counts promptly offered substantial inducements for him to join their service. We have seen the evidence that he did in fact accept Count Philip's offer before his recall to his estranged lord.

Others have well described the sort of things that happened on the tournament fields of the twelfth and thirteenth centuries.[3] I see no reason to go into any great detail here and I will simply summarize some of the main points they have made. The tournaments of the Marshal's day differed very little from war. The same weapons and tactics were used, the same greed for captives and ransoms is evident. About the only thing that distinguished the tournament from war was the fact that the death of a participant was a cause for regret in the tournament. The tournament also allowed the participants to withdraw into roped-off safe-areas called *recets*. Otherwise they were occasions when no holds were barred.

As a sport, tourneying was a most dangerous activity: in the level of violence the participants suffered, it was rather like horseback American football with sharp sticks and no referees.

3 See bibliography of this chapter, page 211.

There were some elements of it which make the sporting analogy as irresistible to me as it was to Duby. There were teams dressed in the same colours and there was a decided team spirit about the game, with captains, team chants (the war-cry) and regional loyalties. In a great tournament, as at Lagny in 1180, teams were grouped into their nominal place of origin by nations: English, Bretons, Flemings, Normans, and so on. In other ways, though, the analogy is inadequate to describe more than the underlying spirit of the tournament. There was no formal objective to be achieved. The winning side was the one which chased the other from the field, or that which amassed the greater number of captives at the end of the day's fighting. Also, the individual went in for it for more than the satisfaction of team-spirit and co-operative endeavour, he went into it to fill his purse.

Few rules governed the tournament field, apart from the feeling that it was generally bad form to slip away from your captor once his attention had been drawn away, or steal the horses taken by another man. The most regulated part of the business was the taking of ransoms. A man once taken must undertake to pay a ransom, but that done should be allowed to rejoin the field if he felt up to it. The *Histoire* is very hot against bad sportmanship where it involved ransom, and very particular that it be paid. On the other hand it is willing to balance this punctiliousness with admiration for the knight, as William Marshal is said to have been at Joigny who tempered industry with largesse. At Joigny, the Marshal took numbers of prisoners as usual, but is said to have distinguished himself by grandly giving away his winnings.

Men conducted themselves on the twelfth-century tournament field with the same brutality and ruthlessness as they did on the battlefield. Since the main justification for the activity was that it offered an authentic training ground for war, we must not be surprised at this. There was no particular objection to deploying whole companies of foot-soldiers to assist in the action, as was done at the town of Anet on the Norman border in 1176. The French baron, Simon, castellan of Neauphle, drew up 300 footmen to cover the retreat of his team. It says a lot for the quality of armour by this date that William Marshal and the Young King were able to ride the foot-soldiers down with impunity. William took advantage of the situation by grasping Simon de Neauphle's reins as they passed him (his preferred method of capturing knights). He and the king rode away, towing Simon behind. He could do no more than flail around helplessly, deprived of his reins. Unfortunately for Simon, he came into contact with a low beam as William dragged him along and was knocked off his horse. When William finally drew rein and looked behind him, he saw only an empty saddle and the king, convulsed with laughter.

Some of the other tactics described as used in tournaments also appear distinctly unsporting, until we remember that the tournament field was no less than a rehearsal for battle. When tournaments began, they began with a general onset of the two sides. When the massed ranks met with a thudding crash, their ranks would often disintegrate and a confused mêlée follow. The most successful company was that which kept close together in the charge and whose cohesion survived into the following scrum. But Philip of Flanders' favourite tactic was to avoid the shock of battle altogether; keep back his men until the tournament had become a milling throng of individuals and small, lost groups; then ride in on the fight in a disciplined company and mop up captives at will. The Marshal observed the Count in action. Liking what he saw, he introduced the same tactic to the Young King's team. At a subsequent tournament the Young King pretended that he did not want to join in and held back from the fray. Later when all the teams were engaged he charged in on the count of Flanders' men with great success. This ploy afterwards became the basis of the English team strategy.

. . .

## THE BATTLEFIELD

The tournament being what it was, we can expect even less of the chivalry of Sidney Painter on the battlefield. Here was a place of real seriousness. Indeed, it was the field of war that gave the aristocracy the only warrant for its privileges in the stock view of contemporary writers. They fought for Christ and for justice while the clerks offered intercession with God. The peasants who worked to provide the necessities for both had to console themselves that they were the foundations of the two shafts which held up the sky.

The Marshal and his class had ways of alluding to their reason for existence. On surviving impressions of the Marshal's seal he appears represented, as do almost all of his lay contemporaries, garbed as a knight on horseback. The common image of aristocracy in the late twelfth century was a military one. Since William I had his new seal cut after conquering England it had been thought increasingly suitable for a great man or ruler to be depicted as a horse-soldier. It did not happen all at once. There was a different, older, idea that a lay lord should be shown in civilian dress, the military display confined to the sword that was to represent his power to discipline the evil-doer. Some seals and all tomb-effigies preserve this more pacific and judicial aristocratic image until the Marshal's time. But in general, from the early-twelfth century onwards, it was the arms and accoutrements of a knight which automatically identified the aristocrat. The association of ideas had advanced so far by 1200 that just to be a knight was recognized as qualifying for inclusion in a superior social group. In the Marshal's own lifetime this idea had advanced to the point where a knight, however poor, could still expect to be addressed as *sieur* or *messire*; a form of public deference extended in the first half of the century only to earls and barons.

Since the great aristocrats had for many generations made war their profession, this conjunction of ideas is by no means odd. The oddity lies in the newer idea that the knight was himself noble just from taking the rite of passage of dubbing; this particular association of ideas was a novelty, and it appeared in the Marshal's own lifetime. He would not have been averse to the idea, however. It was partly through people like himself that the idea came about. Younger sons of barons, such as he was, would have bridled at the thought that they were not as noble as their father. If they took up the profession of arms it did not alter their status, and their presence would enhance the status of the men of meaner origins they associated with in the *mesnies* in which they were employed.

On his seal (and his alleged tomb) we see the Marshal garbed as a knight would have been at the close of the twelfth century. He wears the flowing surcoat on which in real life his arms would have been stitched or embroidered. Beneath are the fine-meshed mail hauberk and leggings which protected him from spear-points, arrows and the sharp edge of swords. Beneath that, we know, would have been a buff-leather or quilted under-robe to deaden the shock of blows which reached his body. About his shoulder, on a thong, was his shield, a construction of wood and boiled leather, painted over with his arms; lighter and smaller than the great kite-shaped shields of the Conqueror's army. On his head was a mail coif, like a balaclava, and over that, by 1200, it would have been customary to wear a light iron cap, less confining than the older helmets with nasal which remained the fashion until the end of Henry II's reign. For full protection in battle and tournament, however, the great helm would have been worn that is depicted on the Marshal's seal. It was an enveloping iron bucket with eye-slits and ventilation holes punched in it, laced tightly to his shoulders. The *Histoire* has the Marshal wearing one in the 1170s, but that is perhaps an anachronism; they do not seem to have been in full fashion till King Richard's reign.[4] His sword and light, ashwood lance completed the Marshal's war gear.

The Marshal at war was a formidable and, we might also say, colourful figure: robes of yellow, green and red linen or silk, the polished steel helmet, gilded clasps and jewels flashing in the sunlight; one could hardly imagine a more impressive military peacock. The effect of a whole, uniform company of such creatures must have been a quite deceiving sight. No wonder that the young Perceval, brought up in ignorance of the world by his mother in a Welsh forest, was made by Chrétien de Troyes to fall in love with such military magnificence at first sight, and mistake the first knights he met for angels.[5] Contemporary writers, such as Jordan Fantosme, preserved stirring descriptions of the effect of a twelfth-century army on the observer. It is colour they often pick on, the overwhelming effect of the strong colours – red, blue and white – at a distance. Then there is the added effect of the uniform accoutrements of the disciplined companies (*conrois* or *constabularia*); the shields, the fluttering pennons and thickets of lances, which hypnotized the eye. In terms of visual effect, at least, the twelfth century fielded more formidable armies than had been seen in western Europe since the time of Theodosius.

We can only wonder, in the moralizing strain adopted by the older and wiser Guy of Warwick, home from the wars and alone on a tower of his castle as the sun went down, whether all this glamour was justified by the result.[6] Indeed there is nothing

4 The great helm, as opposed to the lighter helmet, is represented on the seal of Richard I cut for him in 1189. However an early version of the great helm, an iron cap with a metal mask attached to the front (rather like the Sutton Hoo helmet), was carved *c.*1160–70 on the military tomb effigy of William Clito, Count of Flanders, at the abbey of St Bertin, St-Omer, see F Sandford *A Genealogical History of the Kings of England and Monarchs of Great Britain* London 1677 17; E Warlop *The Flemish Nobility before 1300* (4 vols) Courtrai 1975–6 I pl. fac. 139.

5 *Le Conte de Graal* ll.125–52.

6 *Gui de Warewic* II ll.7568–74.

glamorous in the warfare described by the Marshal's biographer. It is a prosaic business of siege, calculated brutality, waste and trickery. The pattern of the warrior most admired by William Marshal was his father, John. It would seem from the *Histoire* that the Marshal instructed his young followers in war in examples he drew from his father's life. To William, his father provided an admirable example of a captain and lord. If John Marshal was so admirable as a soldier, then we have in his son's stories of him the particular qualities that he admired.

Courage, particularly in adversity, was plainly one quality to emulate. Although the *Histoire* does not admire failure, it could at least praise the desperate stand of John Marshal in Wherwell abbey in 1141, holed up in a tower, engulfed in flame and spattered with molten lead. It was not his fault that he was in such a pass. He was there because the Angevin army he had joined was defeated, and he had for once done the generous thing and covered the retreat of the empress. Such was the reward for the truly self-sacrificing chevalier; he was sacrificed. The *Histoire* preferred that its heroes did not get in such desperate straits. It admired far more the cunning that could turn possible disaster to triumph. John Marshal was admired for his address in luring the dangerous mercenary, Robert fitz Hubert, into captivity in his castle, under smiling assurances that he was in fact planning an alliance with him. The *Histoire* chuckles over John's dawn ambush of King Stephen's force, just as it emerged, unarmed, from its base to destroy him; fooled by his deceptive assurance that he had too few men to resist the king. Most praise went to John for edging out of a losing military situation by a strategic capitulation; putting aside his wife and taking instead the sister of his great enemy to form an alliance. William Marshal himself was a by-product of this particular stratagem, son of this politic marriage.

Like father, like son. John Gillingham has described better than I can the various deceptions and brutalities that the Marshal perpetrated in his long, military career. The Marshal's wars were not usually the sort of full-dress affairs for which tournaments were the preparation. 'The kind of war William fought – and by definition this was the kind of war the best knights fought – was a war full of ravaging, punctuated quite often by attacks on strong-points but only rarely by pitched battles.'[7] The *Histoire* describes seventeen sieges, but only three or four battles (depending on how seriously Drincourt is taken as a battle). The Marshal,

7 Gillingham 12.

only took the field in two pitched battles in all his long life.

The *chevauchée* (the word is employed by the *Histoire*) was the principal horror that war inflicted on the land. It was the systematic pillaging and burning of enemy land by a raiding column of knights and sergeants. It enriched one side at the expense of the other, and put pressure on the enemy. Although, as Mr Gillingham points out, there is good evidence that the author of the *Histoire* was well aware of the idea of the war of attrition and the pressure of economic damage on resources, such warfare was also a denial of the enemy's lordship: he could not protect his people and this was a grief to him (as the plundering of Netherwent by the Welsh was a matter of grief to the Marshal). There was otherwise no feeling that this, the seedy side of war, was anything but honourable.

Self-control in battle, as much as in the king's hall, was also admired in this age. It was a more sophisticated age than it is given credit for being. By the twelfth century warfare was the professed occupation of an aristocracy that was also becoming literate and articulate. It was a century that saw for the first time for a long time magnates as well as kings who turned to the pen and the written word for the purposes of propaganda, administration, correspondence and, indeed, amusement. Even the Marshal did not escape the influence of this movement although, unlike Geoffrey fitz Peter and many of the court of the kings he served, as well as the kings themselves, he was not in any way literate. It may be that the Marshal was untypical among his generation in being unlettered; in which case his biography (again, the product of a lettered laity) may have grossly distorted our picture of the barons of his day. There is every reason to see the twelfth century as the first in northern Europe since the eclipse of Rome in which there was an aristocracy which prized learning amongst its members as much as military proficiency.

A military aristocracy that also cultivated and admired learning was going to find much to interest it in that earlier age. Mr Gillingham, in his writings, has proven how widespread amongst the twelfth-century aristocracy were the maxims of Vegetius, the fourth-century writer on warfare. Intelligent, instructed soldiers would fight with more considered and mannered tactics than the popular picture of all-in knightly mêlées would accommodate. Head-down charges, as we have already seen on the tournament field, were not the way that the leading captains won the day. They held back, deceived their adversaries and probed for a weak point before committing themselves. Only then could the morale of the well-disciplined *mesnie* be used to full advantage. The same was true on campaign. All was feint and movement. A full-scale battle was rarely entered on, for the result might be uncomfortably decisive and irretrievable. Battles, as at Lincoln in 1217, were for desperate men. Otherwise, as when a determined Count Baldwin of Flanders met King Philip of France in 1197 outside an invested city, one did not fight unless the odds were overwhelmingly in your favour. Philip drew off from the belligerent Flemings and left the city to its fate. The *Histoire* did not criticize him for this, it complimented him on his sense. Again, the *Histoire* condemned the Emperor Otto for unnecessarily taking on the retreating French at Bouvines in 1214. If he had just waited he would have obtained as good a result as if he had met and destroyed the French. As it was the emperor's decision, and its unexpected result, cost him his throne and lost Normandy to John for good.

The Marshal knew, partly from his father and partly from experience, the burden of one of Vegetius's maxims as well as if he had read it: 'courage is worth more than numbers, and speed is worth more than courage'. As at Cilgerran in 1204 he knew the value of surprise and the confusion it might cause. To achieve it, he and his contemporaries would march at night, pretend to disperse to deceive the enemy to do likewise, or use the uncongenial winter season to stage unexpected strikes and raids. There was a premium placed on disciplined and reliable reconnaissance to try to minimize the danger of being caught off guard. The Marshal time and again gave lessons on this. Local intelligence and informers were a necessary complement to scouts. As much as could be was done to avoid being taken off guard by the enemy.

This was the way that men fought in the twelfth century if they were wise and experienced. Warfare then was not 'chivalrous' in quite the way Painter and Duby would have us believe. The word 'chivalry' (*chevalerie*) appears a couple of times in the *Histoire*: it describes the action of knighting, and it describes virtuosity in the military games outside Winchester in 1141. The adjective for proper and commendable conduct in the *Histoire*, as Mr Gillingham points out, is *corteis* (courtly); it is an adjective associated by the author with God himself. Used at a more mundane level it appears when King Richard fell in with one of the Marshal's schemes for deceiving Philip and ravaging his lands; he congratulated William with the compliment that he was *molt corteis*. The twelfth century was such an age that could equate ingenious trickery and stern attrition with the word 'courtly'; and it did so because those were the qualities that it admired: sterness to an enemy and cleverness in the craft of war. Giving the enemy a sporting chance was a perversion of a later age. William Marshal would have gaped at the chivalrous French captain at the battle of Fontenoy who invited the English line to open fire first, and would have judged the catastrophic result to be no more than the man deserved.

*Chapter 8*

# LA BONE FIN VA TOUT

The *Histoire* does not in general worry too much about the Marshal's spiritual state. He was a good man, and God loves good men. The Marshal's soul only occupies the author's attention at the point he and his paymasters would have considered appropriate: his deathbed. Nonetheless it is surprising, and unaccountable, that he does not mention any of the Marshal's several, expensive religious foundations, save one. Curiously, the one foundation inspired by the Marshal that the author does see fit to place in his narrative is one that cost him little. After the sea-battle in the Channel in 1217 that destroyed the French fleet, the Marshal expressed a wish that a hospital might be built at the port of Sandwich. It was to be dedicated to St Bartholomew on whose feast day the battle had been fought. However it was neither built on Marshal lands nor with Marshal funds, but with the prize-money taken from the French. I can only guess that the hospital's foundation escaped the editor's knife because it made a neat full stop to the story of the battle that saved Henry III's throne. The Marshal's other religious foundations were but unnecessary digressions to the author.

But pious grants aside, the text of the *Histoire* is nonetheless saturated by remembrances of God, even between deathbeds. We may take this as an accurate reflection of the degree of open religion displayed by the Marshal's circle. There was no mocking (except of the household clerks) nor was there indifference. 'God for the Marshal!' was the cry of the Marshal's men. God was ever present and was particularly to be called on in a crisis, or at the lowest level, invoked in oaths ('By the Sword of God!' was an fittingly military one used by the Marshal). The narrative has occasional asides which demonstrate a strong sensibility of the workings of God in the world: 'My lords, it is no nonsense that God is wise and courteous; ever he gives aid and succour to the man who believes in him'.[1] This is how the *Histoire* comments on the first tournament of the Marshal's career in 1167, which gave him the capital to quit the Tancarville household. When the Marshal knighted the Young King the author says: 'Great honour did God to the Marshal that day'.[2] *Damnedex* (the Lord God) was a good lord to his true vassals and rewarded them as a good lord ought. And if the Lord God was a little slow to answer the Marshal's prayers, there were counsellors near him who could make intercession. The Virgin Mary and the Three Kings of Cologne were approached to assist in vindicating the Marshal of the charge of adultery with his master's wife. The devil too might be invoked in the heat of anger and battle fury. It was to his mercies that the Marshal committed Richard when he had him defenceless at his lance's end in 1189.

The Christian powers sit a little oddly beside the other supernatural force to be found in the *Histoire*. Fortune and her wheel were also credited with affecting the Marshal's fate, as when the Young King died. This streak of fashionable Classical paganism may well reflect the Marshal's own perception of his fortunes. It is an image which could have reached him from the world of the romances. The power of luck and the Fates must have bothered the Marshal, as it would any courtier, for it must often have seemed that his fate depended on the whim of some supernatural agency beyond his control.

The piety of the Marshal, so far as it is open to analysis, seems to parallel that of another seasoned warrior of his day, his younger contemporary, Philip de Navarre. His 'Four Ages of Man' is a prolonged and dour sermon on mortality. Even as he deals with childhood he urges parents to instil as much of piety in their children as infants can bear. To him youth was a time of direst danger to the soul. Youths (that is, unmarried or childless knights up to the age of forty) were heedless and luxurious by their nature, yet they were at a time of life when their inexperience and foolishness might lead them to be carried off without warning. In what state of soul would they then meet God? For Philip, the business of middle and old age was to send ahead riches 'to that other strange isle' to which all must come, that is, to the world beyond this one. Alms and good deeds must make amends for the

1 *Histoire* ll. 1363–66.

2 *Histoire* ll. 2097–8.

folly of youth. For Philip, as for John Wesley and Mrs Thatcher, it was a good thing to acquire riches, but only because it increased one's ability to do good to the poor and the Church. The old man might then approach the end of his life with more assurance, and regard with equanimity the fading of his faculties. Such a preoccupation with mortality was very much present in the Marshal's biography.

William Marshal was still a 'youth' when he first made the acquaintance of sudden death, when his uncle was stabbed to death before him in Poitou. His own survival from this incident was by no means assured and this may have led to reflection. However, the only evidence we have is that it led to distinctly malevolent feelings towards the alleged inspirers of the deed, the Lusignan family. The death of the Young King in 1183 is a different matter. Neither the Marshal nor anyone else could have expected the grim scenes that terminated the Young King's life within a fortnight. 'Caitiff death' had stolen away his lord, and we can well believe the description of the grief and despair of his men that broke out in the chamber. What we cannot know directly is what effect the scene had on the Marshal. How accurate is the poignant dialogue between the two men, lord and servant, as the king died? It is certainly affecting. The younger man sinking, but lucidly dictating his testament to his clerks; the Marshal at his side, undertaking the trip to Jerusalem for him, but still talking of recovery. Were the Young King's last words really for him? We cannot know. What we do know is that the deathbed scene did persuade him to set aside his career and travel to the East, with all the risks that decision involved. We know also from his own deathbed reflections that he had decided in the Holy Land that he would die in the Templar order, and that it was in the East that he purchased the rich silken pall that he intended would one day cover his own dead body. It lay untouched for thirty years in one of his castles or monasteries in Wales until John of Earley was sent to fetch it to the death chamber at Caversham. It was the appearance of this cloth, a little faded, that made him talk of these long-ago thoughts before his curious knights.

The Marshal was around the age of thirty-five or thirty-six when the Young King died. In the reckoning of his time he might still be called a 'youth', but he had come to that time of youth when 'middle-age' was fast approaching and thoughts were more settled and composed. According to the course of life described by Philip de Navarre, he was due for a spiritual crisis, and this is what seems to have happened in 1183. There may have been other contributing causes than catching the dying breath of a master rather younger than himself. His career had not been particularly salubrious for the past ten years. He had recently learned exactly how unstable were the foundations of a life at court. No wonder then that the *Histoire* could not find much material for his time in the Holy Land, despite his two or more years there. William Marshal remained a curiously private man in an age without much privacy for the great. He did not care to share with his later household what he did and thought in the Holy Places; it was between him and God, his chief lord.

His household was also not favoured with his thoughts on the foundation of his various religious houses in England and Ireland. He founded three: an Augustinian priory at Cartmel in 1189 x 90; Cistercian abbeys at Tintern Parva (*de Voto*) and Duiske (or Graiguenamanagh), in the first decade of the thirteenth century. The foundation of Tintern Parva (Little Tintern) was also called forth by a spiritual crisis. We have it from a late, but reliable source that the Marshal resolved to found Tintern Parva when caught in a storm on his passage to Ireland in 1201. The ever-mobile aristocrat of the Anglo-Norman world was as much at the mercy of his nerves on embarking on a sea voyage as a modern businessman on boarding a jet. No doubt there were then too people to reassure them that sea travel was statistically the safest form of travel in the twelfth century. And if there were such people they would have been right, in theory. Fatal wrecks were by no means common in the Marshal's time, but some unnervingly well-known characters had foundered at sea: William Atheling, the son of Henry I, and Richard, Earl of Chester, who both went down with the White Ship in 1120. A storm in the Channel had carried away several well-known courtiers in 1165. King Richard had just escaped drowning on the Dalmatian coast on his return from the Crusade in 1193. As his own ship yawed and plunged in an autumn gale in 1201, it must have seemed to the Marshal a very cruel joke of that ineluctable force of the Fates that he was threatened with drowning at the very height of his fortunes while going to take possession of his wife's great domain of Leinster. But he was not completely helpless; in such circumstances others had successfully bargained with God. In 1148 Waleran, Count of Meulan and Earl of Worcester, had sworn to build a Cistercian abbey if he escaped impending doom in a storm in the Mediterranean while returning from a less than successful Crusade. He escaped and promptly commenced the building of the Cistercian abbey of Le Valasse in Normandy (also called '*de Voto*'; the 'abbey of the vow'). The Marshal made his vow in the Irish Sea and the measure of the horror and relief he must have felt can be seen in the promptness with which he began the foundation. An abbot and monks were in place by 1203, a colony drawn from the original Tintern in his Welsh lordship of Netherwent.[3] It is very likely that he made his wishes known to his monks of Tintern as he passed back from Ireland through Netherwent *en route* to the court of King John.

The foundations of Cartmel and Duiske were more leisurely and considered. Both seem to have been intended to mark his acquisition of new lordships: polite acknowledgements to God of the grace with which he had favoured William Marshal with more possessions. Cartmel was founded in the first year of William's enjoyment of his wife's inheritance, but it was not founded on his wife's lands.[4] Cartmel was his alone, and the gift was in effect a direct one from him to God, owing nothing to his wife's inheritance, although conditional as all English foundations were, on the king's approval. It was executed in a public assembly; the presence of Geoffrey fitz Peter indicating that it was done within the precincts of a royal palace. Although the king did not participate, his brother, Count John, issued a confirmation of the deed as lord of Lancaster. William's relations were present: the Earl of Salisbury, his cousin; John 'the king's marshal' his elder brother; and Philip of Prendergast, his wife's brother-in-law. Also present were nine men who can be identified as the Marshal's knights, and four of his clerks. Amongst the throng was John of Earley, whose memories of this pious scene did not (curiously) make it into the eventual biography of his lord.

The foundation of Cartmel was a considered act and the foundation charter preserves much of the thought behind it. He

3 A copy of the foundation charter survives but it is undated and might have been executed anywhere and at any time between 1201 and 1212, see *Chartae, Privilegia et Immunitates* 80.

4 The date of the foundation charter of Cartmel can be ascertained by its being after the Marshal's marriage to Isabel late in July 1189 and before his departure to Normandy in March 1190. All the witnesses, especially Geoffrey fitz Peter, would have been found in England at this time. The mention of William's 'heirs' (rather than his sons and daughters) is interesting. This indicates that his wife must have been expecting a child, but had not yet produced, and we know that the Marshal's eldest child, the second William Marshal, was born in Normandy in the summer of 1190.

had done it, he said: 'for the widening of the field of Holy Religion' and 'for the soul of the lord King Henry II, and for the soul of the Young King Henry *my lord* [my italics], and for the soul of King Richard; for my soul and the soul of my wife Isabel, and those of my ancestors and successors and our heirs'. Debts were being paid. Principally the debt was to God, who had given him a wife, wide estates, royal favour, and now, it seems, was promising an heir. But there was also a debt to the sad shade of the Young Henry, whom few remembered. A local debt may also have been involved. We know from another source that the personnel of the new priory (already in place at Cartmel when the foundation charter was written) was drawn from Bradenstoke priory in Wiltshire, where the Marshal's father was buried. But the Marshal was firm in stating that his new house was to be completely independent of Bradenstoke, it was to be his alone, and it must always be a priory and never promoted to an abbey (I am not clear why he stipulated this last point). The Marshal was also as punctilious as ever about future relations between himself and his heirs and Cartmel. He was its patron and to him belonged the formal right of choosing the prior of Cartmel, in consultation with two canons sent to him by its chapter. There seem to have been few contacts between the Marshal and Cartmel thereafter, which is not surprising in view of its remoteness from his centres of interest. However, he did transfer to the priory a church and village in Leinster at some time after 1199, the later confirmation of which survives.[5]

The foundation of Duiske, some eleven years after Cartmel, was a not dissimilar exercise. He must have decided to do it before he left for Ireland in 1201, and had already got the approval in principle of the abbot of Stanley, another Wiltshire house, who was to provide a colony of monks. The storm *en route* that precipitated a twin Cistercian foundation at Tintern Parva was an accidental windfall for the white monks; the Marshal increased the stakes with God so that his survival was more desirable to him. He would have announced his foundation of Duiske on his arrival in Leinster, and indeed he secured the assistance of Bishop Hugh of Ossory, the diocesan, before he left again for England. But Tintern Parva took priority over the next few years, understandably perhaps. An abbot and monks were already in place at Tintern Parva while purchases were still being made to provide an

5 *Monasticon Anglicanum* VI 455.

endowment for Duiske in the period 1207–12.[6] The cemetery of Duiske abbey was consecrated by the bishop of Ferns in June 1204 while the bishop of Ossory was in England, and this indicates that the monks of Stanley had a cell there then working at the foundation, but it was a slow process.[7] The formal act of foundation may have been as late as 1210 x 12, for although it was executed in Ireland it features several men who were estranged from the Marshal in the difficulties he had with the king before 1210, notably his nephew, John Marshal.[8] Even then there is an air of a thing half-done about the business. The Marshal had written into the foundation charter his approval of any future grants or sales to the abbey that might come its way. The chief difference between the foundations of Cartmel and of Duiske is the prominence in the latter of his wife. It was on her lands that the abbey was erected and so the Marshal has written into the deed her approval of the foundation. When he died, she would enter into the untramelled enjoyment of her lands, and then any grant he had made would be at her mercy.

One thing that both the Duiske and Cartmel foundation deeds have in common is a concluding passage cursing in his own name and in God's any man who dared to trouble the new houses. In an age which had developed effective church courts to protect pious donations such curses had become uncommon and dated. That they appear in both deeds is remarkable and allows one to picture the Marshal, thinking back to what was done in his younger days, instructing his clerks to be sure to have a good curse written into the acts to put off ill-wishers. It might well have been his idea of how things should be done properly. It certainly tells us something about how he thought God worked in the world.

Apart from these major acts of patronage the Marshal's other grants to the Church were limited. Most are not grants at all, but confirmations of what his predecessors had given. The range of his patronage was narrow and in many ways as old-fashioned as the maledictions of his charters. The orders he patronized: the Cistercians and the Augustinians, and even the Templars, were the orders patronized by his father's generation. The patronage of

6 'Charters of the Cistercian Abbey of Duiske', 16: a deed quitting land to William Marshal, Earl of Pembroke and his monks of Stanley, which is attested by John, abbot of Tintern Parva.

7 Ibid. 23–4.

8 For the text *Facsimiles of National Manuscripts of Ireland* ed. J T Gilbert pt 2 London 1878 pl. LXIX.

the high nobility at this time was beginning to be diverted into the first purposely-founded chantries: chapels of one or several chanting priests singing daily masses for their benefactors' souls: a direct response to the growing influence of the doctrine of purgatory. What major grants were still being made were being directed towards the orders of Sempringham, La Grande Chartreuse, Grandmont and Prémontré; who were tapping a continuing taste for asceticism that the friars of St Dominic and St Francis would exploit to great effect soon after the Marshal's death.

I know of a total of twenty-three chapters of regular or secular clerks which had charters from the Marshal: the bishops and chapters of Winchester, Dublin, Ossory and Glendalough; the Benedictines of St Thomas of Dublin, Gloucester, Lyre and Pembroke; the Cluniacs of Longueville; the Tironians of Pill; the Augustinians of Bradenstoke, Cartmel, Dunstable, Kells, Llanthony, Notley and Waltham; the Cistercians of Duiske, Dunbrody and Foucarmont; the nuns of Maiden Bradley and Markyate; and the Temple. However, most of these charters record not grants, but concessions of grants that his predecessors had made. Despite this impressive dispersal of parchment, in fact the Marshal gave very little to the clergy. It is even possible that he may have had more from them: sums of money paid to him to secure confirmations of privileges. Apart from his three foundations the Marshal made real grants to only six churches. Most of these were unimpressive: tithes to Pembroke (Monkton) and Longueville priories; a few acres and houses at Caversham to Notley abbey; and a church each to the chapters of Christchurch, Dublin, and Bradenstoke, Wiltshire. Curiously, the most striking outright grant to a church other than a foundation was of ten plough-lands to the cathedral of Glendalough in Leinster.[9] If there is any preference to be gleaned from the Marshal's Church patronage it is a thoroughly conventional one towards the Augustinians and Templars, both of whom were much favoured by the courtiers of his father's day. His first foundation was an Augustinian one at Cartmel, and he also favoured its mother house, Bradenstoke, where his father and brother were buried. The Marshal's good friends were Abbot Edward of Notley, an Augustinian house of the

9 For these grants see Christchurch Oxford muns DY 13(a) mm. 3–4; Wiltshire Record Office 9/15/6; *Monasticon Anglicanum* IV 321; *Longueville Charters* 105; *Crede Mihi* 53; *Appendix to the Twentieth Report of the Deputy Keeper of the Public Record, Ireland* 38.

congregation of Arrouaise, and Bishop Hugh of Ossory, an Augustinian canon before he was elected bishop. His chief clerical executor was Abbot David of the Augustinian house of Bristol. The stolidity and respectability of the Augustinians seems to have stirred some answering chord in the Marshal. He was a most conventional man.

This most conventional of men died as such a man must. 'A good end counts for everything' is the proverb that Philip of Navarre quotes again and again. All life should be a preparation for the final act, and the Marshal had been thinking of his death and planning for it for fully half his long life. He had done as Philip said a man must, and sent ahead his fortune to the strange isle, the Avalon to which he must one day sail. Two abbeys of monks and a priory of canons were the ports from which he sent his wealth to the other world, and for generations they and others would send after him cargoes of prayer and intercession. So it was with composure that he made the first stage on his journey. Once he knew that his last illness was upon him, he sent away the futile, self-important doctors, and had himself gently rowed up the Thames and out into the country, away from London and Westminster and the world of affairs which now at the last he found oppressive. Out he went to that very country where his father had manoeuvred and fought in Stephen's civil war. There he settled into his death chamber in the manorial complex at Caversham across the Thames from Reading and nearby Earley, his friend John's home.

His manor at Caversham had for some years been a favourite of his. He had erected a private chapel within the circuit of his residence, served by canons of his abbey of Notley. A hall, private chambers, and a small town of lodgings within the precinct wall made as comfortable a setting as could be contrived for himself and his men to await his death. It was a long time coming and he resisted it steadfastly. He showed no fear of death, just the same patience and determination he had shown all his life. But he was treating death as an adversary right till the end, until he had then to admit it was too strong for him. The only real measure we have of his thoughts at this time – for he was still for the most part as guarded as if he were in King John's council chamber – is the sudden loquacity that came upon him when he saw the silken pall which he had sent for from Wales, the pall he intended to cover his bier. Then his eldest son and his men learned for the first time the plans he had made years before for his burial, and some few details of the man's inner life for once escaped the prison of his discretion.

At Caversham he lingered, often noticeably in pain and eating little, from the end of March to the middle of May. Ever sensible of the approaching end, he said confession weekly. Here, as we have seen, he took on the white cloak of a Templar, but did not yet divest himself of his lordship over men. One wonders whether he was ready as yet to give himself up as lost to life. It is so hard to abandon hope, and with the Marshal we do indeed see that the strongest mind will still turn from the last journey even though it has accepted that it must soon leave. In the days immediately before he died he asserted himself with some asperity, scolding his clerk Philip ('Be silent, rascal!'), who suggested that he sell for alms the robes laid in to distribute amongst his followers at Whitsun. Philip had made the error of reminding his lord of the last and most difficult farewell the Marshal had to make, a farewell to love and lordship. While he lived he remained stubbornly the Earl of Pembroke.

At the end he sank visibly, quite unable to eat and prey to hallucinations. The day before he died he startled his attendant knights by declaring he saw two men in white on either side of his bed. They were quick to conclude that God had sent fitting counterparts of themselves to escort their lord on the journey in which they could not accompany him. John of Earley later told the author of the *Histoire* how much he regretted that he had never asked who exactly his lord thought he had seen. The fascinations of the 'near-death experience' are nothing new. The next day, 14 May, he died in his crowded chamber, a cross held before his face, lying in his son's arms, John of Earley beside him and two abbots signing his absolution. The scene was deeply affecting, and both the young William and John of Earley took good care that their poet should record those last months of the Marshal's life in every detail, even down to the bread-stuffed mushrooms which was all that they could get him to eat. As the late Professor Dominica Legge said, in the death scene as nowhere else, the *Histoire* rings true. Here there is no evasion or explanation. We have been led to the great man's death chamber to see how the good and pious soul that they believed him to be sanctified his life by leaving it as a good lord and a good Christian. There is no moralist's delight in the squalor and wretchedness of the deaths of princes. We had indeed been given a selection of these with which to compare the Marshal's departure: the Young Henry, his father, and then John. But unlike them, William Marshal had lived well and died as he should. The good end counted for all.

*Appendix 1*

# THE KNIGHTS OF WILLIAM MARSHAL

The following is a selective list of the more prominent Marshal knights, as appears from charter attestations and the *Histoire*. Certain men who were attached to the Marshal are not to be found here. Ralph Musard, a Gloucestershire knight, seems to have been a member of the Marshal retinue before the crisis of 1216. Thomas Basset, son of Alan Basset of High Wycombe, Buckinghamshire, was definitely a Marshal protégé (see above), but probably rather late in the Marshal's life.

Other Marshal knights such as William and Hamo le Gros, Richard Siward, Bogo de Knoville, Bartholomew de Mortemer, William de la Mare and Alan of Hyde, belong properly to a study of the younger William Marshal's household. Five charters of William Marshal II in which he is already attended by this *mesnie* some time before his father's death are to be found in *Early Charters of the Cathedral Church of St Paul, London*, ed. M Gibbs Camden Soc 3rd ser. LVIII 1939 175–7; *Luffield Priory Charters* ed. G R Elvey (2 vols) Bucks and Northants Rec. Soc. jointly, 1968–75 I 166; *Curia Regis Rolls* VIII 249–50, 251.

Knights are listed in order of frequency of attestation.

### 1 John (II) of Earley

*17 Attestations. 5 (1189–99) 12 (1199–1219). Dated appearances in the Marshal's entourage: 1188 (Montmirail); 1189 x 90 (England); 1198 (Meullers); 1199 (Rouen); 1200 (England); 1207–8 (Leinster); 1216 (Gloucester); 1219 (Caversham).*

Grandson of John (I) of Earley, chamberlain of Henry I (ob. 1162–3). Son and heir of William of Earley, Kt, chamberlain of Henry II and founder of Buckland priory, Som. (ob. 1181), and Aziria (viv. 1201), daughter of Ralph de Insula. In royal wardship

1181–94, custody granted to William Marshal 1187 x 88. Married Sybil (parentage unknown). Died 1229, before May. Children: John (III); Henry; a daughter, m. Henry de Brehull.

Held in chief: Earley, Backham and Charlton, Berks.; Beckington, Durston, North Petherton and Somerton Erleigh, Som.; held hundred of North Petherton, Som., at feefarm. Patron of Buckland priory. Grant from the Marshal: Newton in Coillach (Earltown) co. Kilkenny. Joint seneschal of Leinster (1207–8); hostage for William Marshal, 1210; named marshal of the royal household, 1212; joint sheriff of Devon, 1211–15; co-executor of Marshal's last testament.

**Sources:** *Calendar of Inquisitions: Miscellaneous* I 321; *Pipe Roll of 12 Henry II* 97; *Pipe Roll of 27 Henry II* 5; *Pipe Roll of 6 Richard I*, 184; *Buckland Cartulary* ed. F W Weaver Somerset Record Society XXV 1909 1–2, 26 30; *Cartularies of Muchelney and Athelney Abbeys* ed. E H Bates Somerset Record Society XIV 1899 172, 190; *Red Book of the Exchequer* I 235; *Book of Fees* II 547; *Curia Regis Rolls* I 256–7; E St J Brooks *Knights' Fees in Counties Wexford, Carlow and Kilkenny* Irish MSS Commission Dublin 1950 243–6; *Rotuli Litterarum Clausarum* I 115, 132; *Excerpta e Rotulis Finium* I 184.

### 2 William Waleran

*11 Attestations. 4 (1189–99) 7 (1199–1219). Dated appearances in the Marshal's household: (1189 x 90); 1198; 1200; 1202.*

Son of Richard Waleran of Melksham, Wilts. (ob. a. 1182). Married (before 1206) Isabel, daughter of Roger (III) of Berkeley, Lord of Dursley, by grant of Earl William Marshal. Knight on Wilts juries, 1202, 1203. Died after 1224. Children: Robert (seneschal of Henry III), William, John.

Held in marriage from Berkeley of Dursley: Siston, Omberley and Deerham, Glos.

**Sources:** *Rotuli Litterarum Clausarum* I 615; *Three Rolls of the King's Court, 1194–95*, ed. F W Maitland P.R. Soc. XIV, 1891; *Curia Regis Rolls* II *103,* III *2,* IV *298,* VII *264, 294; Pipe Roll of 28 Henry II* 84.

## 3 Geoffrey fitz Robert

*11 Attestations. 3 (1189–99) 8 (1199–1219). Dated appearances in the Marshal's household: 1189 x 90; 1202, 1207, 1210.*

Possibly the Geoffrey fitz Robert *camerarius* who succeeded his brother William in his Wilts. lands *c.* 1190. Married (1) 1189 x 1199, Basilia sister of Earl Richard Strongbow, widow of Raymond le Gros (ob. c. 1188); (2) 1203 x 9, Eve, daughter and heir of Robert of Birmingham. Founder of Kells priory and borough 1203 x 10. Died 1211. Children: William, John (presumably by his second wife for Basilia could not have been less than 42 years of age when they married).

Grant from king (1199) of 5 knights' fees at *Radoger* in the cantred of *Huhene*, and a burgage in Limerick. Held of Marshal: Kells, co. Kilkenny; by right of his wife, Eve, Offaly, co. Kilkenny.

Seneschal of Leinster (1199 x 1210); hostage for the Marshal, 1210–11.

**Sources:** *Register of the Abbey of St Thomas Dublin* ed. J T Gilbert Rolls Series 1889 112–13, 125; *Chartae, Privilegia et Immunitates* Irish Record Commission 1829 17; *Rotuli Chartarum* 28; *Rotuli Litterarum Patentium* 59; *Pipe Roll of 2 Richard I*, 123; *Pipe Roll of 5 Richard I*, 81; *Irish Monastic and Episcopal Deeds* ed. N B White Irish MSS Commission 1936 300–13; *Calendar of Ormond Deeds, 1172–1350* ed. E Curtis Irish MSS Commission 1932 14–16, 134.

## 4 Jordan de Sauqueville

*10 Attestations. 1 (1189–99); 9 (1199–1219). Dated appearances in the Marshal's entourage: 1200; 1207; 1208; 1210.*

Descendant of Herbrand, constable of Arques and steward of Earl Walter Giffard (viv. 1086). Son and heir of William de Sauqueville. Died 1227 x 35. Child: Bartholomew.

Held of the Marshal: Fawsley, Bucks. Granted by the Marshal: *Clanavelay, Clanbeg, Arglas* and *Sanctum Boscum* (Ireland).

Joint-seneschal of Leinster, 1207–8; hostage for the Marshal, 1210–13; attorney at Westminster for William Marshal (II), 1214; seneschal of Pembroke, 1216.

**Sources:** J H Round 'Tales of the Conquest' in *Peerage and Pedigree* (2 vols) London 1910 I 284–9; *Rotuli Litterarum Clausarum* I 271, 304; *Curia Regis Rolls* VII 100; *Book of Fees* I 464; *Calendar of the Justices in Eyre in Buckinghamshire, 1227*, ed. J G Jenkins Bucks. Arch. Society VI 1942 36.

## 5 William Jardin

*10 Attestations. 0 (1189–99) 10 (1199–1219).* Dated appearances in the Marshal's entourage: *1196.*

Knight on Bucks jury 1203. Brother of William of Crendon. Married Cecilia (who later married Gilbert Marshal). Died 1220 x 23. Children: William.

Held of the Marshal land in Sundon and Chalton, Beds; South Mundham, Suss.

Seneschal of the honor of Crendon (1199 x 1219). Attorney for the Marshal at Westminster (1194).

**Sources:** *Curia Regis Rolls* II 217, XI, 189, 231, 500–1; Bodl. Libr. ms Dugdale 39 fos. 68r, 69v–70v; *Rotuli Curiae Regis* I 63.

## 6 Ralph Bloet (III) or (IV)

*9 Attestations. 2 (1189–99) 7 (1199–1219). Dated appearances in the Marshal's entourage: 1189 x 90.*

**Ralph Bloet (III)** eldest son of Ralph (II). Brother of Walter Bloet of Raglan and Robert Bloet of Daglingworth. Follower and tenant of Richard Strongbow, Earl of Striguil (died 1176). Keeper of the honor of Striguil (*c.* 1176–88). Married Nest, daughter of Iorwerth ab Owain, lord of Caerleon, (sometime mistress of King Henry II). Died 1198 x 99. Children: Ralph (IV); Thomas; Roland; William; Petronilla, m (1) William of Feltham; m (2) Diarmait mac Carrthaig, king of Desmond.

**Ralph Bloet (IV)** eldest son of Ralph (III). Died 1241 x 42. Married Eve (parentage unknown). Children: William; Ralph.

Held of the honor of Striguil: Silchester, Hants.; Yeovilton, Hinton Blewitt, Som.; Lackham, Hilmarton, Clyffe Pipard, Wilts.; Duntisbourne, Glos; Langstone, Whitson, Mon.

Grants to Ralph (III) and Nest by King John: Wiston, Pemb.

**Sources:** Domesday Book I fos. 47a, 71d, 96c, 166d; *Pipe Roll of 21 Henry II*, 194; *Pipe Roll of 22 Henry II*, 193; *Pipe Roll of 31 Henry II*, 8; *Pipe Roll of 34 Henry II*, 2; *Pipe Roll of 1 John*, 170; *Rotuli Litterarum Clausarum* II 23, 59; *Lacock Abbey Charters* cal. K H Rogers Wiltshire Records Society XXXIV 1978 18; *The English Register of Godstow Abbey* ed. A Clark (2 vols) E.E.T.S. 1906–11) 11–12, 134–5; *Durham Annals and Documents of the Thirteenth Century* ed. F Barlow Surtees Society clv 1945 1–2; *Close Rolls, 1231–34, passim; Book of Fees* II 724.

## 7 John Marshal

*9 Attestations. 4 (1189–99); 5 (1199–1219). Dated appearances in the Marshal's entourage: 1196, 1197, 1198, 1205, 1216, 1219.*

Illegitimate son of John Marshal (II). Nephew of the Marshal. With king in Normandy (1203), in Ireland on William Marshal's service (1204), with king at Woodstock and Tewkesbury (1207), Ireland (1210), Runnymede (1215), ambassador to Rome (1215), at Newark (1216), at battle of Lincoln (1217). Married (1199): Aline, heiress of Hubert (III) de Ryes, lord of honors of Ryes and Hockering. Marshal of Ireland (1207). Died 1235. Children: John; William.

Held of king: Honor of Ryes in Normandy (1203–4); Honor of Hockering, Norf. (1200) by marriage, and other grants.

**Sources**: references collected in *Complete Peerage* VIII 525–6.

## 8 Hugh of Sandford

8 Attestations. *4 (1189–99); 4 (1199–1219). Dated appearances in the Marshal's entourage: 1196, 1200.*

Son of John of Sandford, marshal of King Henry II? Younger brother of Adam, Richard and Thomas of Sandford. Squire of King Henry II (1189). Married (before 1208) Joan de Chesney, heiress of Missenden, Bucks. With king in Poitou (1205), Durham (1212), La Rochelle (1214). Keeper of Bradenstoke Forest (1223). Advocate of Missenden Abbey. Died 1234. Illegitimate child: Juliana, hermit of Missenden.

Held of king: one-tenth fee in South Moreton, Berks. Had by marriage: Great Missenden, Bucks. Held as rent charges of king: £20 of land in Risborough, Northants (1204); £30 of Norman lands in Bucks. Grant from the Marshal (1189 x 99): share of knight's fee in Wittenham, Berks. King Henry III established chantry in his memory at Missenden (1234).

**Sources:** *Monasticon Anglicanum* IV 492; *Book of Fees* I 105, II 857; *Red Book of the Exchequer* I 144; *Rotuli Chartarum*, 188, 201; *Rotuli Litterarum Clausarum* I 12, 44, 49, 109, 122, 552, 565; *Curia Regis Rolls* VI 358; VII 216; *Cartulary of Missenden Abbey* ed. J G Jenkins (3 vols) Bucks. Rec. Soc. II, X, XII 1938–62 I 21–2, 50–1; BL Add charter 21164.

### 9 Henry Hose (IV)

*8 Attestations. 0 (1189–99) 8 (1199–1219). Dated appearance in the Marshal's entourage: 1207.*

Son and heir of Henry Hose (III) of Harting, Suss (died 1213). Patron of Durford priory. Married: Cecilia, daughter of Emma of Stanton. Died 1231 x 35. Children: Henry, Matthew.

Held of the Earl of Arundel: Harting and Chithurst, Suss. Held of king: Stapleford, Wilts.; Standen Hussey, East Hendred, Sparsholt, Berks; Littleton, Hants. Grant from King John: Eling, Hants.

**Sources:** References collected in, W. Farrer, *Honors and Knights' Fees*, III 83–7.

### 10 Henry fitz Gerold

*7 Attestations. 0 (1189–99), 7 (1199–1219). Dated appearances in the Marshal's entourage: 1202, 1205, 1219.*

Son of Henry fitz Gerold, chamberlain of King Henry II. Younger brother of Warin fitz Gerold (II), also chamberlain. Born 1173. Married (*c.* 1203): Ermentrude, widow of (1) Quentin Talbot of Gainsborough, Lincs.; widow of (2) William of Grendon. Executor of William Marshal. Died *c.* 1231. Child: Warin fitz Gerold.

Held of king: Iffley, Oxon. Held of the chamberlain's fee: Kingston-Lisle, Berks; Nettleton, Wilts.

**Source:** References collected ibid, 168–74.

## 11 Alan de St-Georges

*6 Attestations. 6 (1189–99); 0 (1199–1219). No dated appearances in the Marshal's entourage.*

Son and heir of Ralph de St-Georges of Didling, Suss. and Agatha, daughter of Ralph fitz Savaric of Midhurst. Married: (1) (?Beatrice) widow of Richard de Guize (c. 1177); (2) Sybil. Knight (elector) on Sussex juries: 1204, 1206, 1212, 1226. Constable of Knaresborough castle (1214). Died 1226 x 31. No children, his sister Agatha his heir.

Held of Earl of Arundel: Trotton, Didling and Dunsfold, Suss.

**Sources:** Cartulary of Durford BL ms Cotton Vespasian E XXIII fo. 40v.; Cartulary of Wymondham BL ms Cotton Titus C VIII fo. 20v.; *Chartulary of the Priory of Boxgrove*, ed. L Fleming (Sussex Record Society, LIX, 1960), 72, 146–7; *The Chartulary of the High Church of Chichester* ed. W D Peckham Sussex Record Society XLVI, 1942/3), 89–90; *Calendar of Patent Rolls, 1358–61*, 535; *Pipe Roll of 23 Henry II*, 99; *Pipe Roll of 2 Richard I*, 129; *Pipe Roll of 7 Richard I*, 37; *Pedes Finium, 1195–1214*, ed. J Hunter (2 vols) London 1844 II 91; *Curia Regis Rolls* III 173, IV 157, VI 282, XII 449, XIV, 421; *Rotuli Litterarum Clausarum* I 206

## 12 Roger d'Abenon

*4 Attestations. 4 (1189–99); 0 (1199–1219). No dated appearances in the Marshal's entourage.*

Son and heir of Enguerrand d'Abenon. Married Adelina, daughter and heir of William Peverel. Died childless 1216.

Held of the Earl of Hertford: North Mousley, Albury, Stoke Daubernon, Surr. Held of king: Lessham, Hants.

**Source:** references collected in, C.S. Perceval, 'Some Account of the family of Abernon of Albury and Stoke D'Abernon', *Surrey Archaeological Society* V 1871 53–58; C A F Meekings 'Notes on the de Abernon Family before 1236'. ibid CXXII 157–73.

## 13 Philip of Prendergast

*4 Attestations. 1 (1189–99); 3 (1199–1219). Dated appearances in the Marshal's entourage: 1189 x 90, 1205.*

Son and heir of Maurice of Prendergast. Married (1172 x 76) Mathilda, daughter of Earl Richard of Striguil. Died 1226 x 29. Children: Gerald, David.

Held of the castellan of Wiston: Prendergast, Pembs; held of the Marshal: The Duffry, Ayrmellach, co. Wexford; grant from King John (1207): *Benneer, Dufglas*, co. Cork.

**Sources:** *Knights' Fees in Counties Wexford, Carlow and Kilkenny*, 129–41, 145–51; *Rotuli Litterarum Clausarum* I 171; *Rotuli Litterarum Patentium* 123, 144; *Close Rolls, 1227–31*, 208.

## 14 Thomas of Rochford

*4 Attestations. 4 (1189–99); 0 (1199–1219). No dated appearances in Marshal's entourage.*

Father unknown, brother of Robert of Rochford. Married (before 1204) Isabel, daughter of Roger of Berkeley. Daughter and heir: Alice, m. . . . de la Bere. Died 1206.

Held in marriage: Dursley, Glos. Held of Berkeleys of Berkeley: Ozleworth, Glos. Held also Rochford, Herefs.(?).

Constable of Bristol castle (1204); under-sheriff of Glos. (1201–4)

**Sources:** Berkeley Castle Muniments, Select Ch. 185; PRO JUST1/273 m 2d; *Rotuli Litterarum Clausarum*, I 6, 645; *Rotuli Litterarum Patentium*, 39; *Curia Regis Rolls* IV 298.

## 15 Thomas (II) de Colleville

*4 Attestations. 4 (1189–99) 0 (1199–1219). No dated appearances in the Marshal's entourage.*

Son of Thomas (?). Knight on Yorkshire juries: 1236, 1241. Knight on Lincolnshire jury: 1227.

Held from the honor of Mowbray: Coxwold, Yorks. Grant from William de Colleville: land at Bytham, Lincs (before 1230).

**Sources:** *Red Book* I 420, II 734; *Curia Regis Rolls* XIII 37, XIV 145–6, XV 126, 487, XVI 24, 311.

## 16 Nicholas Avenel (II)

*4 Attestations. 2 (1189–99) 2 (1199–1219). Dated appearances in the Marshal's entourage: 1189 x 90, 1196.*

Son and heir of Nicholas (died 1212 x 14) and Hilaria, co-heir of the barony of Curry Malet, Som. Died after 1220. Son: William.

Under-sheriff of Gloucestershire: 1192–94, 1199–1201.

Held in chief: Sheepwash, Chilton, Devons; Warminster, Wilts; Curry, Holcombe, Som. Held of grant of King Richard (1194), *Lalega*, Gloucs.

**Sources:** Cartulary of Christchurch, Twynham, BL ms Cotton Tiberius D VI, pt I, fo. 46v; *Pipe Roll of 6 Richard I*, 238; *Red Book of the Exchequer* I 261; *Book of Fees* I 96, II 96, 717, 782; *Curia Regis Rolls* VI 142, IX 365; *Rotuli Litterarum Clausarum* II 238.

## 17 Stephen d'Evreux

*4 Attestations. 0 (1189–99) 4 (1199–1219). Dated appearances in the Marshal's entourage: 1207.*

Son of Walter (died after 1193). Married Isabel de Cantilupe (sister of William?). Died 1228, before March. Son: William (II) d'Evreux.

Justice of gaol delivery at Hereford (1220).

Held of honor of Weobley: Lyonshall Castle, Holme Lacy, Stoke Lacy, Herefs.; Lower Hayton, Salop; Temple Guiting and Oakley, Gloucs. Held from bishop of Worcester: Crowle and saltworks at Droitwich, Worcs. Grant from Walter de Lacy: Frome Quintin, Herefs. (1205). Grant from Gilbert de Lacy *pro eo quod sit in familia mea* land in Staunton on Wye, Herefs. (1219 x 28). Grant from William Marshal II of Wilby, Norf. (1219 x 27).

**Sources:** PRO E210/1363; Hereford County Record Office, Hopton Collection no. 107; Hereford D & C Archives, mun. no. 3235; Cartulary of Wormley, B L ms Harley 3586 fo. 89r; *Red Book* I 282, II

602; *Book of Fees* I 439, 440, II, 808; *Collectanea Topographica et Genealogica* II 250; *Monasticon Anglicanum* VI 399–401; *Curia Regis Rolls* VII 51, IX, 198; XII 343; *Rotuli Chartarum* 156; *Rotuli Litterarum Clausarum* I 167, 168, 219, 437, 623; *Rotuli Litterarum Patentium* 91; *Pipe Roll 8 Richard I, 91; Excerpta e Rotulis Finium* I 168; *Cal Charter Rolls* I 43; *Flaxley Cartulary* 134.

## 18 Eustace de Bertremont

*3 Attestations. 1 (1189–99) 2 (1199–1219). Dated appearances in the Marshal's entourage: 1183, 1214.*

No personal details known.

*Appendix II*

# THE MARSHAL AND THE EARL MARSHAL

From his earliest appearances in the *Histoire*, William son of John Marshal is invariably William *li Mareschal*, or often just *li Mareschal*. Yet he did not inherit the office of royal marshal until the death of his brother John in 1194. We cannot dismiss this as a retrospective elevation, however. Other evidence, particularly the government list of the rebels of 1174, preserved by Roger of Howden, tells us that he was called by contemporaries William *Marescallus* (the Marshal) in the lifetime of his brother. In the exchequer records of 1165–66 both William's elder brothers, Gilbert (II) and John, are called *Marescallus*. In 1189 his younger brother Henry was also called *Marescallus*. From this it is clear enough that all the sons of John Marshal (I) took their father's office as a surname.

The transformation of hereditary offices into surnames was by no means uncommon in the twelfth century: there were then numerous families who took the names of Butler, Chamberlain, Steward or Seneschal, or Despencer, who traced their origins to a man who was an actual office holder. Sometimes the office continued to be hereditary in the family, but quite often it did not; nonetheless the name continued to be used. The example of the Marshals is more interesting in that it is rather early to find several sons taking their surname from the father's office. I can only think of one comparable example, the Despencer family of Leicestershire. The family descended from Geoffrey, the despencer of Earl Ranulf II of Chester in Stephen's reign. By John's reign all five of his grandsons were sporting the name 'Despencer'. There may well be other instances, however, of which I am unaware.

The office of marshal was an ancient one. The Latin word *marescallus* or *marescalcus* preserved two ancient Frankish elements meaning 'horse-slave'; it seems very likely that the word was being applied to the unfree grooms of the ancestors of the Merovingian kings of the Franks. The office was well in evidence at the court of the Carolingian kings and emperors, although it was not a high one. The titles of the Carolingian court were transmitted to the courts of its later imitators, the kings and princes of France. The Normans brought them to England where the royal court contained all the functionaries who had surrounded Charlemagne centuries earlier. According to the *Constitutio Domus Regis* (the Organisation of the King's Household), a treatise compiled early in 1136 for the information of King Stephen, the English court then had a Master Marshal 'namely John' (William Marshal's father). John Marshal headed the department called the Marshalcy (otherwise called the Marshalsea), and received fees and provisions ranking him with the other great officers, the seneschal, the constable and the master chamberlain. His duties then involved the keeping of certain royal records. Besides this there was his department to oversee. The Marshalcy contained four other lesser marshals; both clerks and knights; assistants called sergeants; the knight ushers and common ushers of the royal hall; the usher of the king's chamber; the watchmen of the court; the tent-keeper and the keeper of the king's hearth. From this information it seems that the marshal was then responsible for the good order of the court, and the supervision of movements both within and without the palace.

The *Constitutio* assumes that John Marshal actually carried out the functions ascribed to him. Certainly the evidence of royal charters of 1135–8 place John in close attendance on the king. But it is very unlikely that any of his sons did so, and unlikely too that he carried out his office about the court and Exchequer after his breach with Stephen in 1138. After that the office (like the chamberlainship held by the Earley family) became purely honorary. Thirteenth-century evidence tells us that the later Marshals did indeed occasionally take over the supervision of the hall, but only on great state occasions such as a king's or a queen's coronation. Similarly, the function of the keeping of the records of debts and settlements reached in the exchequer devolved on to a nominee of the Marshal, a deputy marshal (a clerk called in Henry III's reign 'the marshal of the Marshalcy of the royal court'). The earliest so far known of these is Master Joscelin (occasionally called Joscelin Marshal or Joscelin of the Exchequer) rector of Tidenham, Gloucestershire, and a long-serving clerk of William Marshal (see Chapter 5). The one aspect of the Marshal's office in which he may have kept some active concern was the keeping of the records of service done in the royal army.

The Marshal's office as held by William Marshal, and probably also his elder brother, was an honorific, the work being done by someone else. That does not mean that it was unimportant honorific, however. The *Constitutio* already reveals that there was the idea at the courts of Henry I and Stephen that certain officers (seneschal, master chamberlain, master butler, constable and master marshal) were raised above others. In Henry II's reign we begin to find the baronial families who held these hereditary offices were using them as titles in their own right. Thus the heads of the Hereford family (after it lost the earldom of Hereford in 1155) fell back for its dignity on the secondary title of 'royal constable' (*constabularius regis*). John Marshal (II) on occasion had himself described as 'royal marshal'. The Mauduit family were similarly 'royal chamberlains'. In the thirteenth century the offices were in the hands of great earls: the chamberlainship went to the Earls of Warwick; the seneschalcy to the Earls of Leicester; the constabulary (once more) to the Earls of Hereford. All these earls took the office as part of their style: Henry de Bohun was 'earl of Hereford and constable of England'. Such styles were much sought after. Lacking an English one, the Quincy Earls of Winchester fell back on their constableship of Scotland. The Irish hereditary offices of state were paraded in a similar way.

The Marshal Earls of Pembroke very rarely called themselves 'marshals of England', although their successors, the Bigot Earls of Norfolk made it part of their routine style after 1245. What did happen however, was that the Marshal Earls of Pembroke came generally to be called the 'Earls Marshal'. Their surname, title and office were run together in common usage to appear to create something quite new. This was already happening at the time of William Marshal (I). He and all his Marshal successors called themselves consistently 'Earl of Pembroke'. But on several occasions William was called by others *Comes Willelmus Marescallus*. What this meant was that his title of earl was simply preceding his full name, rather in the same way as the contemporary Earl of Surrey was called *Comes Willelmus Warenne*. To talk of the 'Earl Marshal' rather than the 'Earl of Pembroke' was simply the next step after this, and a personage called the *comes marescallus* certainly appears in the time of William Marshal II. Thus because of laziness in the thirteenth century we still have an 'Earl Marshal' in the English peerage; since the late-fourteenth century a title combined with the duchy of Norfolk.

(For this see in general, studies in, J H Round *The Commune of London* Westminster 1899; J H Round *The King's Sergeants and Officers of State* London 1911; *The Complete Peerage* x Appendix G.)

# GENERAL BIBLIOGRAPHY

The following is a brief guide to works of use on the general topics covered by each of the chapters.

*Chapter 1: Childhood and Squirehood*

For the political background of Stephen's reign the finest general study remains R.H.C. Davis, *King Stephen* 3rd edn London 1990. However his views on the causes and nature of the anarchy have been questioned by: E King, 'King Stephen and the Anglo-Norman Aristocracy', *History*, LIX (1974), 180–94; and in a rather difficult article by the same writer 'The Anarchy of King Stephen's Reign', *Transactions of the Royal Historical Society* 5th ser. XXXIV 1984 133–53. See also D Crouch 'Robert, earl of Gloucester, and the daughter of Zelophehad', *Journal of Medieval History*, XI (1985), 227–243. For the best recent general study on the general background of Norman and Angevin England, see M M Chibnall, *Anglo-Norman England, 1066–1166* Oxford 1986.

*Chapter 2: The Household Knight*

For the reign of Henry II the only general modern study is, W.L. Warren, *Henry II* London, 1973, but see also, K. Norgate, *England under the Angevin Kings* (2 vols) London 1887. T K Keefe *Feudal Assessments and the Political Community under Henry II and his Sons* Berkeley 1983 contains new ideas on relations between the king and his magnates. J Gillingham *The Angevin Empire* London 1984 offers a fine general study of the problem posed by the Angevin dominions. For the kingdom of France at this time, see E M Hallam *Capetian France, 987–1328* London 1980; J. Dunbabin *France in the Making, 843–1180* Oxford 1985. The only published study on the Young Henry is, O H Moore, *The Young King Henry Plantagenet, 1155–1183* (Columbus, 1925), but this is disappointing on his political career. The essays translated and reprinted in, G. Duby *The Chivalrous Society*, trans. C. Postan (London, 1977), particularly 'Youth in aristocratic society' (pp. 112–22), and 'The Structure of Kinship and Nobility' (pp. 134–48) are to be recommended as stimulating introductions to the medieval family.

### *Chapter 3: The Making of a Magnate*

For the reign of Richard there are several good general studies: K. Norgate, *Richard the Lionheart* (London, 1924); J. Brundage, *Richard Lionheart* (New York, 1973); J. Gillingham, *Richard the Lionheart* (London, 1978). For the duel between Philip and the Angevins the best study remains, F.M. Powicke, *The Loss of Normandy* (2nd edn., Manchester, 1961); but see also, J.C. Holt, 'The End of the Anglo-Norman Realm', *Proceedings of the British Academy*, LXI (1975), 223–65.

### *Chapter 4: The Making of a Regent*

For the reign of John there are several worthwhile studies: K Norgate, *John Lackland* London, 1902; S. Painter, *The Reign of King John* Baltimore, 1949; J T Appleby, *John, King of England* London, 1960 W L Warren *King John* 2nd edn. London 1978. For Ireland at this time, still valuable is G H Orpen *Ireland under the Normans* II 1169–1216 Oxford 1911; more dense and difficult is J Otway-Ruthven *History of Medieval Ireland* Dublin 1968). For Wales a recent book has overridden all previous work, R.R. Davies, *Conquest Coexistence and Change in Wales, 1063–1415* Oxford 1987. For the Barons' War and Magna Carta, see J C Holt, *The Northerners* Oxford 1961; J C Holt *Magna Carta* Cambridge 1965; F M Powicke *Stephen Langton* Oxford 1928; C R Cheney *Pope Innocent III and England* Stuttgart 1976; H G Richardson and G O Sayles, *The Governance of Medieval England from the Conquest to Magna Carta* Edinburgh 1963. For the Minority, see particularly, K. Norgate, *The Minority of Henry III* London 1912; F M Powicke *King Henry III and the Lord Edward* Oxford 1947; M T Clanchy *England and its Rulers, 1066–1272* London 1983; D Carpenter *The Minority of Henry III* (forthcoming) 1990.

### *Chapter 5: The Marshal's Men*

For the status of the knight in twelfth- and thirteenth- century society, see generally G Duby *The Three Orders: Feudal Society*

*Imagined* trans. A Goldhammer Chicago 1980; F Gies *The Knight in History* New York, 1987. More particularly English studies are: S Harvey 'The Knight and the Knight's Fee in England' *Past and Present* no. 49 1970 3–43; P R Coss 'Knighthood and the Early Thirteenth-Century County Court' *Thirteenth-Century England* II ed. P R Coss and S D Lloyd Woodbridge 1988 45–57. For the clerical household the nearest approach to a general study is, C R Cheney *English Bishops' Chanceries, 1150–1250* Manchester 1950. For contemporary baronial administration, see N. Denholm-Young, *Seignorial Administration in England* London, 1937.

*Chapter 6: Love and Lordship*

The classic statement of the structure of twelfth-century English society is F M Stenton, *The First Century of English Feudalism, 1066–1166* 2nd edn. Oxford 1961; D Crouch *The Beaumont Twins: The Roots and Branches of Power in the Twelfth Century* Cambridge 1986 offers some modifications to the Stentonian view. There is no corresponding work for thirteenth-century society, although the following studies offer some insight: J C Holt *The Northerners* Oxford 1961 chs 3–4; R H Hilton, *A Medieval Society: The West Midlands at the End of the Thirteenth Century* Cambridge 1966; K J Stringer, *Earl David of Huntingdon* Edinburgh 1986; D Crouch 'Strategies of Lordship in Angevin England and the Career of William Marshal' in *The Ideals and Practice of Medieval Knighthood*, II ed. C Harper-Bill and R Harvey Woodbridge 1988. Much to be recommended as a study of aristocratic mores of the time, is C S Jaeger *The Origins of Courtliness* Philadelphia 1985.

*Chapter 7: The Chivalry of the Marshal*

For the knight and chivalry generally, see above all, M Keen, *Chivalry* New Haven 1984; see also S Painter *French Chivalry* Baltimore 1940; R W Barber *The Knight and Chivalry* London 1970; J Flori *L'Essor de Chevalerie* Geneva 1986. For the tournament, see N Denholm-Young 'The Tournament in the Thirteenth Century' *Studies Presented to F.M. Powicke* ed. R W Hunt and others (Oxford, 1948), 204–68; L D Benson 'The tournament in the romances of Chrétien de Troyes and *L'Histoire de Guillaume le Maréchal*' *Studies in Medieval Culture*, XIV 1980 1–24; G Duby *Le Dimanche de Bouvines* Gallimard 1973 100–44, 'La Guerre'; J R V Barker *The Tournament in England, 1100–1400* Woodbridge 1986. For warfare generally, see P Contamine *War in the Middle Ages* Oxford 1984; and for some revisionist comments J Gillingham 'Richard I and the science of war in the Middle Ages' in *War and Government in the Middle Ages: Essays in Honour of J O Prestwich* Woodbridge 1984, 78–91.

*Chapter 8: La Bon Fine Va Tout*

On the monastic orders generally D Knowles *The Monastic Order in England* Cambridge 1949. On the subject of monastic patronage at the time of the Marshal, see E M Thompson *The Carthusian Order in England* London 1930; J C Dickinson *The Origins of the Austin Canons and their Introduction into England* London 1950; S Wood *English Monasteries and their Patrons in the Thirteenth Century* Oxford 1955; E M Hallam 'Henry II as a Founder of Monasteries' *Journal of Ecclesiastical History* XXVIII 1977 113–32. For the Marshal's Irish abbeys, see A H Thompson and others, 'The Cistercian Order in Ireland' *Archaeological Journal* 88 1931 1–36; R Stalley *The Cistercian Monasteries of Ireland* London 1987.

# MAPS

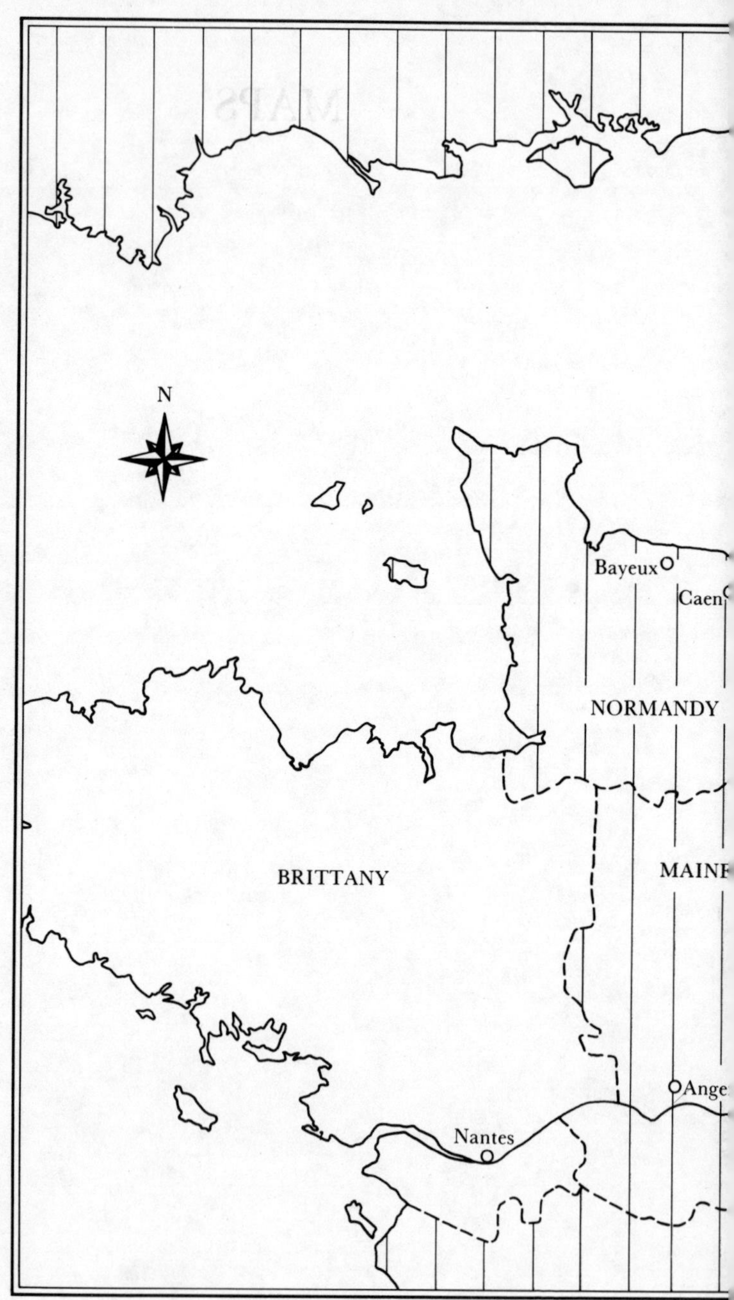
N
Bayeux
Caen
NORMANDY
BRITTANY
MAINE
Nantes

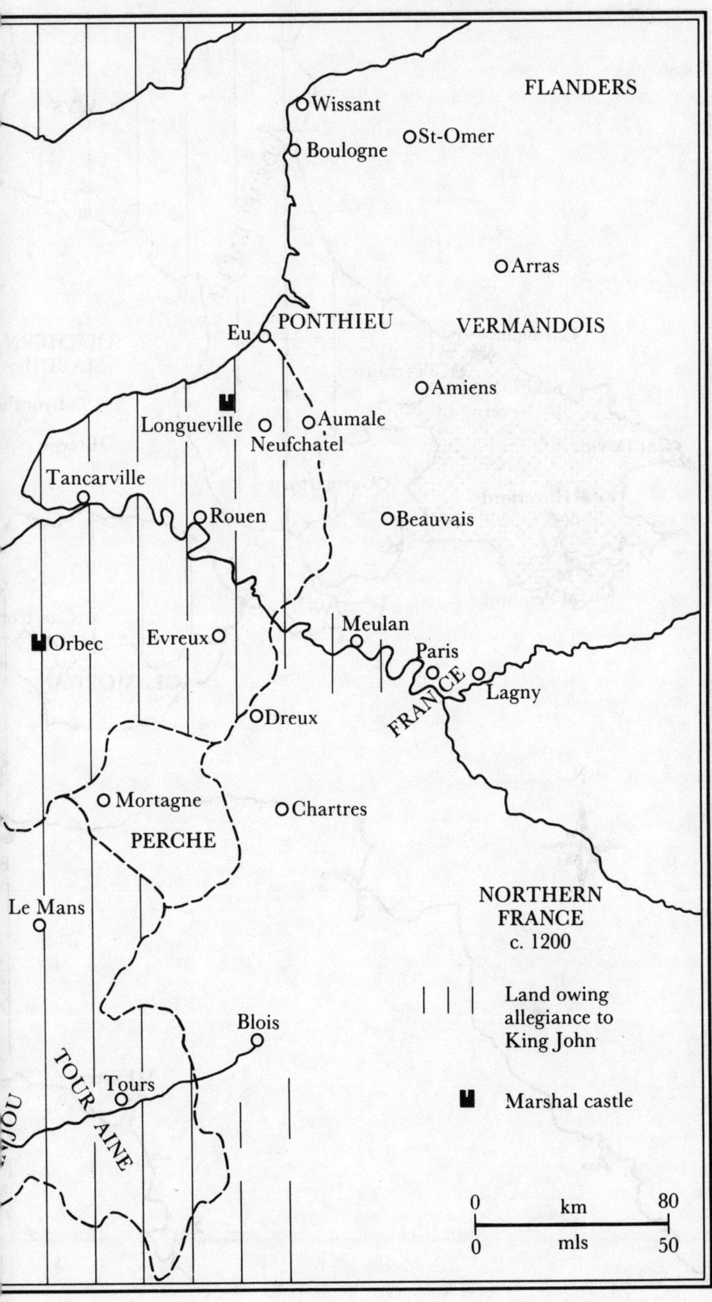
FLANDERS
Wissant
St-Omer
Boulogne
Arras
PONTHIEU
VERMANDOIS
Eu
Amiens
Longueville
Aumale
Neufchatel
Tancarville
Rouen
Beauvais
Meulan
Paris
Orbec
Evreux
FRANCE
Lagny
Dreux
Mortagne
Chartres
PERCHE
Le Mans
NORTHERN
FRANCE
c. 1200
Land owing
allegiance to
King John
Blois
TOURAINE
Tours
Marshal castle
0
km
80
0
mls
50

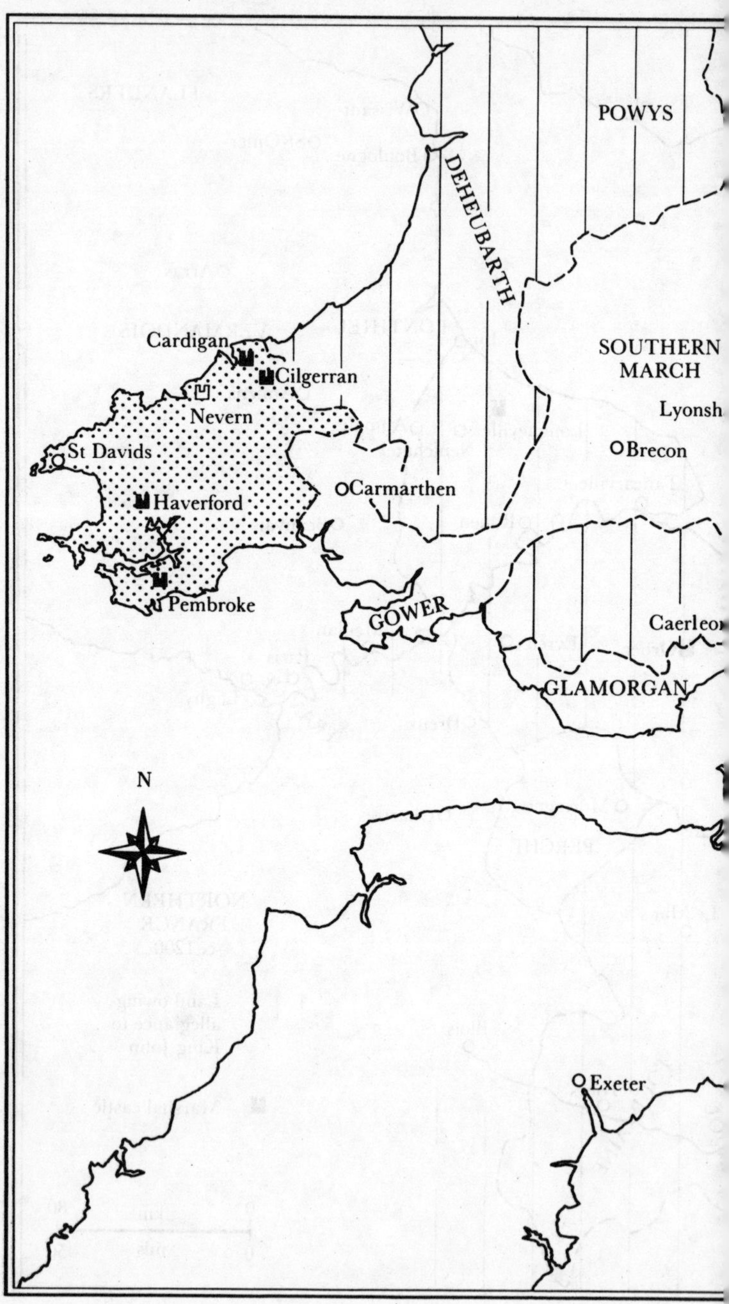
POWYS
DEHEUBARTH
SOUTHERN
MARCH
Lyonsh
Brecon
Cardigan
Cilgerran
Nevern
St Davids
Carmarthen
Haverford
Pembroke
GOWER
Caerleo
GLAMORGAN
N
Exeter

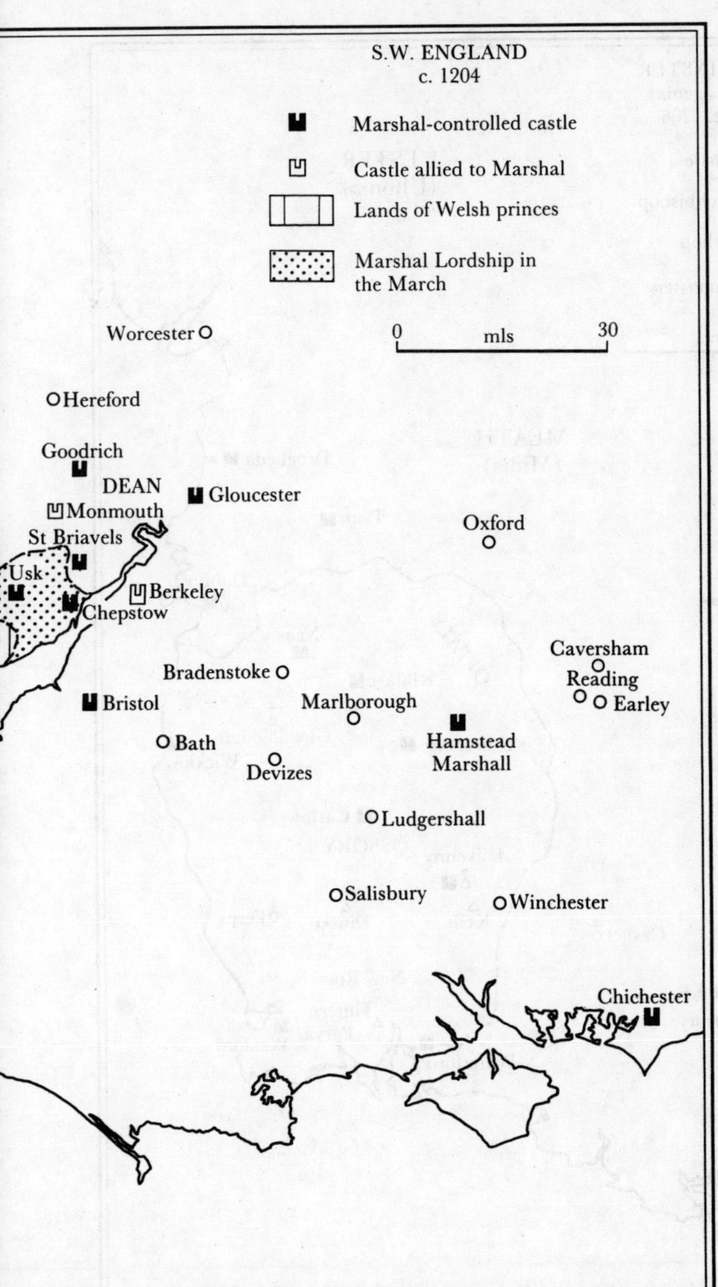
S.W. ENGLAND
c. 1204
Marshal-controlled castle
Castle allied to Marshal
Lands of Welsh princes
Marshal Lordship in the March
0
mls
30
Worcester
Hereford
Goodrich
DEAN
Gloucester
Monmouth
St Briavels
Oxford
Usk
Berkeley
Chepstow
Caversham
Reading
Earley
Bradenstoke
Bristol
Marlborough
Hamstead Marshall
Bath
Devizes
Ludgershall
Salisbury
Winchester
Chichester

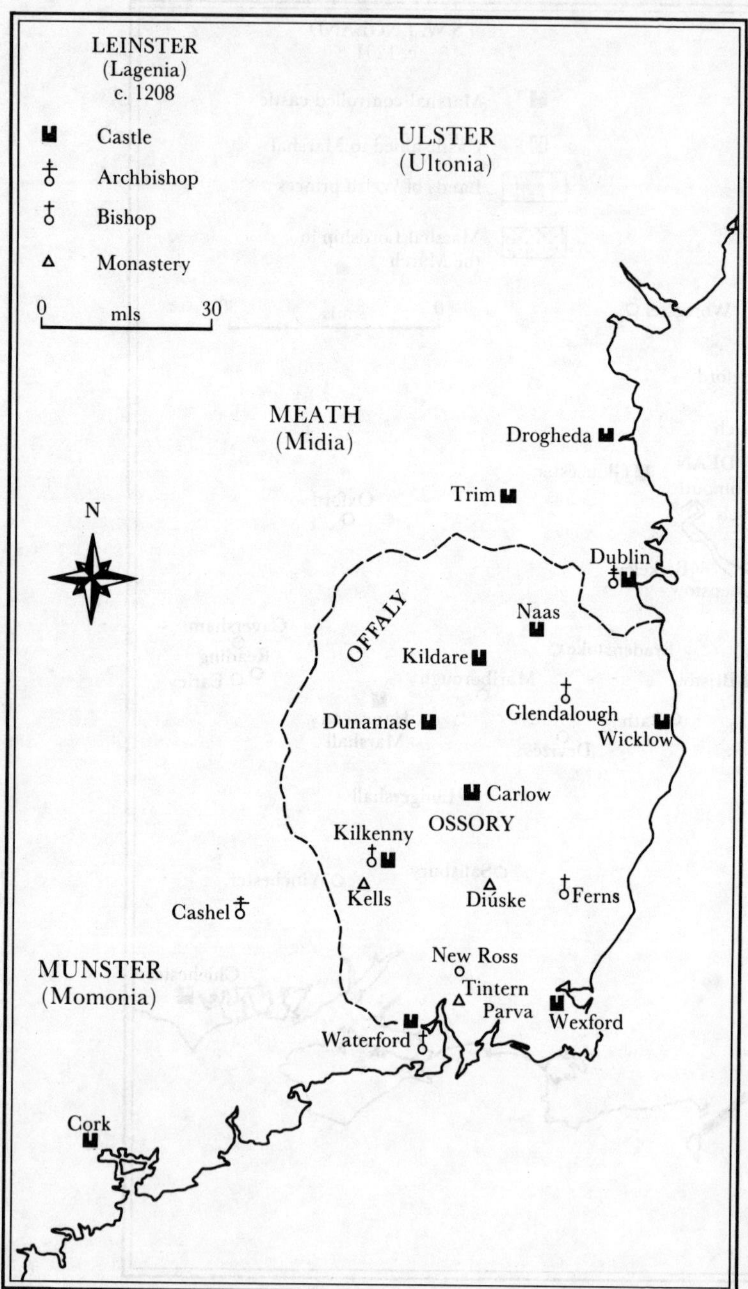
LEINSTER
(Lagenia)
c. 1208
Castle
Archbishop
Bishop
Monastery
0
mls
30
ULSTER
(Ultonia)
MEATH
(Midia)
N
Drogheda
Trim
Dublin
OFFALY
Naas
Kildare
Glendalough
Dunamase
Wicklow
Carlow
OSSORY
Kilkenny
Kells
Diúske
Ferns
Cashel
New Ross
MUNSTER
(Momonia)
Tintern
Parva
Wexford
Waterford
Cork

# GENEALOGICAL TABLES

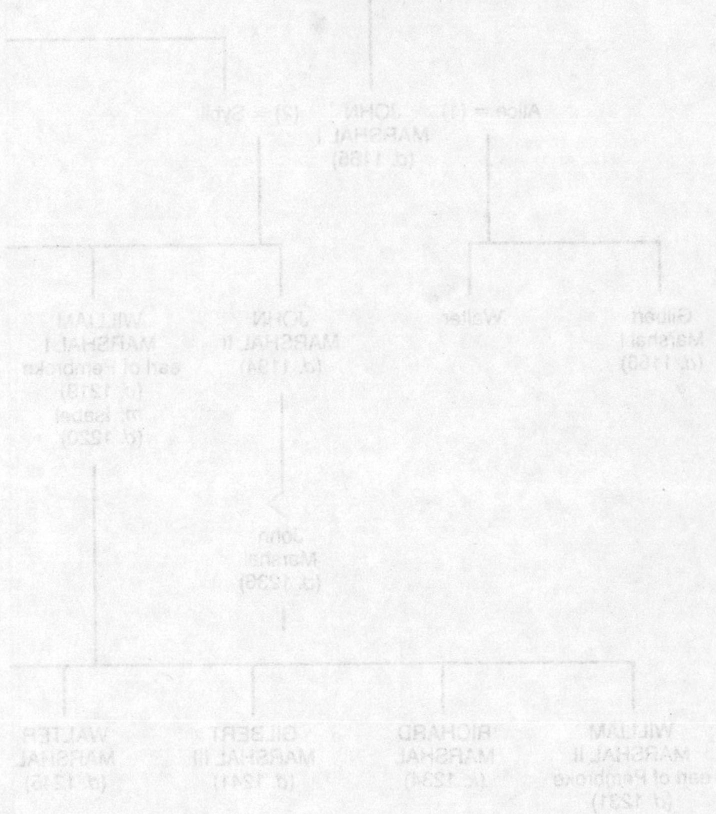

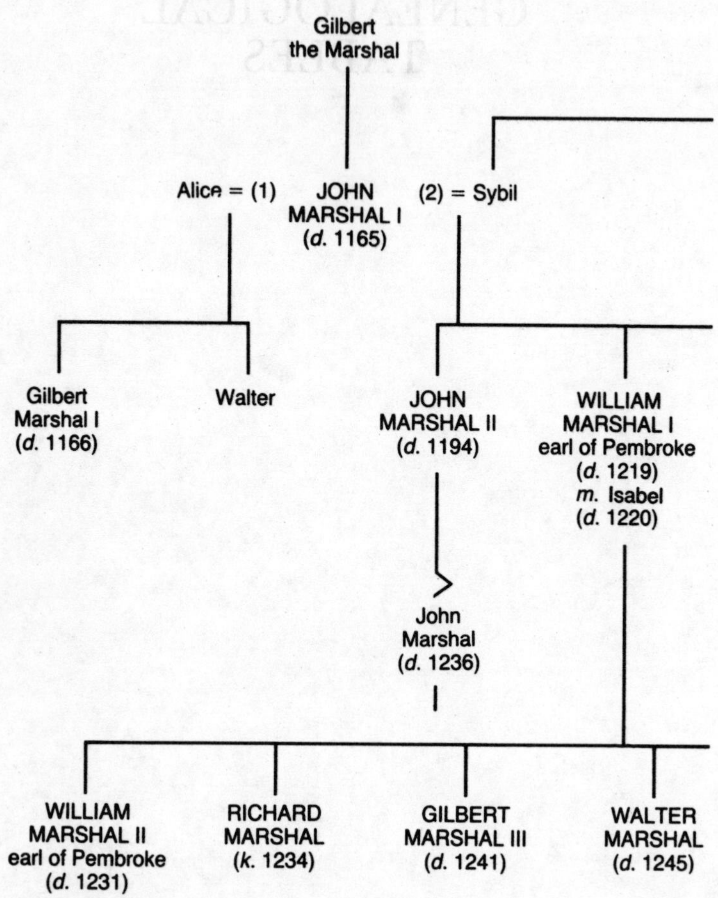


Fig. 2 Selective genealogy of the Marshal and Salisbury families

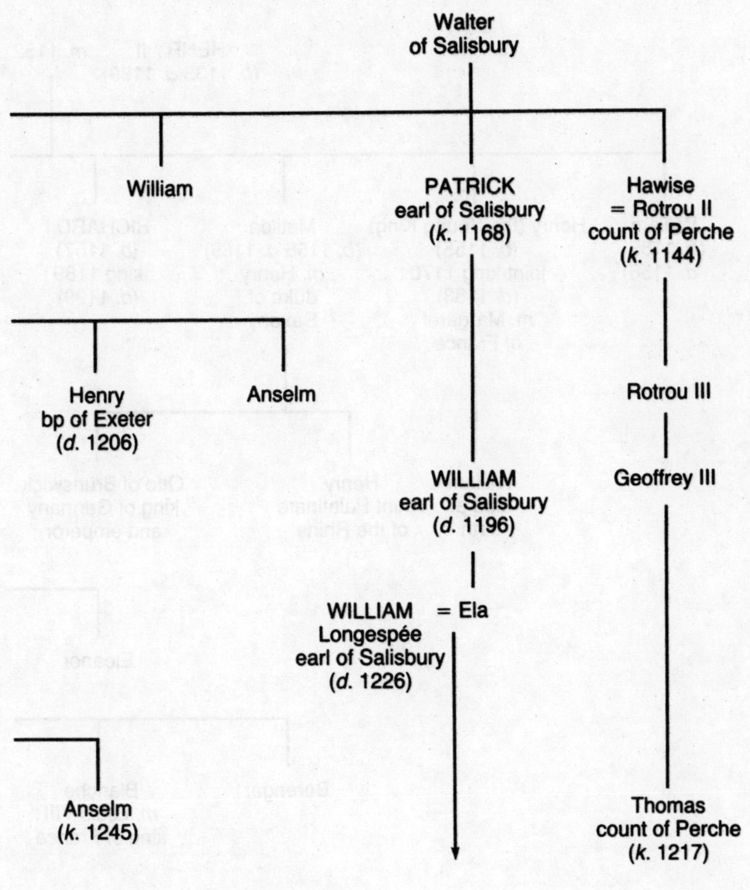
Walter
of Salisbury
William
PATRICK
earl of Salisbury
(k. 1168)
Hawise
= Rotrou II
count of Perche
(k. 1144)
Henry
bp of Exeter
(d. 1206)
Anselm
Rotrou III
WILLIAM
earl of Salisbury
(d. 1196)
Geoffrey III
WILLIAM
Longespée
earl of Salisbury
(d. 1226)
= Ela
Anselm
(k. 1245)
Thomas
count of Perche
(k. 1217)
d. = died
k. = killed

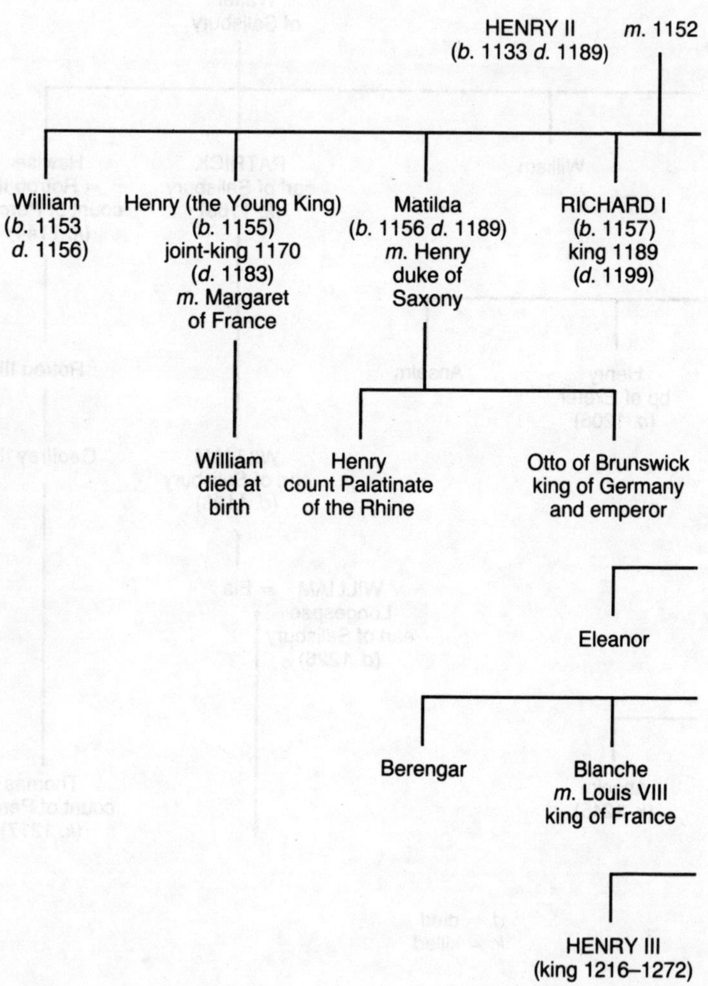


Fig. 3 The children and grandchildren of Henry II and Eleanor of Aquitaine

Eleanor of Aquitaine
heiress of William X duke of Aquitaine
(*b.c* 1122 *d.* 1204)

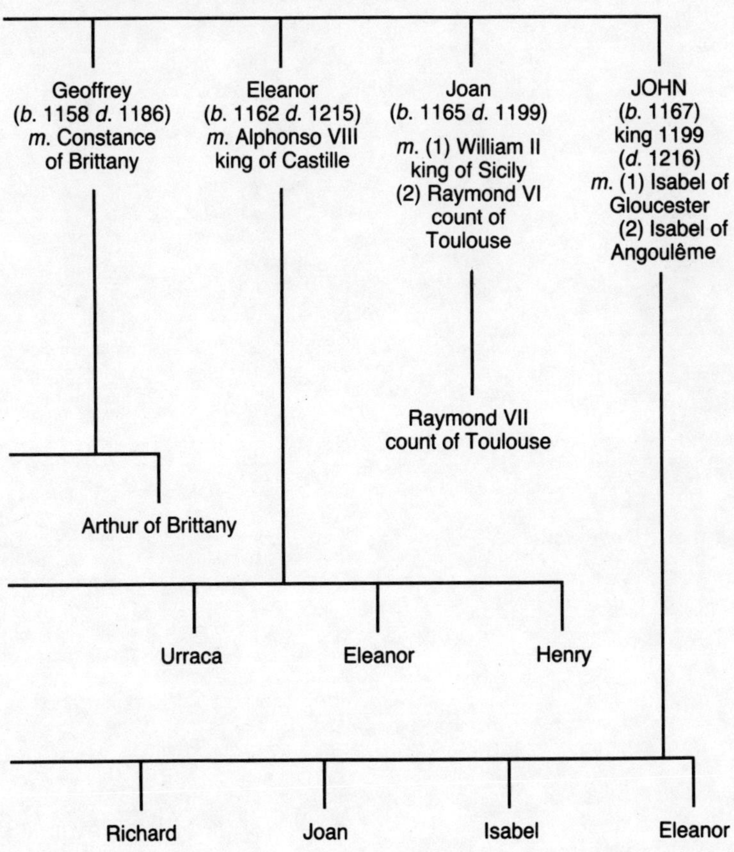

# INDEX

The following abbreviations have been employed: abb = abbot; abp = archbishop; adn = archdeacon; bp = bishop; br = brother; css = countess; ct = count; d = duke; dr = daughter; e = earl; k = king; pr = prince; qn = queen; s = son; ssr = sister; w = wife.